THE
SELF-RELIANT
MANAGER

John Cowan

THE
SELF-RELIANT
MANAGER

amacom
A DIVISION OF AMERICAN MANAGEMENT ASSOCIATIONS

Library of Congress Cataloging in Publication Data

Cowan, John.
  The self-reliant manager.

  Includes index.
  1. Supervision of employees.   2. Self-reliance.   I. Title.
HF5549.C747   658.4   77-12145
ISBN 0-8144-5447-X

Second Printing

Contents

Introduction

This book is written for you who because of excellent technical work have vaulted to the responsibility of managing a group of people.

Chances are you have had virtually no management training and your promotion had nothing to do with your managerial ability or inclination. Your own management probably doesn't even know your managerial capability and, unless you belong to a highly sophisticated corporation, has no way of assessing your aptitude. What they have evaluated is your technical ability. They are impressed with your skill and delighted with your zeal. They have noticed that you don't alienate people often or irrevocably. Your seniority is comparable to that of others, so they have made their decision, and *you are a manager.*

No longer the engineer, but now the section chief. No longer the librarian, but now the branch supervisor. No longer the maintenance man, but now the maintenance foreman. No longer the lead person, but now the boss.

With the assumption of that title your world has altered radically. First came the congratulations and the honeymoon months. Everyone assured you how far superior you were to your predecessor, who did not truly understand the needs and the finer qualities of this group of people. At first you may even have remained one of the gang in spite of your new position.

But then, some six months later, symptoms began to develop. The situation had changed. There was a sudden hush as you entered the coffee room. There was a party, and you alone were not invited. Was the axiom "once a supervisor never again a friend" to be true for you too?

Then came the inexplicable crises. Your budget was being threatened, but you had no idea who was threatening it. Why was your group under fire? What could you do to change their minds? How could you be held responsible when you hadn't a clue as to what was going on?

The next problem was the complaint about Elwood's personal hygiene. It was quite apparent that you, his manager, were to confront him about it. Your stomach still churns when you recall it.

This book is written for you who are facing the isolation, ambiguity, and stress of the first-line manager's position. You are the sergeant of your army, responsible for making the organization work, no matter what the obstacles. You hold the position that is crucial to your organization's success. It is at once the most pleasurable and creative position on the management ladder. Above your level, it becomes difficult to see results. Below your level, the excitement of planning and creating is often outweighed by the drudgery of carrying out the plans.

I decided to write this book because of the number of people I have seen in your position who were both well intentioned and technically well trained, yet were in the process of failing or of succeeding only marginally. The basic problem was their failure to realize that they alone would determine their own success or failure. They were waiting vainly for someone else to lead them to the right goals, the correct methods, and the desired results—like the *deus ex machina* of a Greek play waiting to descend in the last act and make all things right. If such a god exists in management, she surely remains in the wings.

The approach to management taken by the naturally successful is based on being self-reliant and encouraging self-reliance in others. Instead of waiting, I recommend doing. Instead of depending completely on management's guidance, I encourage taking risks. Don't wait for the world of work to begin running correctly—initiate a program to sort out and improve the part of the world nearest you.

Everyone is depending on you to bring it off. You must depend on yourself. If you don't, you risk joining the ranks of those who have lost the battle and, in the words of T. S. Eliot, join the "living, and partly living."

You will lose "not with a bang but a whimper." Short of sabotage, drunkenness on the job, or clearly immoral acts, most organizations will not fire you. They are quite willing to let anyone of your proven caliber hold a position and draw pay. Losing the battle does not mean leaving the organization. Losing the battle means:

Having little influence.

Being told what to do more often than telling others what to do.

Taking on the boring tasks instead of creative ones.

Making few decisions.

Preparing the reports to be used in others' decisions.

In a sense, the rare organization that fires the mediocre manager does that person a favor. The message is clear: The person may have failed but can learn from that failure and succeed in the next job. The tolerant organization that supports marginal performance for the sake of avoiding personal harm or offense lets you waste your life in favor of a consistent paycheck.

This is a workbook for the energetic reader. If you are content to put your feet up and doze as I preach the maxims that will guarantee success, you have the wrong book. Every chapter gives you the diagnostic instruments to help you analyze your own approach to management. I also suggest exercises to give you practice in new behavior. Try to pace yourself, making a conscious effort to test what you've learned in your own work environment. Many people are tempted, when knocking down a wall, to get a running start and lower their heads. The exercises in this book are designed to help you knock down the wall a brick at a time.

I believe that your success as a manager—or lack of it—depends on how you feel about yourself—on what was once called strength of character. I believe this, despite the fact that managers invariably assure me that the problem bothering them is located at least one level below themselves. This book is based on the principle that your first problem (or your first opportunity) is you, not those who report to you. More often than not, work groups reflect their manager's self-image. If your unit seems bedraggled and beaten, look in the mirror. If it is successful, happy, and productive, the odds are that you have set the pace. Where else do you think they have learned what it means to be employed in your organization, if not from you?

Since managing yourself must precede managing others, this book begins with you. Part I—40 percent of the book—focuses on helping you become a more self-reliant person. Part II gives you some techniques for getting your employees to become more self-reliant. In Part III I discuss approaches that will help you and your employees interact successfully with others, both outside and inside your organization. Part IV makes some final comments on just plain enjoying the practice of self-reliance.

According to the Sufis, a Mideastern religious group, people cannot be taught what they do not already know. They believe that all knowledge is innate.

Once a village invited a Sufi sage to come and teach them. The wiseman's first question was, "Do you know what I am about to say?" They answered, "No." He said, "Then there is no point in speaking to you, because you cannot learn what you do not already know."

Convinced that he had something to offer, they reinvited him to the village. Again he asked, "Do you know what I am about to say?"

This time, a little wiser, they answered, "Yes."

He said, "Then why should I talk to you, if you already know?"

They gave it one more try. This time, in answer to his opening question half the village answered yes and half answered no. To which he said, "Then let the half that answered yes tell the half that answered no."

The educational philosophy of this book lies midway between the Sufi principles and the Western presumption that people can be taught what they do not know. If you recognize that a book on self-reliant management is important for you to read, then you do know what I am about to say, although you do not know it clearly. You have the experience that has taught you that self-reliance is the successful approach to management. But you probably haven't articulated that experience.

This book provides the words and concepts with which to order and express your own experiential knowledge of self-reliance. Very little of what I say will be completely new to you. The responses I most expect and hope for are: "He's right. I never thought of saying it that way," or "So that's how that fits into the total picture," or "Yes, that's a clear way of saying what I'm trying to do."

PART I

THE
SELF-RELIANT
MANAGER

A key indicator of an organization's potential for success is the strength of its first-line managers. No amount of executive cleverness can overcome weakness at your level. On the contrary, if you are strong, you can often turn impossible situations into success. So, before talking about anybody else, this book begins with you and your self-reliance.

1

Why be self-reliant?

What is self-reliance? The problem is not to find the words to describe self-reliance, but to have those words mean something common to you and me. There are two semantic reasons for this difficulty: first, the stereotype of the self-reliant person and second, the fact that the term "self-reliant" is heavily loaded as a positive value.

THE STEREOTYPE

In looking for a model—one who exemplifies self-reliance in action—most people go back at least a century to figures like Daniel Boone and Buffalo Bill, the pioneers and the mountain men. These were self-reliant people. For the most part they spent their existence alone, depending on their own hands and their own tools to protect their lives and snatch sustenance from an unfriendly environment.

But is it essential to be alone to be self-reliant? Is it essential to live in poverty to be self-reliant?

Many people seem to think so. In a blind rush to avoid becoming organization people—wearers of the gray flannel suit with all the implications of conformity—many of our young and some of the middle-aged have abandoned our institutions and sought the privacy of the wilderness or the economic independence of the commune. They feel that in order to be self-reliant they must do everything for themselves and have nothing done for them.

I submit that they have misread the model by taking an incidental fact and making it essential. A person can be self-reliant and live in the midst of our society. There is no virtue in being poor. Pioneers did not choose poverty. As a matter of fact, most of them were struggling to become comfortable, if not rich. Nor did most of them find joy in being alone. Usually they organized wagon trains for travel and formed villages as soon as they were settled.

If making their own clothing and utensils was prized, why did they so willingly respond to the arrival of shopkeepers, tinkers, and other trades-men? Even Daniel Boone started a family and established a town as quickly as possible.

Standing on your own two feet does not mean that you must be either poor or alone. Paying for food with money you have earned is no less self-reliant than growing the food yourself. Discussing with your neighbors how to control crime in your area is no less self-reliant than moving to a rural commune to avoid crime.

In my definition, self-reliance will be an attitude you can assume for yourself without abandoning the amenities of society. As a matter of fact, in view of today's technology and today's problems, I consider those who seek solitary solutions as undeserving of the title *self-reliant.*

The modern man or woman who refuses to use the specialized skills of others is like a buffalo hunter who refuses to use a rifle or a pioneer who refuses to use an iron plow. This is not self-reliance; it is foolishness.

To understand my definition of self-reliance, you must first put aside the commonly held stereotype of the self-reliant person. Besides making it difficult to understand my meaning, the stereotype causes a further problem. Many people, perhaps yourself, would like to be more self-reliant, but the stereotype is too extreme a model for imitation. Roaming the woods is too far removed from busing into work every morning.

First flickering desires for increased self-reliance are quickly quashed when it appears that so much will have to be sacrificed. The definition of self-reliance provided here, and the model developed throughout the book, is achievable without going beyond the bounds of our normal society. My self-reliant person lives with others, interacts with them, and even depends on them. He or she does not try to make it isolated from others.

THE VALUE-LADEN TERM

Because this country was settled and developed under conditions of great hardship, and because it was founded on principles that permitted social and economic mobility, this society has always encouraged self-reliance. We therefore place high value on self-reliance. Now when you ask someone to define a term as loaded as this one, you'll find that its meaning is given in very personal terms, often bent way beyond its intended sense.

That's even true on a national scale. For instance, does communist Russia have a democracy? Because "democracy" is valued worldwide, Russia claims to be a democracy. It would seem that the Russian version of democracy has little to do with our definition.

Is my son a good boy? He thinks so, although he has had to stretch my originally quite tidy definition of "good boy" to include shouting at his father, spilling milk on the table, and, on occasion, repeating language he wasn't even supposed to have heard.

So, are you self-reliant? Of course you are! No matter how you distort the definition in order to shape it to fit you, you will see yourself as self-reliant. It is the human thing to do with a highly valued quality. How else would we describe ourselves? The alternatives are too socially disrespected for you to accept them readily as even partial definitions of yourself.

My definition
Self-reliance is the continuing act of taking responsibility for applying your own judgment, capabilities, and resources and those of others to solving problems and capturing opportunities.

Self-reliance is distinguished from *other-reliance* in that the other-reliant person allows his or her behavior to be dictated by the judgment of others and places the responsibility for success or failure on the shoulders of others. For example, when given a difficult assignment, the other-reliant person points out that the objective is impossible unless he or she is assured the full cooperation of several other departments. The other-reliant person waits for management to line up that cooperation.

Self-reliance is also different from *isolationism*. The isolationist does not utilize the opinions, capabilities, or resources of others but attempts to solve all problems independently. In the foregoing example the isolationist takes the objective back to the office and tries, somehow, to get it done without making internal support functions provide assistance, even if it means buying services from outside the company. The self-reliant person recognizes the need for help from others and *does* put pressure on management to line up such assistance. Moreover, the self-reliant person takes on the responsibility of pursuing that assistance.

What happens if the objective is not met? The other-reliant person of course blames the "uncooperative" departments and management. The isolationist blames himself or herself, for who else is there? The self-reliant person feels responsible for not having succeeded in influencing others for assistance.

The other-reliant person seeks advice so that the responsibility for action falls on the other person. This is a ploy to multiply the fingerprints on the murder weapon. There is no intention to use the advice. "I did what you told me and now look what happened."

Isolationists neither seek nor desire advice. They do what they do on their own, uninfluenced by the opinions of others. Self-reliant people seek advice depending on many aspects of the situation itself and on their own need for information. In the last analysis, even when totally dependent on the advice of others, the self-reliant person takes the responsibility for following the advice he or she sought.

Two quick tests will tell who is self-reliant and who is not. If you wish to know whether someone is self-reliant or other-reliant ask, "Whom do you hold responsible for success or failure?" The self-reliant person holds *self* responsible. The other-reliant person quickly shifts the responsibility to *others*. If you wish to know whether someone is isolationist or self-reliant ask, "Do you seek help?" The self-reliant person does; the isolationist does not. The table below shows the prototypical approach to several issues.

Characteristics of the Three Approaches

	Position		
Issue	Other-Reliance	Self-Reliance	*Isolationism*
Whom do I hold responsible?	I hold others responsible.	I am responsible for taking action and for getting others involved.	I am responsible for myself.
Where do I find resource?	I look to others.	I look to myself and others.	I am my only resource.
How do I make judgments?	I depend on others' judgments.	I consider others' judgments in making my own.	I make my own judgments.
How do I accomplish work?	I wait for others to do it.	I share it with others.	I do it myself.
How do I handle failure?	I blame others.	I accept it.	I accept it.
Do I initiate individual projects?	No, I don't.	Yes, but I will quickly get help.	Yes, and I will do it myself.
Do I initiate group projects?	No, I don't.	Yes.	No, I do things myself.

An exercise

To what extent are you self-reliant? As it's pretty hard to be objective about this kind of question, here are some suggestions to help you delve further into the issue.

1. Take everything from your "in" and "out" baskets. Sort the contents of each basket into two piles, which represent: My initiative and someone else's initiative. How much is going out because you decided it should go out, and how much is going out because someone else requested it? How much is coming in in response to your initiative, and how much is coming because someone else decided to send it to you without your asking? If you are self-reliant, a major portion of the contents should be there on your initiative or as a response to your initiative.

2. Pull out last week's calendar and review all the meetings and appointments you had. List them down the left-hand side of a blank piece of paper. On the right-hand side of the paper make five columns. The first is headed: "I called this meeting"; the second, "They called this meeting"; the third, "I had no hope of accomplishing anything"; the fourth, "I had hope of accomplishing something"; the fifth, "I actually did accomplish something." After each meeting or appointment put checks in the appropriate columns. (See Figure 1 for a sample format.)

Analyze the total picture and ask yourself, "Does this square with my image of myself as a self-reliant person, or do I avoid taking responsibility for my time, wasting it at the whims of others?"

3. Do you have a personal agenda for today or for tomorrow? Are there things you want to get done, or will you show up for work and go through the motions demanded by the normal routine phonecalls and visits of others? Examine today's calendar. What is on it as a direct result of your personal initiative?

4. Who is lined up to help you with a project or task during the next week? In particular, have you lined up anyone to help you who does not report directly to you? If you are not using others, you may not really be self-reliant at all. You may tend toward being an isolationist, trying to handle complex jobs on your own.

5. Who has lined you up to help them? Others recognize an isolationist very quickly. Because isolationists do not seek their assistance, out of common courtesy they cease to ask isolationists for their assistance. If nobody has asked for your assistance during the next week, consider the fact that you may be pegged as a person who prefers to work alone.

WHY BE SELF-RELIANT?

Although as a society we place high value on self-reliance, we are not, on the whole, self-reliant as individuals. In administering and scoring his

Figure 1. Analysis of daily appointments.

Appointments	I Called	They Called	No Hope	Had Hope	Did Fulfill	Comments

Personal Orientation Inventory, Dr. Everett Shostrum, the author of *Man, the Manipulator,** discovered that most people are significantly more other-directed than inner-directed when compared with a population of people judged by a group of therapists to have the appropriate balance. (The terms *other-directed* and *inner-directed* compare roughly to my use of other-reliant and self-reliant.)

Other-directed people look to other people for direction, and they are more concerned with the needs and feelings of others than with their own needs and feelings. By contrast, inner-directed people are more concerned with their own needs and feelings than with those of others; they look to themselves for direction. The therapists compared test scores on apparent state of happiness, personal strength, and ability to interact with the rest of society. From that comparison they were able to construct an ideal score for a well-balanced individual. The score indicated that well-balanced people were more inner-directed than other-directed.

Over the years large numbers of people have used the test. Their average score indicates that, despite our social values, most Americans are significantly more other-directed than the ideal.

Leaving the scientific tests aside, your own experience should indicate that few people seem to be in control of their own lives, in comparison with the many who have abandoned the rudder to someone else. Let's try to understand why.

Self-reliant people accept accountability for their actions. That means

*Everett L. Shostrum, *Man, the Manipulator: The Inner Journey from Manipulation to Actualization* (Nashville: Abingdon, 1967).

that if they succeed they will be rewarded, and if they fail they will accept the results.

Many people expect failure. They doubt their own competence. If they take a self-reliant stance they expect that over a period of time they will be taking the responsibility for many more failures than for successes. But if they stand around until someone else takes action, the chances are that they will witness, without having to bear responsibility, many more failures than successes. This witnessing of failure reinforces skepticism and certainly undermines self-confidence.

Self-reliant behavior irritates other people. It irritates those who understand it, and it irritates those who don't understand it even more.

I was once in a group, in the lobby of a motel, with a very self-reliant friend. He said, "I want a scotch and water." This caused quite a debate. Some people wanted a drink, but not in that particular bar. Some wanted to wait and have a drink with supper. Others preferred to adjourn the group and return to their homes for the evening. In the midst of the cacophony someone asked, "Where's Henry?" He was in the bar finishing his scotch and water. There was a general miffed feeling that although he had in no way harmed others or hindered their freedom of choice, he really should not have done that. He should have waited for the group to decide whether this was the time and place for his drink. If it is important to be liked by others, some people would rather not take the risk of offending them by showing such independence.

Many people prefer to believe that their destiny is in the hands of someone much mightier than they. Like children who depend on their parents, they rely on the agency director or the corporate president to guard their well-being. Conversely, taking a self-reliant stance is an indirect assertion that the distant father figure is quite fallible. If this is so, the self-reliant person may be gambling with his or her job security. This is more personal responsibility than many want.

Society is so organized that feelings of weakness and dependency are enhanced. There is an inadequate base for self-reliance. First, society is itself complex. It's hard to get things done. It's difficult to find the sources of power in a complicated bureaucracy. It's difficult to know the right answer when the answer requires in-depth understanding of sophisticated fields of knowledge. Second, the priests of society—the bureaucrats and the technicians—assume a leave-it-to-us attitude in dealing with "lay people." Some do this in order to protect their own economic interests, some out of simple frustration over the difficulty of communicating complicated information to others. Either way, the final impact is that most "lay people" feel helpless and do leave to the experts many crucial decisions that affect their own lives.

For example, my accountant says, "I have figured your taxes out correctly." Helplessly I stand dependent on him. I do not possess the knowledge he possesses. I do not have the computers he has. And I am absolutely bewildered by the tax laws. I am on weak ground for being self-reliant. I give him my trust, until the federal government informs me that he has made a mistake. The doctor says, "You are too nervous. Take these pills, they'll calm you down." I bow to professional wisdom, although prior to that moment it hadn't even occurred to me that I was nervous.

It's hard to be self-reliant when you feel overwhelmed. Yet daily we are overwhelmed by the difficult decisions of modern life. And daily the new magicians—the accountants, the lawyers, the doctors, the psychologists—encourage us to give up our self-reliance and trust them to handle our problems.

Can you add a number of your own reasons for not taking on a self-reliant stance? It will be a useful prelude to listing some reasons for being self-reliant. Put your objections on the table.

The exercise is very purposeful. I will assume that your reasons for not being self-reliant are valid. In some situations they may even be overriding. However, after you have finished making your list of reasons for not being self-reliant, examine the list of reasons I have prepared for being self-reliant. Then you can decide which seems to carry the most weight.

Have you ever tested the depths of your own resources? Perhaps you have run in a long-distance race and pressed yourself to the finish line a full minute faster than you have ever done in practice. Perhaps you misjudged the mileage on a canoe trip and found yourself still paddling hours after your body told you to stop. Perhaps the labor of giving birth to one of your children went beyond the normal bounds, and you truly doubted that you would be able to continue the pressure and survive. Perhaps someone you loved died and you were forced, despite your own grief, to be the source of stability and strength for others. In those moments you tested your own resources. You were reliant on yourself because you had no other choice. Were you surprised at your strength? Were you surprised at what you could do?

It is possible to go through life in an other-reliant stance and not know what you can do, not experience your own depths, not feel the individuality and power of your own uniqueness. Therefore, the first reason for being self-reliant is that it forces you to tap your own resources and allows you the pleasure of experiencing your own strength.

One of the problems in being either other-reliant or isolationist is that you simply don't get much done. The other-reliant person spends time waiting for others to do the job. Since most of them are in turn waiting for someone else, it adds up to a lot of waiting and very little doing. Because complex organizations have complex problems, the isolationist seldom possesses the technical skill as an individual to do the job. Consequently, the isolationist is usually unable to complete an important piece of work. If you want to see tasks competently finished, you must take on a self-reliant stance and see them through.

There is satisfaction to be gained through self-reliance in being able to put your autograph on the work and know that it is your creation. My two-year-old son began taking on small tasks and then answering the question "Who did it?" by crowing: *"Ben* did it." Haven't you felt the immense satisfaction at the end of a work day when you were able to point to even a very small accomplishment and announce: "I did it"? Self-reliant people experience that pleasure.

Boethius, a Roman philosopher, defined a person as the "center of attribution of a rational nature." Other-reliant people, by continually setting up situations so that they can avoid attribution and responsibility, actually deny personhood. Others learn that although this person occupies a desk and has a position on the organization chart, practically speaking he or she can safely be ignored. These people may be rational, but as no responsible acts can be attributed to them, others do not feel the impact of having a real person to contend with.

Usually such people put a great deal of energy into maintaining social contacts as a desperate attempt to remember that they really do exist. In contrast, the self-reliant person, by chosen style, demands attention and others soon know. If you don't encounter the self-reliant person, the self-reliant person will encounter you.

A story comes from the Korean War of a colonel who was quietly moved to one side, with a title and secretary but with no mission or job responsibilities. A lesser person would have settled down to wait out the war and hope for more productive days when it was over. However, this man began taking normal memos that crossed his desk and stamping them "Do nothing until you have consulted with me," signing them with an authoritative flourish. Soon he was back in the mainstream of activity. Instead of one secretary, he had an office staff of 25. He was consulted on matters of high importance and was regarded as an essential cog in the local army's machinery, although people weren't exactly sure what he was supposed to be doing.

Exaggerated perhaps, but organizations do respond to people who declare themselves as "centers of attribution." These people experience life at a depth at which others do not.

It usually takes much more energy and creativity to avoid work than it takes to do the work in the first place, particularly when other-reliance is used as a ploy for ducking. Elaborate constructs and excuses must be built and maintained to prove that it is really the other guy's problem that I am not getting things done. Endless hours are wasted in cocktail party conversation explaining the incompetence of peers, the bureaucratic weaknesses of management, the uncooperative spirit of other departments, all in the dim hope that the other person, who can't know the facts, will commiserate and support your contention that it is not you but others who are responsible for your lack of success.

A final, unarguable reason for self-reliance is that that is how the cards have been dealt. Any attempt to live life as if someone else is in charge is simply to duck the obvious rights and responsibilities that are your birthright. When you retire, who will accept your successes and failures? When you die, who is going to claim responsibility for your mistakes? Can you afford to let the years tick away and lay no claim to personal control of them? It is *your* life that's ticking away. No one else knows your needs, your desires, the balances and stresses of your situation the same way you do. Only you can know what you want. Only you can make the right decisions for yourself. That's the clincher.

Although I believe you should be self-reliant because it is a stance you want for yourself, in Chapter 2 I will review several reasons why organizations are coming increasingly to need self-reliant managers. True, many corporations and agencies discourage self-reliance, but I am convinced that it is destined to be the management style of the future.

You have already jotted down some reasons of your own for avoiding self-reliance. To close this chapter, now write on the same paper your personal reasons for increasing your self-reliance. Then compare lists. Don't you agree with me that self-reliance will actually be more rewarding? Why risk losing the most valuable things in life by allowing yourself to rely on others, or by isolating yourself from their help?

> Here are two titles worth looking into. The first of these is a novel, and the second a psychological study. Both books describe the attitudes and style of self-reliant people, although neither uses that term. Both also make a case for being self-reliant.
>
> Aldous Huxley, *Island* (New York: Harper & Row, 1962).
> Abraham Maslow, *Toward a Psychology of Being* (New York: Van Nostrand, 1962).

2

The organization of today

The best reason for developing self-reliance is the personal joy and interest it will allow you in your work life. No other reason will keep you going quite so well during those occasional periods in which your judgment seems to be proving a less reliable source of direction for you than the judgment of others is proving for them.

Self-reliance is not a "no-risk" stance. It demands that you take your own risks. You will land on your nose less often than "other-reliant" people do, but unlike them you will have no one else to blame when you fail. Also, since your tumbles occur separate from those of the group, they will be more obvious. Because there are always some who resent anyone taking the risks they refuse to take, your tumbles may even be greeted with a certain amount of glee. The motive that will continue to sustain you during these difficult periods is the understanding that you are doing things in a way you find personally satisfying.

But there are other motives, as well as other reasons, in favor of the self-reliant attitude. Organizational needs are shifting radically and swiftly. Organizations that previously encouraged "other-reliance" or encouraged "isolationism" are now finding themselves increasingly in need of self-reliant managers within the organization. The case against running an organization on an "other-reliant" model resembles the reasons for no longer allowing an "isolationist" management philosophy, but the two types differ enough to deserve separate treatment.

Self-reliance will be the organizational value of tomorrow; for many it is already a reality.

THE MOVE TO DEMILITARIZE

The normal cooporate organization chart of the 1970s differs only slightly from that designed by Julius Caesar, a corporate leader before the time of Christ. The persistence of Caesar's military model in corporations is neither accidental nor simply a carryover from centuries past. Love it or hate it, the model has worked! Despite the grumblings of subordinates trapped in the cogs of its grinding machinery and the curses of community groups struggling to avoid being crushed beneath its treads, the corporate legion continues to fire out products and conquer new holdings for its stockholders.

Although in some ways despised, the military-styled corporation is also emulated; its concept and approach have been adapted by even the most nonmilitary of people. Organizations dedicated to health, education, and welfare have *target* populations and *battle* plans and are managed by *objectives*. The most peaceful—the peace corps—is a corps, not a group, association, or brotherhood. Julius Caesar or George Patton would be comfortable with the terminology, thinking, and approach of just about any organization in the Western hemisphere, particularly any corporate organization.

The military organization is based on a system of total other-reliance. Do what you are told. Depend on your superior to determine what is right, as that person will depend on their immediate superior. This completely other-reliant approach has proved effective in the past. There are three major reasons for its success.

First it provided massive pressure against its chosen objectives. The other-reliant corporation can decide clearly and quickly on its own priorities and then organize to "get there firstest with the mostest," to quote General Grant. The sheer proportion, violence, and single-mindedness of its attack preclude defeat. What wild-eyed, small entrepreneurial firm wants to compete with Honeywell for the thermostat business?

Advertising, investment, engineering development, and mass production have meant success and profit on a grand scale.

The small firm can work longer hours, have smarter people, and be twice as dedicated as the large firm—yet it will probably lose. The self-styled, small-business gladiator is no more than a petty annoyance to the large organization.

Second, it tapped the dependency needs of the work force. The basic education of much of the work force included two to four years of military service, which followed immediately on the heels of a military-style education in high school and elementary school. The drill instructor's demands differed only in degree from those of the principal. Both relied heavily on vested authority. The recruit did not march because he saw it as beneficial to his own development—He marched because the drill instructor said, "March!" The pupil didn't study algebra out of a sense of joy, but because it was required of all sophomores.

Almost anyone entering the organization world after so thorough an indoctrination is geared to expect management to give orders as well and to see a clearly defined line of authority from the general down to himself, the buck private. Any other approach would be considered disappointing, vague, and inadequate.

Finally, military organization filled the national need for quantity, not quality. For the last 50 years the American people have called for large quantities of cheap goods. The question has not been "How good is the refrigerator?" but "How many can you turn out?" The Model T Ford was never the best car, but it cost little and was plentiful. So what if assembly-line craftsmanship rapidly deteriorated? The public still bought. The gravestones of the Hudson, Studebaker, and Packard were tributes to the folly of doing it any other way.

The other-reliant military organization is on the way out. Although it fit the needs of past eras extremely well, it is beginning to be inappropriate to the needs of the present. There are sure signs that in the immediate future the other-reliant military organization will be as out of place as a dinosaur on a subway. The situation is changing; organizations must rethink both their structure and their management style to fit this emerging situation. Here are the differences:

The situational nature of decisions

Most organizational generals would be embarrassed and offended to hear themselves described as merciless. Most of them are personally well bred and courteous. But corporations run on a military model, by their nature, show little respect for those unfortunates who get between them and their objectives. The battalion preparing to take the hill has little consideration for the village at the foot of the hill. The steel-making corporation has had little concern for Lake Erie. The economic-minded government architect has little concern for the privacy needs of the welfare client. The corporation seeking a cheaper labor force pays minimal attention to the jobless left behind.

The corporate manager needs to remember, however, that when Gulliver awoke, he found that the Lilliputians had tied him down. The Occupational Safety and Health Act, the Environmental Protection Agency, and tax laws are among the strings that the little people are using to make it impossible for the corporation to remain single-minded.

Government managers are finding that citizens and taxpayers are becoming increasingly unwilling to accept shoddy returns on their investments and are demanding care and consideration to their varied needs. Because they are managed in response to the needs of elected officials, government organizations have always tended to be more concerned with multiple priorities than have organizations in the private sector. The supposed superiority of the private sector's method of conducting business is often based on its willingness to be blind to the effects of more than 50 percent of what it is doing. For instance, the private sector can indeed deliver mail more cheaply than can a government agency, but they certainly would not deliver it to such poor customers as farmers spread out through the grain plains of Montana.

With every new administration, former vice-presidents of industrial corporations show up in Washington to run the federal government properly. Two to four years later, depending on their durability and their capacity to see the handwriting on the wall, they return to industry. Now they know that you cannot fire a civil service employee. Now they know that reorganization has no impact on the informal bureaucratic network. Now they know that if the senator from Utah wants to know what is happening on any particular program, all other work had better stop until the senator is informed.

The government itself is having more and more trouble sorting its multiple priorities as it becomes clearer how the work of one agency affects the work of another. The health department in one city announced to the local hospital that they would have to remove and replace all their new piping. This announcement was made 24 hours before the Department of Public Works was to obtain the director of the hospital's signature on a permission to run a badly needed road through hospital property. Needless to say, the hospital treated the roadbuilders as roughly as the city's health inspectors had treated them. The head of the health department preferred to run his organization with an eye to the health care and ethics of his profession. He hated getting involved in petty politics. After this incident, the city manager made the point that although enforcing the code was no less important than before, the department head was to hold "petty politics" in equal esteem with the code from that time on. The city couldn't afford to have its departments causing one another trouble, each zealously pursuing its own narrow objectives.

If organizations are not to be single minded they must find new ways, less other-reliant ways, of organizing. A vice-president of environmental concerns cannot turn the monolith from its appointed tasks single-handedly. Nor can a coordinator of minority affairs de-Caucasianize county government. Warren Avis made millions by getting his organization to focus on a single mission: "Lease driverless cars." How can his successors write that mission now? Lease—for only a small profit—in ways that enhance the dignity of the employees, advertised on recyclable media, cars relatively free from pollution, economical in the use of energy, even safer than required by federal standards, and stored in lots not offensive to the local community.

It would be impractical, if not impossible, for the general to send so complex a command. The only answer is to disband the army and re-form it into a flexible organization of self-reliant people who will ascertain what is the right course and choose the appropriate action to fit the multiple priorities of their present situation. This may involve taking only half the hill in order to spare the village.

The rate of change

The other-reliant organization depends on having the world standing still until it catches up. It takes a long time for a command to filter down from the top of a 10,000-person organization. There was a time when things progressed much more slowly. Buggies needed buggy whips for centuries.

Ours is a period of rapid change. The catalytic converter is at this writing required by law; by the time this book is published the odds are that catalytic converters will be in disfavor, for one reason or another. Black-and-white TV's have come and gone before my father went from his fifties to his seventies. The new math became the old math before those who were taught it in junior high graduated from high school. Anyone who is waiting for the boss to tell them what to do risks falling behind the pace of the times. All of this presumes that even the boss is able to keep up with the changes, while in fact she or he is close to drowning in the rapid flux.

By the time the director has figured out an adequate response to the senator from Utah, the senator has changed his mind. By the time the new school has been built, the baby boom is over. By the time the engineering department has figured out a practical way to produce item x, the research department reports that item y, x's replacement, is now available—and marketing reports that competitors are coming out with item z, which may outdate everything. With the world of rapid-fire change, there is little value in the large, lockstep, other-reliant organization.

Increasingly sophisticated technology

At one time the superintendent of a mill was expected to be an expert on all jobs performed within his area. The right to supervise depended on his ability to do any job better than anyone else in the plant. As technology is applied even to common mill operations, the expertise required for every job is such that only a full-time student of the machine can be expected to use it to its optimum. I know a manager of a research group who has only limited understanding of the technology of every one of his 15 subordinates. In such a situation, who relies on whom? The best judge of the quality and quantity of their work other than themselves is the marketplace. If their clients continue to hire and pay them, most likely they are doing something right, which should please him. If not, something must be wrong. He can help them analyze what's wrong, but he is certainly ill equipped to tell them their errors from his own knowledge.

The technology explosion is having an impact on all levels. The omnipotent executive everyone used to rely on doesn't understand how computers work or what they can do for him; he doesn't understand how memory typewriters work and has only a minimal idea of what they can do for him.

Will the glue stick? The research lab says so. Is the action legal? The law department says so. Will it sell? The marketeers say no. All these instances of the executive's inadequate grasp of the technology indicate that they do not rely on him, but it is rather he who relies on them.

What's the best way to do the job? Self-reliant professionals who understand the technology must answer the question for themselves. Their management cannot be relied on to control their activities because management lacks the technical knowledge.

New training methods

The educational system is changing rapidly. The new graduates have been geared to ask what they want out of life since the first grade. More and more men have avoided military service and aren't interested in whether a drill instructor can be a maturing influence. They not only don't obey the stentorian voice of authority, they don't even hear it. To them, George Patton is not a hero, but a mixed-up windbag who never worked out his adolescent conflicts.

This is not to say that members of this new breed are uncreative, lacking in initiative and drive, or incapable of being influenced. But they have been educated to be self-reliant. They are more influenced when presented with worthwhile tasks, by feeling that the corporation respects their dignity, and by their own respect for the intelligence of their management than by authority pure and simple.

For instance, consider the lovely young college graduate who has just joined your accounting department. Last year, as president of the student body, she challenged the college's fee structure before the board of direc-

tors and won. Don't expect her to sit meekly at her desk waiting for anyone's orders. She may look as sweet as her mother looked 25 years ago,
but she comes from a different mold.

New approaches to family life

One of the first moves of the Chinese communists in their attempt to
reprogram the Chinese people away from the older, Confucian, Buddhis-
tic models of behavior was to launch a direct attack on family life. Alternatives to family living were provided. Children were encouraged to ridicule, betray, and correct their parents. The policy backfired. Once taught
that they should not respect the authority of parents, the children lost
respect for all authority, including that of the Communist state.

It is in the family that each of us learns our relationship to authority.
The family of today is different in its views on authority and in its application than the family of 25 years ago. Extend the span to 50 years and the
days of Clarence Day's *Life with Father* and the difference becomes even
more radically apparent.

The increasing rate of change makes it increasingly difficult for parents
to predict the right or successful modes of behavior. My father's father
provided him with a model for manhood which, if slavishly followed,
would have—and for that matter did—provide a modicum of success. If I
were to follow some of my father's ideals for me, I would surely court disaster. And with the rate of change picking up, I have nothing but a feeling of helplessness in discussing ideals for my son and daughter.

As our concept of the earlier ideal becomes outmoded, so our ability to
take on an air of authority weakens. Increasingly, like it or not, we are
forced to discuss and compare our ideals with the ideals of others. In the
last analysis, we can only hope that our dialog and relationships with our
children will help them to build their ideals, develop them, and even
bend them as the world places new demands on them.

As these children of dialog enter organizations, their own inbred self-
reliance will demand a similar attitude among their supervisors and managers. If their parents couldn't tell them what was right when they were
13, they certainly won't be prepared to have their boss tell them what is
right now that they are 30.

The increasing need for craftsmanship

The consumer already has a car that falls apart. He doesn't need
another. If he can help it, the next car he buys will be one that will hold
together.

To continue to supply the American consumer, the American corporation must encourage craftsmanship. People who take pride in their work

do not take orders blindly, perform simple routine tasks, or work at continuous high speed.

Service may also be seen as a "product," for which skill and care are essential. The welfare client has no use for the demeaning clumsiness of well-meaning but inept social workers. Nor the efficient callousness of petty bureaucrats. How will America's poor be affected when they know they can count on meeting a social service person who not only possesses skills but whose own needs for respect are well taken care of? This will be a person who can give the clients' needs the attentive care and concentration of the craftsman.

It is in the personal dignity of self-reliance that the true craftsman is formed, whether the craftsman's object is a thing, such as a car, or a person, such as the welfare client. Only organizations that foster such self-reliance will have true craftsmen.

For the six reasons enumerated earlier, organizations that formerly used the heavily other-reliant organizational form and style of the military unit are shifting to more flexible forms of organization that depend on the self-reliant skills of managers and members. Even the military is no longer a particularly other-reliant organization. The same forces that affect other organizations are also affecting them. Some of the more creative experiments in self-reliant organization are now taking place within the military.

THE MOVE FROM ISOLATIONISM

In order to perform their functions, a number of professions, such as medicine, law, and education, used "isolated" professionals.

Although many professions have used this model, the most apparent and successful is the profession of medicine. That's why I've labeled this approach the "country doctor" model. This was an entirely different strategy from that of the military organization. The military strategy cared little for the type of person who actually performed the task and relied instead on the direct control of that person's behavior to assure that the task was performed properly. In contrast, the professional college concentrates on the formation of the person. The type of task to be performed by their graduates, the healing of the sick, the ministering in churches, the teaching of the young, the practice of law, could not be done on a mass scale but had to be done by a single person who lived at some distance from his or her colleagues. Rather than rely on controlling the person from outside, the professional college relied on controlling the person from within. Professional training included an ethic for members of the profession. For instance, doctors do attend patients at all hours.

Doctors do not criticize other doctors. Teachers remain up to date in their fields. Teachers take advantage of the credulity of students.

It may seem strange at first to think of this strategy as purely "organizational," since organizations are usually thought of as providing daily opportunity for people to interact. This is precisely the point. The country doctor strategy provides organizational control when you cannot have daily interaction with colleagues or management. Within this system the idea of review, or command, or even contact with an outside authority became repugnant. For a lawyer to be called in for a hearing on his professional behavior is an attack on his integrity in itself, no matter what the outcome of the actual hearing. On the other hand, in most corporations employees are regularly reviewed under the title of appraisal with minimal fanfare. They are not only given—they demand—a regular review of their management's opinion of them. To the lawyer, educated to be an isolated professional, the idea of a review would be an affront; to the corporate employee educated to be an other-reliant organization member, it is viewed as a right.

Doctors are extremely reluctant to offer their opinions on their colleagues' performances and judgments unless directly asked by that colleague. On the contrary, in most government organizations it is extremely unwise to take anything beyond a draft form until you have the opinions of everyone in your organization who may have expertise to offer on the subject. When your plan finally hits print, no one will be shy about offering their comments, even without solicitation. Under the cover of academic freedom the classroom has been the exclusive domain of that teacher, who has been assigned to that classroom. What the teacher says has gone relatively unchallenged.

Over time, these isolated professionals are increasingly coming together under one roof. However, instead of abandoning the country doctor model, even under one roof they have successfully remained isolated. Lawyers are partners, but the partners seldom seek one another's opinions. Fundamentally they tend to be partners because as individuals they do not need a full-time secretary, or cannot as individuals afford the rent, or one of them is starting and hopes to make a living off of the lowgrade work discarded by the senior partner.

Large medical clinics and hospitals do not have managers—they have administrators. The term manager implies a type of control which the medical profession isn't prepared to tolerate. One administrator I know was finally allowed to attend the doctors' meetings if he promised to take notes and write up the minutes. So much for the power of his position relative to theirs.

These professions are in a period of transition. The country doctor model worked relatively well, but it is now becoming a thing of the past. There are several reasons why professionals are being forced to form professional groups and turn from isolationism to self-reliance.

The reach of knowledge can no longer be mastered

Research has deepened our knowledge of every field. What was considered definitive twenty and thirty years ago is now simply an historical footnote. "The Atom" used to be a chapter title in college physics; now it is a semester course. Medicine has gone through similar expansions. At one time pediatrics was a specialty; now there are subspecialities within that specialty. In order to make a service available to clients and utilize the full reach of professional knowledge, practitioners are using a team approach. The generalist cannot understand all that must be understood, and the specialist knows only his or her own area in any depth. The team approach presumes that there is some kind of organization, which begins to erode the stance of the isolated professional.

The target of change is too broad for one specialty

I participated with a team of professionals in preparing an environmental impact statement for the U.S. Corps of Engineers. Engineers specializing in mineral deposits, water pressures, and dam construction were merged with specialists in wildlife, water runoff, scenic beauty, and the history of the region. Twenty years ago any one of them would have been the sole technician called in to study the problems of that area. However, since the possible impact of the change has such widespread effects the target of change becomes too enormous for any one of these specialties.

The question formerly asked of the hydroengineer was relatively simple, as the foreseen impact was simple: "If we build the dam this big, how much water will we retain?" However, as the ability to build the dam increased, so did the potential impact of building the dam. The hydroengineer can no longer predict the effects of doing what he was hired to do. What about the ducks? With more water will they continue to fly in here? If they do not fly in here, can they survive? Are there alternate sites? What will be the effects on the local economy of having all this land underwater? Are there any historic sites? What will happen to them? How about the coal in the area? Will it be covered? Will the shafts be flooded? Will the flooded shafts collapse? What will that do to the lake? To the ducks?

In medicine the old question, "How do we cure this person of the disease?" has been expanded to: "How do we eliminate or drastically reduce disease in this community?" The sheer size of the question and volume of the problem is drawing professionals out of their niches and forcing them to develop special ties in order to work together toward solving these problems. They are being forced to form professional teams.

Cost effectiveness

Equipment is too complicated and too expensive. Significant cost savings can be achieved by buying together and ending duplication. However, if we are to buy together, what will we buy? What brand? What specifications? And if we have avoided duplication, which of us will use the new machine when? Formerly isolated nomads are meeting at the well of limited funding to form the professional groups that make cost-saving decisions.

The freeing effect of transportation

One reason for placing isolated professionals out in the community was the inability of most people to travel very far. The one-room schoolhouse took in any child of school age who was able to hike or ride horseback to school. In other words, the professional came to the local community of the child. With modern busing and with 16 year olds driving, it is now possible for one school and numerous teachers to service a few hundred square miles of countryside.

The general practitioner either cured you or you risked dying en route any major center. Today, your only limitation in selecting a hospital is the money available for transportation.

Control Data Corporation is investing in a home computer system. It won't be long before adults who wish to further their education will be able to put this computer in their home and rely on a CDC professional group of educators to reach them anywhere in the country.

As these examples illustrate, increased mobility and ease of communication render the country doctor obsolete.

The speed of change

The primary driving force behind specialization in education and the medical profession is the same as that which is exerting so strong an influence on the military organization. Just keeping up with the field involves limiting the professional's personal endeavors to an ever narrower spectrum.

WHY THE SELF-RELIANT ORGANIZATION?

Although professionals are associated with a group, why is it imperative that they select the self-reliant form of organization? Why not select the

more military form of the other-reliant organization? There are a number
of reasons.

First, nobody became a doctor or lawyer because of an urge to wait on
the orders of others. Most of these professionals enjoy the independence
of wheeling and dealing offered by their fields. They are not about to give
up that independence, even if it were to prove more effective, efficient, or
cost effective.

Second, the situations faced by such professionals are far too risky to
be subjected to an unwieldy military model. Whereas most of us would
have no difficulty in tailoring a sales presentation to direct orders,
whether we agree with it or not, we would not be willing to perform an
operation that could prove fatal to a patient under similar duress.

The military model does not function well in the industrial sector, but it
won't work at all among professionals. Professional groups will lose their
capacity to perform sophisticated functions if other-reliant organizational
controls are applied effectively.

Neither groups nor governments can afford a margin of freedom in
times of near-starvation. Artistic freedom is precluded when all hands are
needed to wield the hoes. In the United States the risks in being self-
reliant have been greatly reduced by conditions of plenty. As a nation,
we can afford to allow individuals to experiment with their own lives—we
already have 8 percent more workers than jobs.

The American standard of living is such that the average welfare recipient's dole is equivalent to what an employed person earns in India. A
newspaper deliverer here earns more money than what 75 percent of the
world's population works for. A person can afford to fall to the bottom of
our economic ladder and still manage without too much difficulty. So
sticking your neck out and getting it nicked occasionally doesn't mean
you won't be able to make ends meet. We have a safety valve for self-
reliance.

On the next pages are two exercises to help you locate your group
or organization at some point on a continuum of self-reliant behavior.
The first exercise measures the degree to which your organization is self-
reliant or isolated. The second exercise predicts what kind of organization
yours should be based on a number of variables. Circle the numbers and
add up your scores in each column. By comparing the results of the two
exercises and discussing your own results with those of your peers, you
will be able to see if you are (1) at the vanguard of a trend toward self-
reliance, (2) moving inevitably toward self-reliance, or (3) stuck in an organization that holds no chance whatever for making self-reliance an inte-
gral part of your act.

For further reading on organization models, I suggest Schumacher's book. The assumption is that our world is organized as if people didn't matter. The author sketches new organization models designed to meet the real needs of people.

E. F. Schumacher, *Small Is Beautiful: Economics As If People Mattered* (New York: Harper & Row, 1973).

EXERCISE 1: PRESENT STATUS OF EMPLOYEES

Are employees other-reliant?	Are employees self-reliant?	Are employees isolated?
They wait for direction.	Wait for direction—varies with situation.	Employees never get directed.
|0|1|2|3|4|5|	|0|1|2|3|4|5|	|0|1|2|3|4|5|
false *true*	*false* *true*	*false* *true*
Know nothing about what management does.	Know a great deal about what management does.	Know nothing about what management does.
|0|1|2|3|4|5|	|0|1|2|3|4|5|	|0|1|2|3|4|5|
false *true*	*false* *true*	*false* *true*
Never influence the organization.	Often influence the organization.	Never influence the organization.
|0|1|2|3|4|5|	|0|1|2|3|4|5|	|0|1|2|3|4|5|
false *true*	*false* *true*	*false* *true*
Employees feel unimportant compared to management, but would like to become managers.	Employees feel on equal par with managers—willing to someday become managers.	Feel more valuable than manager—will try to avoid becoming one. Real work at their level.
|0|1|2|3|4|5|	|0|1|2|3|4|5|	|0|1|2|3|4|5|
false *true*	*false* *true*	*false* *true*
Employees possess no important information unknown to management.	Employees possess some important information unknown to management	Management knows next to nothing about what employees do.
|0|1|2|3|4|5|	|0|1|2|3|4|5|	|0|1|2|3|4|5|
false *true*	*false* *true*	*false* *true*
Total ____	**Total** ____	**Total** ____

EXERCISE 2: FUTURE STATUS OF EMPLOYEES

Employees should be other-reliant if:	Employees should be self-reliant if:	Employees should be isolated professionals if:
A product (widget) is manufactured in response to a consistent, nonvarying need.	A sophisticated function is performed in a complex environment (aerodynamics).	There is a collection of individuals whose work is aimed at individuals (country doctor, barber).
|0|1|2|3|4|5| *false* *true*	|0|1|2|3|4|5| *false* *true*	|0|1|2|3|4|5| *false* *true*
Once task set up, no further real decision making (military model).	There are some rather complex tasks for individuals.	There are some rather complex tasks for individuals.
|0|1|2|3|4|5| *false* *true*	|0|1|2|3|4|5| *false* *true*	|0|1|2|3|4|5| *false* *true*
There is an easily grasped, simple technology.	There is an increasingly sophisticated technology (new training needed).	There is an increasingly sophisticated technology that keeps shifting.
|0|1|2|3|4|5| *false* *true*	|0|1|2|3|4|5| *false* *true*	|0|1|2|3|4|5| *false* *true*
There is a slow rate of change. Easy to keep up.	There is a rapid rate of change. Hard to keep up.	There is a slow rate of change.
|0|1|2|3|4|5| *false* *true*	|0|1|2|3|4|5| *false* *true*	|0|1|2|3|4|5| *false* *true*
Economy is of prime importance.	Economy has some importance.	Economy has little importance.
|0|1|2|3|4|5| *false* *true*	|0|1|2|3|4|5| *false* *true*	|0|1|2|3|4|5| *false* *true*
Total ____	**Total** ____	**Total** ____

3

The psychology
of self-reliance

Only recently have business people come to appreciate the value of the science of psychology in their corporations. Government managers and the organizers of volunteer agencies are also beginning to experiment with applying the behavioral sciences to their field of management. Although individuals have sought the help of psychology for some time, managers of organizations have been much slower to obtain its assistance. There are a number of reasons for this reluctance.

The science of psychology is still in the process of being established. During the past 20 years, as the field has developed, what was one day considered a sure cure has in another day been seen as a poison. Not so long ago electroshock therapy was indiscriminately applied as a panacea for a generally vague disorder known as schizophrenia. Electroshock is now used far less frequently, and the generalized diagnosis of schizophrenia has been replaced in many cases with other more exacting descriptions.

Anyone with an ounce of skepticism is reluctant to use the methods of a science with tenuous axioms. Many have, of course, used psychology and psychological counseling to their personal betterment, even during this period of dismaying growth and development in the field. But for the most part they have grasped it because of the desperation of their personal situations as opposed to the certainty of its effectiveness. If you own an old clunker that wheezes, gasps, threatens to conk out at every stop-

31

light, and barely climbs the next hill, you may be willing to dump some new additive into the gas tank on the principle that things can't get worse. Any change in equilibrium may bring an improvement. However, you examine the same additive with a more skeptical eye if you own a race car that is showing a slight tendency to miss 100 miles per hour. Most organizations, at least in the minds and hearts of their managers, resemble the race car, not the clunker. Impartial outsiders may disagree with the managers' estimate of organizational well-being. But impartial outsiders are not in charge of what goes in the gas tank.

An invalid reason for avoiding applying psychology to management and managers is the fear that the people involved may experience psychological collapse as a result of such application. When I first began working with industry I was concerned that the personally confrontative training groups I was running would have devastating effects on the personality structure of some of the participants. I trembled at the thought of having word spread through the company that someone had had a "nervous breakdown" at one of my seminars. I soon found I had little to worry about. Anyone who could stand the normal stresses of management could easily withstand the stresses of the training group. The person who had just been rejected for a million-dollar contract and was trying to figure out the replacement source of salaries for 20 engineers was not about to fall apart at the seams because someone in a training group took exception to his bull-in-the-china-shop management style. Most managers can cope with a great deal of psychological stress; otherwise they wouldn't be managers.

Another reason for avoiding psychology is that psychologists have been pegged as appreciating only the side of human behavior that emphasizes softness, understanding, compassion, and caring. Managers have mistrusted the one-sidedness of such an approach, suspecting that it is the psychologist who wants the world oriented totally toward saving those who are weak. The manager neither feels weak nor believes that the organization that tolerates weakness is likely to have financial success.

A number of things have changed that now make psychology much more appropriately applied to organizations. Many organizations have begun to put psychologists on their payrolls, some managers having taken the risk of allowing the "shrink" in the door. As the psychologists have gained organizational experience they have also learned that the value structure of the naturally successful manager also tends to be healthy and health-producing. A psychologist friend once described the joy he experienced when he first began to understand the cleanness, the definiteness—the relief—of being able to fire a negative, recalcitrant employee. As a counselor and therapist, the psychologist would not have considered it a kosher option. Now, as a consultant to managers, it suddenly became legitimate. And he found that most people preferred to work in an environment in which total unwillingness to collaborate was given its appropriate dessert. Managers are teaching the psychologists the value of toughness in human interaction.

The psychologists are also refining their own tools. Research has expanded, not only into the psychology of sickness, but also into the psychology of health. No longer do theories represent the thinking of one practitioner and his or her particular clientele, but theories are supported by mountains of clinical data. The development of psychology as a science is far from complete, but it has proceeded a long way from its recent origin.

Now, instead of offering a secret, untested formula to put into the gas tank, psychology can offer advice on what might be subtly out of place or minimally out of tune in the behavior of an otherwise high-performance manager. You will benefit if you apply psychology to yourself and to your behavior.

THE PSYCHOLOGICAL UNDERPINNINGS OF SELF-RELIANCE

Here is a quiz. It is intended to help you understand yourself a little better as you read the rest of this chapter. This is not a professionally validated test. Enjoy taking it, but accept its results with a grain of salt.

I have found that most people have difficulty dealing with psychologists because they fear giving themselves to these priests of the new order. The doctor is to some extent a fraud. The assurance the doctor projects is all part of the act. They may be more right than wrong, but they are also more often slightly wrong than perfectly right.

1. When I was a child I could count on my parents.

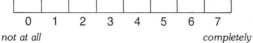

    0   1   2   3   4   5   6   7
not at all   *completely*

2. When I was a child I used to worry that my parents might leave me.

    0   1   2   3   4   5   6   7
often   *never*

3. When I was a child I didn't know if my parents really loved me.

very unsure   very sure

4. When I was a teenager I used to have fights with my parents.

never   often

5. When I was a teenager I had very different values from those of my parents.

not at all   radically
different   different

6. When I was a teenager, even in the midst of disagreement, my parents and I still understood that we loved one another.

doubted   sure

7. When I was a young adult I felt capable of handling almost any situation I faced.

never   usually

8. As a young adult new situations frightened me.

never   always

9. When I was a young adult, I enjoyed the challenge of difficult tasks.

avoided   sought

10. Now I enjoy working in organizations.

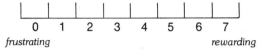

     0   1   2   3   4   5   6   7
frustrating   *rewarding*

11. I like helping others.

     0   1   2   3   4   5   6   7
not at all   *very much*

12. I like being helped by others.

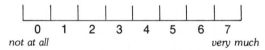

     0   1   2   3   4   5   6   7
not at all   *very much*

13. I don't like to see people in disagreement and will do whatever I can to smooth it over.

     0   1   2   3   4   5   6   7
yes   *no*

14. I enjoy arguments. I find that it makes things interesting and I learn from them.

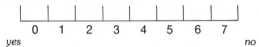

     0   1   2   3   4   5   6   7
yes   *no*

15. I feel I must explain to people when I am going to do something different so that I neither surprise nor upset them.

     0   1   2   3   4   5   6   7
seldom   *always*

Was your reaction to these questions, "What does this have to do with me as a manager?" During each stage of your life you develop perceptions and strategies for living. These perceptions remain a part of you as you go on to the next stage. Since you have been selected to be manager, your own developmental process must have been at least adequate, as you have learned how to solve the problems of life and seek its opportunities well enough to deserve promotion. But in your developmental process all may not have gone quite that well. You can improve your management approach through understanding where your own growth pattern varied from that of a pattern that would lead more directly to a healthy situation. Every issue that was inadequately solved during your growth that has not been addressed since stands between you and a self-reliant approach to management. It may be a minimal hindrance, or it may be a major block. But it is an impediment to increasing your competence.

Stage One: Learning to Depend on Others

During the earliest period of your life, from infancy to ten years, the biggest issue you face is learning to depend on other people, particularly your parents, to care for you, to love you, to provide the necessities of life. What were the perceptions you formed at that time? Did you feel that you could count on those around you? (See questions 1–3.) The same perception you built then tends to remain unless something radical has happened to change it. If you felt you could depend on others then, you will also feel that you can depend on others now.

When you ask your management for a reasonable increase in budget, you expect a fair hearing, and will be openly disappointed if you do not get it. When you call a client for an appointment, you do not worry about being rejected. You expect that, all things being equal, you will get the appointment. When you ask your employees to take on a task, you expect that they will do it. When you work on a project you expect that your results will be appreciated.

On the other hand, the person who as a child learned that others could not be counted on takes a very different, much less direct and open, approach to managing. The boss is consulted as little as possible, as he is expected to be capricious and uncaring; the boss must be manipulated, tricked, or threatened into doing what is right. There is no reason in the world for peers to cooperate. Enormous force must be brought to bear to get them to help with anything. Every time this person picks up the phone he expects rejection. Employees must be watched constantly and carefully.

The person who does count on others finds self-reliance an easy and natural stance. If he does what he wants to do, he fully expects that he can depend on others not to be offended. If he fails, he fully expects that others will pick him up and give him a fresh start.

The person who learned that he could not count on others moves toward either isolationism or other-reliance. He becomes an isolationist if in seeking his own ends he feels he cannot depend on others for support. Or he becomes "other-reliant." In desperation, he gives up his right to fulfill his own needs and lives his life according to the needs of others. Because he feels he cannot count on others, he attempts to curry favor by giving in to the will of the majority.

Stage Two: Learning to Fight

Between the ages of 10 and 20 there ensued the struggle to determine your own destiny, yet maintain ties with your family. How much could you depend on the family and at the same time disagree with it, rebel against it, be loyal to other groups, hold to different standards?

If you felt as a small child that you could count on your family, you had a head start as you entered your teens. In learning to battle, the battles were therefore less acrimonious, less unreasonable, although not necessarily less rigorous. You could fight, but you knew your parents would be there. Even with this sound beginning in stage one, there is the potential for a serious error in stage two. You may never have learned to fight at all. You continuously expect the world to treat you well and see no need to differentiate yourself from it. You turned out to be a "nice" guy, but without much character, the organization's patsy.

Early in my own career, as a clergyman, I worked with a number of families who were seriously pursuing excellence in family life. I began to notice that those families who most successfully met my own standards of Christian life were not particularly fun to be with. Often I sought the less placid environment of families in which major disagreements existed between parent and child. As the years passed, I noted that the "ideal" children faded into comfortable societal roles which they performed well, but without either creativity or excellence. On the other hand, where parent and child had fought through their differences the child grew into an adult unique in person and strong in character. Each of us is unique. Society tends to attack our uniqueness in many unintentional ways, trying to make us fit on its keypunch cards. If we are to remain ourselves, we must learn to struggle for our individuality. Apparently, adolescence is the period during which nature intended for us to initiate that struggle. Our own parents are designated, not so much as opponents, but as sparring partners to ready us for even stiffer opposition later in life. Many parents miss this distinction and think that they are supposed to win. They are not supposed to win. They are to provide useful opposition and then to gracefully lose. This understanding of defeat makes the winners strong young adults and the losers contented and proud parents.

If you felt as a small child that you could not depend on your family, adolescence was unbearably traumatic. Every move toward independence made you feel you were risking everything that was important in life. You felt that you either had to obey or, at least psychologically, leave your home and all its values behind. The struggle in your adolescence may have been resolved by your giving up, leaving you unwilling to engage in conflict with your peers or your management for anything you consider important. Or you may still be involved in the struggle. You see everything demanded of you as an affront to your dignity. You are still struggling symbolically with your father and mother for your own independence.

Questions 4–6 attempt to pick up the character of your adolescent struggle. Questions 4 and 5 ask if you had such a struggle. It is better to be able to answer those questions somewhere in the middle ranges. Question 6 asks if you felt loved in spite of your attempt, or perhaps even because of your attempt, to be your own person.

Stage Three: Learning to Be Independent

Because of the amount of training and nurturing required in our society, stage two can last for many years. In a more temperate climate and in a low-technology society, a man could make a living and a woman perform the work of wife and mother quite adequately by the middle teens. In our society the preparation for work life usually lasts until the 20th year, and in some graduate students, close to the 30th year.

Stage two is not a real reach for independence since the adolescent still intends to depend greatly on parents for tuition, board, and room. It is a reach for uniqueness of person while maintaining dependence of livelihood. During stage three you learned the thrill of standing alone. You learned that you could find your own job, that you could maintain your own apartment, plan and run your own life, fill you own needs for friendship, and all this without the material assistance of schools, churches, or even your own family.

Questions 7–9 inquire into the satisfaction you experienced during stage three. Unfortunately, many people skip this stage entirely. Women have traditionally gone from financial dependence on their father to financial dependence on their husband. Men go from emotional dependence on mother to emotional dependence on their wife. These people miss the satisfaction of realizing their inner strength.

Although the stage of independence passes quickly, it is invaluable in that you learn that you can do it. A woman who knows that she can support herself financially is in a much better position to allow a husband to support her. Although our society is not accustomed to it, the reverse is true for men. Certainly, the man who knows that he can survive quite well without a woman around to bolster his ego is certainly in a better position to enjoy having his ego bolstered. The proved ability to be in-dependent lowers the desperateness of having to have your needs met by others.

If you never had a period of successful independence you may be overly reliant on others for things you are really quite capable of obtain-ing for yourself. You may be afraid to confront, because you don't know that you could find another job if confrontation resulted in being fired. You may be afraid to alienate others because you don't know that you can make new friends. You may not know how far you can carry a proj-ect without the help, approval, or knowledge of others.

Stage Four: Becoming Dependable

Prior to the stage of independence, you belonged because you had to. During the stage of independence, you prove that you don't even have to belong. During the fourth stage, you seek out belonging, not because you have to, but because it brings a greater sense of peace and satisfac-tion and a richer sense of accomplishment than going it alone. You become someone others can depend on. In the third stage, you see your-self as separate from others; in the fourth you relax to once again work-ing with and through others. Competitiveness and the need to excel are reduced.

The independent person is good at starting new things, new ventures, new enterprises. The dependable person is good at keeping them alive and well over the decades, rather than over the years. For example, the "yippies" were young independent types who were able to confront a society that was not moving down a course consistent with humanity and its own ideals. However, their effect was short run, although extremely useful. The Hubert Humphreys and Gerald Fords are looked on to keep the nation running over the long haul.

The person in stage four does not belong out of a need for the organi-zation to keep him alive, but because of the joy he receives from con-tributing to the life and health of the organization. Questions 10–12 refer to this stage.

Stage Five: The Approach of Wisdom

There is a fifth stage—the period when energy begins to slip, interest wanes, and death approaches. The affairs of life, such as birth, marriage, and death, take on new importance, whereas the affairs of work, such as production, profit, and return on investment, are given a much less cen-tral position. Unfortunately, this fifth stage has little bearing on a book on management, since we quickly retire those who are entering it to places where their wisdom cannot have any impact on our behavior. If we did not, our work habits would change radically. Would not an old man who had had little to do with the birth of his sons feel differently than a middle-aged one about allowing maternity leave for fathers? Would not an old woman who had had to choose a career over a family feel differently than a younger one about providing day care close to the work setting? If older people maintained their ties with the world of work, such feelings as these might cause different corporate policies that would better integrate the world of the family and the institutions of work.

The bearing that it does have is that as the end stage of life is so little appreciated, so also the intermediate stages are entered reluctantly. Why the fear of turning 40? Is 40 so bad? I have found 40 to be so far the best age. But the issue is not being 40. The issue is being 65 and being tossed out to pasture while the young go on with the business of running the world. That is what we all wish to avoid, and in wishing to avoid it we only reluctantly move from one stage of growth to the next. If we cannot stop chronological time, we can at least stop developmental time. If we can't stop the clock, at least we can stop growing up.

A second bearing that it does have is that the whole of life is often kept at a distance from the life of work. I worked with a management team that finally diagnosed its "problem" as "middle age." They were holding themselves to a set of criteria not unuseful for the young. They were wondering why they no longer enjoyed trips, why they no longer saw sales as life-and-death issues, why they were no longer interested in staying up til midnight to get a proposal out the door. And then, the obvious hit them. They had, in the last 10 years, become middle-aged. And yet they had been unwilling to make way for the changes that had come with having children, holding positions of responsibility in the community, loss of muscle tone, impact of their work life, because they did not want to see that they were growing older.

The self-reliant manager is either in the fourth or fifth stage of personal development. None of the stages may be skipped if you are to reach full maturity. To the extent that the issues of these stages have not been resolved, it is impossible for you to be a self-reliant manager. You lack the emotional strength.

Here is a recap of problems that result from inadequate resolution.

Stage One: Dependence: To the degree that you have not successfully completed this stage you are unwilling to trust other people. You have to do everything for everybody. "Without your pulling it, the sun won't rise!" Fundamentally you are not very relaxed. You live with too much anxiety to be self-reliant.

Stage Two: Counterdependence. To the degree that you have not successfully entered this stage you are unwilling to assert yourself. Whatever the world wants, the world gets. You always feel that you must remain agreeable. Since other people can have what they want from you for the asking, you cannot be self-reliant. Or you may still be locked in it, testing your muscles against every authority figure who comes along. You tend to be feisty and challenging in nonproductive ways.

Stage Three: Independence. To the degree that you have not successfully completed this stage you are unwilling to test your own limits, to push yourself. You call for help all too quickly. You are reluctant to take on challenges. You are using only a percentage of your potential.

Stage Four: Dependability. To the degree that you have not successfully completed this stage you are unwilling to take on the responsibility of being an essential part of the organization. You are afraid to allow others to depend on you. You are unwilling to set aside the freedom of youth for the stability of maturity.

Stage Five: The approach of wisdom. Stage five does not occur until after retirement and therefore has no direct bearing on work life. However, indirectly it has a powerful impact. To the degree that you are unwilling to recognize that age and death are inevitable, you become insensitive to yourself and others as human beings. Instead of people, you see organizational roles. Instead of men and women attempting to live meaningful lives, you see organization charts. Instead of yourself, you experience a wind-up toy designed to spend certain hours, certain days, certain years jerking its way through the prescribed motions of organization life.

The nature of these blocks to development is such that no amount of wishing or intellectual understanding will make them go away. However, there is a technique that can have an excellent effect on the type of minor imbalance you may be facing. Awareness of the problem at the moment of its occurrence often has a gradual curative effect. If you can check your hand as you reach for the phone to find out if Sam has picked up the mail again, just as Sam had picked up the mail for the last three years, you can become aware of your inability to trust Sam to do the job. Even though this time you may still feel compelled to complete the call, after you have repeated this exercise 20 times, you may be able to skip a few calls, or even do without calling at all.

If you find yourself giving in too easily to someone else's needs and desires and you allow yourself to feel your fear of fighting, your fear will lessen. Gradually you will find yourself capable of picking small fights, and eventually of holding your own in normal conflict situations.

The secret to healing psychological wounds is gentle, patient care. If you feel that you have a severe problem, consider the use of a therapist to assist you in your development. A good therapist is neither better nor worse than any other good consultant. They have a specialty that may make your management life easier.

THE PSYCHOLOGICAL REWARDS OF SELF-RELIANCE

The fun of life is the fun of experiencing yourself in contact with your environment. If you and everyone around you move as one person, there is neither a feeling of contact nor any experience of movement. But as soon as there is movement in even slightly different directions, there is a sensation and, if it is done right, a pleasurable one. We make love by making contact and then moving our bodies against one another.

If the movement becomes severe, the result is not pleasure, but pain. Both the other-reliant person and the isolationist have had pain-producing contacts with people. The other-reliant person has decided to destroy the bad sense of contact by settling in with others and moving with them at all costs. The isolationist has decided to get as far away from others as possible, to a place where both the pleasure and pain of contact are unlikely. If, however, you can loosen yourself into a self-reliant stance, the work day's constant contact with people can bring you the same pleasure as dancing and playing basketball. You will then have a sense of being alive.

Reasonable disagreement and difference become spice, adding interest and change to what would otherwise be a dull and unproductive world, since these psychological rubbings put you in touch with others, and contribute to your feelings. (To check how you feel about this, refer to questions 13–15 at the beginning.)

Doing well on anything requires a commitment, diving into the task at a level where even the necessities of life don't seem as important as the task. Most of our great geniuses and leaders have given themselves to their roles with an ardor that permits no compromise. Although you may not seek the same level of intensity, in order to be intense at all you must decide what is worth your whole-hearted involvement. The other-reliant person cannot commit or be intense because nothing seems worth such dedication. Everyone gives a slightly different message about the value of a particular task. Who shall the other-reliant person believe? The other-reliant person will do something only after getting everyone else to agree.

The isolationist commits himself easily to a task. With so little contact with people, there is little to distract him from it. However, this type of commitment is a blind risk, similar to pulling the handle on a one-armed bandit. Since he has never checked out the worth or value of what he is doing with others, the odds are that what he does will not be valued. For every great artist who was left starving in a garret by humanity, there were probably 1000 hacks who were too isolationist to realize that their lives would have been more fulfilled had they painted billboards instead of abstractions, welded fenders instead of sculptures, written clear prose instead of obscure poetry.

A final psychological reward derived from a self-reliant stance is a deeper creativity. You have only your own judgment to rely on for the value of the initial germ of an idea that can later become a monumental enterprise. Germinal ideas frequently look slightly crazy. The creative person must be self-reliant. He knows that the initial idea must have time and energy invested in it before others can accurately judge it. The other-reliant person stifles the idea quickly or brings it up either in an awkward manner designed to get it rejected or prematurely, before it has been developed to the point where others can understand and appreciate it. The isolationist, of course, doesn't bring it up at all. Undoubtedly, somewhere an isolationist is hard at work designing a buggy whip holder, who intends to surprise the market with the timeliness of the idea.

WARM-UP EXERCISES

In the last two chapters you have been thinking about self-reliance and self-examination. It is now time to try some self-reliant activity. There is no way to tell how the water is without getting into the pool. Get into the shallow end of the pool. If you have never fought with anyone, don't start with a career-endangering battle with your corporation president. If you have never trusted anyone, don't begin with shifty Sam, the used car man. When I was a swimming instructor I had a rule, "Do not drown the student. It makes the later lessons dull." I want you around for Chapter 4, and preferably still employed.

Several exercises follow. You may wish to create your own. You must first decide whether you tend to be isolationist or other-reliant. The exercises give you steps toward arriving at a more self-reliant balance.

WORKING TOWARD SELF-RELIANCE

For other-reliant people:
—Initiate something you think needs doing, without checking it with anyone.

—Cancel your attendance at one meeting or appointment you do not think is useful.

—Think of something you need from someone, and then get it without regard for their feelings or needs.

—Do something without explaining to anyone where you are going or what you are doing.

For isolationists:

—Invite anyone to lunch and try to get to know them well during that one hour.

—Have a small party at your house.

—Ask your boss his or her opinion.

—Get help on your favorite project from your colleagues.

Here are four books I recommend for their unique insights into what it means to be a self-reliant human being. Rogers is a straightforward psychologist whose theories of behavior are based on the assumption that people are fundamentally worthwhile. Perls and Stevens are Gestalt therapists. Both present their feelings and thoughts in an autobiographical manner—interesting but a bit confusing. Sheehy will give you a full look at personal developments from childhood to death.

Frederick S. Perls, In and Out of the Garbage Pail (New York: Bantam Books, 1972).

Barry Stevens, Don't Push the River (Lafayette, California: Real People Press, 1976).

Carl Rogers, On Becoming a Person (Boston: Houghton Mifflin, 1961).

Gail Sheehy, Passages (New York: Dutton, 1976).

4

Establishing
a self-motivating cycle

Many executives and managers have a profound distaste for what they term "navel-gazing." Repelled by taking time to examine the "why" of their own behavior, they are convinced that the more you concern yourself with the whys of what you are doing, the more you risk defeat. The time for a defensive lineman to be wondering why he plays football is not in the fourth quarter of a hard-fought football game with the score close and the ball on his three-yard line.

While the action is taking place is a poor time to ask why. But, the more stressful the game, the higher the stakes, the more vital the success, the more useful it is to know the answer at the critical moment. If the answer to why he plays football is that success at football is vital to his family's financial survival, the defensive lineman will make a very firm stand indeed. I would prefer to run the play away from him and toward the lineman who is asking the question for the first time or the lineman who doesn't know the answer, or the lineman whose reason for playing is that football is fun.

Self-examination is valuable if it occurs during periods of leisure; it leads to answers and action, not simply to more introspection. I have worked with people who continued to ask the question "Why am I doing this?" long after the answer stared them in the face. They feared that if they accepted the answer they would have to change their life-styles. Such people give self-examination a bad name.

WHY IT PAYS TO KNOW WHAT MOTIVATES YOU

You learn to motivate yourself

I doubt there's a sillier or more futile complaint than to bemoan your organization's failure to motivate you. Self-reliant people motivate themselves. If you are of incomparable talent or outstanding intelligence the organization may decide to take an interest in raising your level of motivation. If you are closer to the ordinary mold of human, few people really care if you have any drive or not.

The skin isn't off their noses. You're the one who's unhappy. You're the one who feels unproductive. You're the one who's going nowhere. You'll have to be the one who does something about it.

But what can you do if you don't even know what motivates you? You must know what makes you happy if you are to tinker with your own situation and increase your incentive.

You increase your personal strength

Have you ever met a person who has experienced a religious conversion? Or have you experienced one yourself? Whether or not I agree with the particular philosophy to which someone has been converted, I have always been struck by the personal strength of the new convert. Part of that strength is based on the fact that they now have a mission—to fulfill the wishes of their Messiah, whoever He may be. The contest between the Christians and the lions, despite numerous temporary setbacks, was won by the Christians. They had a reason for winning—the lions did not.

If you know why you are on this particular job and what you intend to get from it, the odds that you'll succeed are greatly increased. You will have tapped the inner strength of your motivations.

You increase the efficiency with which you use your energy

If you know your goal, you can set your sights and not waste energy pursuing those things you really don't want. Get someone else to work on the budget if you enjoy closing a sale. If you enjoy playing with numbers, work on the budget and get someone else to close the sales. If you can't completely ignore tasks you find distasteful, you can at least minimize the energy you expend on them. My wife and I struggled over who was to do the dishes for the first year of our marriage. Then we discovered that she didn't mind washing them, and I didn't mind putting them away. Since then, what used to take a major effort is now routinely tucked into the important events of the day.

Often the marketing media and the general pressure of others within our culture confuse us as to what we want or what motivates us. I am not motivated by the need to have the sensuous young women of the nation struck with intense physical desire by my teeth, clothes, hair, shoes, or car. For one thing, the odds are slim that I will succeed in so striking them. For another, neither my wife nor my bank account will tolerate much indiscretion. Yet ad after ad presumes that I share these needs with everyone. So much so, that over time I risk the achievement of more realistic middle-aged goals simply because I have lost sight of my own motivation. I may start putting my energy into working at things I don't want because someone else told me I want them.

You reduce the need to avoid work

The trip to the cafeteria for a cup of coffee; the early break for the neighborhood bar; the extended lunch hour; the ever-lengthening conversations about last weekend, or bowling scores, or the vagrancies of top management are often misdirected attempts to satisfy legitimate needs. The needs are legitimate; the methods are ineffective. The real need may be for companionship, meaningful conversation, respect and affection from others, a chance to influence the fortunes of the organization—all commendable, worthy, genuine motivations, but unlikely to be fulfilled around the water cooler.

These very needs are much more likely to be fulfilled through doing work than through avoiding it. Companionship arises more from shared accomplishment than from shared proximity. Conversation with a purpose is more likely to be found meaningful than conversation about past events. Respect and affection follow what you have done, not what you are talking about doing. One well-written, factual memo to management will have more results than hours of grousing at the local pub. Understanding your own motivation will help you find more effective ways to implement it. Instead of avoiding it, you can use work to get what you want.

You eliminate confusion

At one time I was a member of a small consulting firm. During very tough days we often held late-night meetings to deal with business issues. Much of what we dealt with could have been left undone. My hindsight diagnosis is that we were all uncomfortable, nervous, and afraid that we weren't going to make it as a company and were desperately in need of one another's companionship. The meetings were our way of enticing one another to continue to keep each other's company. Had we known our own motivation, we could have found more pleasant ways to have maintained that companionship. An occasional game of volleyball together would have been much more helpful.

You increase your sense of success

If you know what you're trying to do, you can rejoice when you've done it. If you don't know your motives, it's hard to experience a sense of accomplishment. A business acquaintance of mine claims that he gets no joy from managing. Yet, for some reason, his empire continues to grow and grow. He treats every new annexation as if it were a happenstance addendum to his list of problems rather than a delightful conquest by a brilliant and deserving manager. I insist, to his violent disagreement, that if he could admit the obvious motivation that others pick out quite readily, he could quadruple the pleasure he gets from working. On the other hand, another business associate delights in her ability to understand the politics of working life and make the end results come out her way. Her unabashed acceptance of her own desires to gain more power and influence allows her to feel successful as she gets what she is driving at. If you don't understand your own motivation, you'll probably feel most like a failure when you've achieved what you've been working for.

AN EXERCISE

Later in this chapter I describe three areas of motivation—the "real" motivation—which I think can be the driving forces for your improved functioning as a manager. Using descriptions, I will help you analyze your own motivation. To prepare for that analysis now, before I have confused you with more information about motivation, take the following personal survey:

1. Write down your major activities for the last week. Include everything you did a fair amount of during business hours or leisure time—meeting, writing, interviewing, partying, watching TV, hobbies.

2. After each item write a number from 0 to 4, depending on the degree to which you enjoyed each of the things you did. Zero indicates active dislike, 1 mild dislike, 2 neutral, 3 mild enjoyment, 4 great enjoyment. Average these numbers and put that number at the bottom of the page. Save your answers; you will want to refer to them later in this chapter.

OVERRATED MOTIVATIONS

There are several reasons for being a manager which, although valid in themselves, probably won't motivate you highly in the long run.

How much does pay really count?

Pay is much overblown as a motivator. That is not to say that most of us don't prefer money—as much of it as we can get our hands on. All that is true. In that sense it is better to be a manager than a laborer. But you may be able to do as well as a bricklayer as you can as a manager. An aluminum stormdoor salesman who knows how to close a sale can probably afford a bigger house and a better car than you.

Even most bonus systems are influenced by too many other factors for you to expect that your work will result in any direct reward. Everyone else must work equally hard, and the marketplace must be favorable, for the bonus pot to be worth dividing.

Pay does have some motivating aspects. If a person earns only enough to pay for necessities, pay will motivate highly. Few managers, however, find themselves in so tight a condition.

Keeping the paycheck large enough to cover the bills will motivate the manager not to fail, but it won't be motivation enough to succeed. Consider the situation this way. If you really need the paycheck desperately, you can't afford to fail. If you can't afford to fail, you can't afford to take risks. But if you don't take risks, you won't accomplish that something extra we call success. In the end, if you really are desperate for pay, it will motivate you not to take the risks necessary for success.

If your pay is radically less than what comparable professionals earn you may find it a demotivating force. One of my client organizations has the problem that foremen (who are exempt from collecting pay for overtime) complain that their checks are on a par with their highest paid laborers after a normal week which does include overtime. Although their pay has not been diminished, the foremen feel cheated that they have to carry management responsibility and yet get paid no more for bearing that burden.

What about prestige?

In the above example, none of the disgruntled foremen wanted to return to laborer status. As managers, they wore white protective helmets instead of green, they had an office, they gave more orders than they took, they had some freedom, and they went home with their hands a shade cleaner, none of which would seem enough to make a man or woman bear the burdens of management. Yet, for some reason these men and women bore their burdens for little else. They had the prestige of being foremen.

The desire for prestige is a strong motivating force. However, the persons motivated by prestige may be more wrapped up in the symbols than in the job itself. They may chase the accoutrements of power, not power itself. Instead of working, they spend their time devising ways to get plant engineering to give them carpeting for their office. Or, in imitation of

Captain Queeg, they make sure that every subordinate's floor space is at least three square feet less than their own.

The outward sign of success

Most of us like to be rewarded for good work. If you win a race, you get a trophy. If you write the best essay, you get a plaque. If you're an excellent employee, you get to be manager. This is a misconception— people do not run races to win trophies, write essays to earn medals, and work hard to become manager. The runner and the writer run and write because they enjoy doing it well and appreciate having their talent recognized by others; otherwise they would run on a secluded path and write in a private diary. The statue and medal don't act as motivating forces; they symbolize recognition by others.

Most people who become managers have an excellent record of past performance because they enjoyed what they were doing. They are promoted to the office of manager as a sign of their success, as the trophy was given to the runner and the plaque to the essayist.

For those who insist on awarding management status for past performance, without regard to the person's managing ability, I advise that they consider another symbol—one that neither bears the responsibilities of management nor requires skills that the gifted employee may not possess. A simple person-to-person statement of appreciation will probably work well as a symbol of recognition and have fewer costly side effects.

All the above attempts to motivate, as well as many other potential methods, share the same limitations. They are rewards for past performance, but they are not built into the performance itself. It is one thing to be motivated by the results of writing a book and quite another to experience a reward from the process of writing it. For instance, Isaac Asimov, a prolific author of fiction, science fiction, and general science, enjoys seeing the words appear on the page in his typewriter. He finds the process of writing a pleasant experience. For that reason he writes more books and better books than authors who hate writing but enjoy being published.

There are managers who are willing to perform the distasteful tasks of their jobs because they receive more pay, or because they are treated with more respect, or because it is the obvious thing they should do to cap an already excellent technical career. Of course, it is possible to be an adequate manager and to be motivated by such feelings. But an excellent manager has a completely different starting point. Successful managers enjoy managing for itself; many have taken a pay reduction just to have a chance to be one. The deepest need we all have is simply to be allowed to be ourselves.

An associate of mine collapsed one day from a bleeding ulcer to awake in the psychiatric ward of the local hospital wrapped in feet of tubing designed to put nourishment in and take waste out. While in this captive state, he was gently assisted by a psychiatrist working to build a more leisurely, less frenetic approach to the process of existence than he had taken before. When he was dismissed from the hospital, he was given a variety of pills not only to ensure tranquillity for his mistreated stomach, but also to regulate his moods to more nearly match those of the normal population. After three months of unhappiness, he pitched the pills into the wastebasket and, except for finding a less rigorous job, went back to his normal routine. He said, "The doctor made a serious mistake. I've always been crazy. And I'll probably remain crazy. The doctor should have concentrated on curing my stomach, instead of trying to change my personality. That's just the way I am."

A terrible consequence of many motivators is that they tempt the wrong people to try to be managers. Fundamentally, these people don't like managing and would really be much happier elsewhere. The Western philosophical tradition is based on distrust of human nature. We have been taught to distrust our own feelings and thoughts in favor of either the king's (or state's) law or the church's law.

Even the first psychologists treated the unconscious mind and repressed feelings as sources of potential evil, a slumbering volcano of destructive lava to be dealt with tentatively and cautiously. Verbatim accounts of people in therapy are replete with statements of their frustrated rage at other people—incestuous desires for mothers, death wishes for fathers, urges so dangerous and twisted that only a producer of X-rated movies would risk putting them on the screen.

Faced with the potential dangers of unleashing these powerful negative fantasies, our social engineers of the past—priests, teachers, philosophers—recommended that humanity ignore feelings in favor of "doing the right thing." Only recently have such humanistic psychologists as Carl Rogers led us to a deeper understanding of human nature. He, and others like him, has developed a new style of therapy, one that doesn't attempt to impose a better order on the client, but which allows clients to reorder their own life from within.

This approach to therapy has shown that it is not within the depths of human desire that frightening quirks occur. The depths have been shown to be, for most people, pure and good. It is usually after the basic desires have been frustrated that a person's will to have what he wants is bent to dangerous extremes. In other words, it is only after having tried for years to do "the right thing," instead of the thing he or she wants to do, that a person's desires and urges become twisted and dangerous.

Salinger pointed out in *Franny and Zooey* that if you were to get under the skin of many a cross, incompetent, and arrogant college professor you would probably find one hell of a good auto mechanic. Somewhere along the line, the professor was told that with her intellectual gifts and feminine physique she should not enjoy nuts, bolts, carburetors, tires, and oil, but should enjoy poetry, works of literature, and clean classrooms. But before she could be taught this, she had to be taught not to trust her own feelings and desires, as evidenced by the fact that until her parents embarrassed her out of it, she spent her childhood taking things apart and putting them back together again.

I watched the chagrin and rage that occurred around a manager friend of mine when he announced that he disliked his managerial role and planned to return to technical work. It would have been one thing had he managed poorly, but he managed well. His own management tried to get him to stay, making dim threats about the general direction of his career. His employees applied moral pressure; they informed him that without him at the wheel, their department couldn't survive. In the midst of all of that, somehow he managed to trust himself enough to continue with the move. His judgment was accurate. He was much happier in the new position. And, incidentally, his replacement was delighted to take able control of his group.

With the spread of a philosophy of self-trust and the demise of the philosophy of self-repression, it is becoming increasingly easier to listen to your own feelings and desires, and to follow them to their logical conclusions. Easier, but still not easy.

The man or woman who enters management because of a genuine sense of pleasure in the process of management itself is much less likely to build the sour, crusty characteristics of older managers who never really enjoyed the job to begin with.

THE REAL MOTIVATORS

What are the real incentives for being a manager? The most complete work on the subject was done at Harvard by David McClelland and his associates. They distinguish three potential sources of motivation, each of which is operative in all of us to varying degrees.

Achievement Motivation

The achievement-motivated person enjoys turning out end products in the quickest, most efficient way. Deftness is the virtue of the achievement-oriented person. Although not necessarily energetic, he is perceived that way because of the size and quantity of his results. The achiever receives a personal reward from the clever method invented and not from the achievement itself.

Now, return to your survey. How many of the things you enjoyed involved creating some new approach to solving a problem efficiently? In those instances you were responding to your achievement motivation. Examples of achievement motivation that could have appeared on your list are (1) making a change in the planning process, (2) finding a way to increase filing efficiency, (3) reordering the work flow.

Some worthwhile questions to ask yourself about your results on the survey are: Was there high (or low) potential for an achievement-oriented person to be happy? Do my present patterns of work interface with my own needs for creating efficient ways to do things? Would this job be better filled by a more achievement-motivated person? Should I get out of this job and find one that will satisfy my own needs for achievement? Can this job be tailored to fit my personal needs better without ruining or severely damaging the needs of my organization?

Achievement motivation, like self-reliance, is a valued attribute in our society. The Yankee tinkerer, the entrepreneur, and the promotor are well rewarded in our legends and our pay scales. However, Harvard research indicates that achievement motivation is counterproductive in most management jobs. The odds are that if you are achievement oriented, you will be neither happy nor very good as a manager.

The achievement-oriented person is well suited at getting a group or a task started, but in the long run he is better off moving on to another group and another task. One inescapable difficulty for the achievement-oriented manager is not being able to leave well enough alone. Most employees would prefer to settle into some kind of comfortable routine. But about the time the routine has become clear, the achievement-oriented manager has developed a new and truly better way to get from here to there. Often amazed at the lack of obvious delight on the part of other employees, the achievement-oriented manager still persists in bringing one unwanted change after another into their lives.

Another affliction of the achievement-oriented manager is a bad case of the "here, let-me-do-thats." They find the fumblings of those who are less deft irritating and quickly by-step them to do the job right. To the annoyance and further demotivation of the subordinate, an achievement-motivated boss probably can and will do the job better than the employee.

I once played a handball doubles team with a man who had racked up a couple of state championships. After the first game, which we lost by a substantial margin, he designated a spot in the center of the floor. I stood there, and any balls that came right at me, I hit. Any other balls, behind, before, or beside me, he hit. He put on a dazzling display, and we won the next two games. The next week when I declined to be his partner he was hurt. He couldn't understand why I didn't enjoy his deft solution to the problem of my incompetence.

Affiliation Motivation

The person who is motivated by affiliation likes to be around people and enjoys having close relationships with them. This person strikes others as being caring and sensitive. Given a choice, nine times out of ten the affiliation-oriented person prefers to be with people rather than be alone.

What kinds of things do you enjoy doing because they bring you closer to other people? These activities indicate the extent to which you are motivated by this need. Furthermore, they indicate the extent to which your job rewards this motivation in you. It is important that you make the distinction between the simple pleasure you take in finding out what others feel in establishing relationships, and the desire to influence others to do what you think needs to be done. The affiliative person associates with others out of a liking for being close to other people. The ability to influence or be influenced is not a factor in affiliative motivation. People are enjoyed in themselves and for no other motivation.

The highly affiliative manager is extremely useful in small groups facing ambiguous and risky situations. If people are unsure as to what they should be doing and don't know the effects of their work, they feel helped by the manager who supports and likes them simply because they are people.

However, Harvard research indicates that being affiliatively motivated, except in the instance cited above, will have little or no positive influence on the effectiveness of the group of people you manage. As a matter of fact, if your desire to like and be liked by people is too great, you may not be able to perform effectively such management tasks as directing, reprimanding, and controlling. Management can be a daily bed of nails for a highly affiliative person as the manager is caught in the dilemma of friendship versus effectiveness.

The affiliative person often chooses the wrong tools to get the job of managing done. An employee who asks "What do I do today?" doesn't want to be asked about the family's health and fortunes. An employee who asks for feedback on a particular job prefers clear statements of strength and weakness to a general but passionate proclamation of the person's worth. On the whole, most people do not seek love from their boss. The affiliative manager often gives personal support when other things are needed.

Power Motivation

The best managers are those people who truly enjoy influencing others. How many of the things you enjoy doing involve getting others to do things, influencing the course of future events, advising and convincing others of the appropriate course of action? Remember, the desire of the power-oriented person is to have a strong impact on what happens. Many people confuse influence with control. Control is successfully demanding that others do exactly what you want. Influence involves making some change in the approach taken by others, while probably changing one's own approach too.

It may seem that this research contradicts the other trends I have mentioned, which are for a self-reliant stance among people and their organizations. Does a self-reliant person prefer a power-oriented manager? The self-reliant person would shun the authoritarian person, but the power-oriented person is rarely authoritarian.

The power-oriented person cares more about extending his own influence than having the right answer implemented. He will be quite willing to live with a "wrong" answer or two if the politics of maintaining or extending power are at issue. Also, he realizes that too many excursions into the specific domain of technical issues will rob him of the time needed to spread his influence even further.

Although this approach of the power-oriented person does not fit in perfectly with the values of our achievement-oriented society, it does allow those individuals who work for the power-motivated ample freedom to pursue their own ends and make their own mistakes, within limits.

Actually the achievement-oriented person is most likely to come across as authoritarian. The achievement-oriented person will enter situations in quite specific detail, in an effort to discover and implement the "right" answer. In so doing, he takes direction and control away from employees.

To some extent, motivation develops in early childhood. If you don't enjoy influencing others, or if you don't enjoy influencing others more than you need their affection, it is wise that you carefully examine the likelihood of your ever really enjoying a management job. On the other hand, you may be blocking motivation you already have because of your own fears.

If you found that you don't enjoy influencing other people, take a sheet of paper and list all the reasons you have for *not* influencing others. Perhaps you are afraid to be responsible for the results and prefer to leave others responsible. Perhaps you don't want to risk making others angry with you. Or perhaps you feel ignorant compared to most people, and don't value your own opinion enough to trust it. List your own reasons. Even if the exercise doesn't change your attitude, it may give you a perspective on your reluctance to influence which, in the long run, may bring about some change in your willingness to influence others.

Perhaps you found that you avoided close relationships. Although it is not the primary characteristic of a good manager, the willingness to be close to others and to understand their needs is a very valuable tool. Perform the same exercise again, only this time list your reasons for not getting close to others. Are you afraid that their needs will overwhelm you? Are you afraid that in the process of your getting to know them they may come to know you? Are you afraid to reveal that you're basically a sentimental person?

HOW TO HARNESS YOUR OWN MOTIVATION

Understand what motivates you

What motivates you will do you little good unless you can identify it. A person who doesn't know what he wants is like someone trying to fly a jet plane without understanding the controls. Such persons undoubtedly go somewhere, but they probably won't be satisfied with either the place or style of their arrival.

Consider changing your job

It is possible that your motivation simply doesn't fit the job you're in. If you are highly achievement oriented, for example, you may be facing the choice of either frustrating your own natural talents in favor of helping your employees grow or risking the ruin of their motivation and self-confidence as you plunge in to correct their mistakes. If you are highly affiliatively oriented, you may find that the nasty management decisions are made at too great an emotional price for your peace of mind.

I have known three men who stepped down from management when they were finally able to put enough distance between themselves and all those who insisted that managing is the obvious goal of all workers. The first realized that he preferred being a scientist. The second recognized his preference to being a trainer than to managing trainers. The third saw that none of his needs was effectively filled in organization life, and at the age of forty, he started a marina. In each case, the organization lost only a disheartened and partially successful manager. Each of these people was able to throw himself into the next job wholeheartedly and success- fully. Fortunately, each was replaced by a person who found that man- agement job exciting and fulfilling.

Manipulate your days to fit your own needs

If you are highly motivated to achieve and don't want to change jobs, maneuver things so that at least some of the technical work is done by you. Try to let the other guy make his own mistakes, but give yourself the treat of a special project or two. After all, you have as much right as any- body to have fun. However, be clear with yourself. You are not doing these projects because you are the boss, you are doing them for your own pleasure.

If you like being with other people, call meetings, schedule team proj- ects, pair up and solve problems with other people. There is always more than one way to skin a cat, so why not select the way you enjoy.

Learn to savor your accomplishments

Food bolted is not food enjoyed. Most of us don't take time to sit back and take pleasure in our daily accomplishments. Take time at the end of the day to rejoice over the things you have done that filled your own needs; think through the things you will do tomorrow that will allow you to put your own motivation to best use. It may sound selfish, but your employees will be delighted to see the boss happy.

Earlier in the book I mentioned the joy with which my son reviews his accomplishments: *"Ben* did it." Every day set the time aside for your own "Mary did it" or "Sam did it" session with yourself.

"I convinced them the budget was inaccurate."

"I got them to replan."

"Mary and I were a good team today."

One of my clients recognized that the nature of his business was such that his team never had a chance to celebrate its successes. Sales were closed over a period of months. At first, it would be premature to cele- brate because the deal could still collapse. And once the deal was closed, it was old hat and not worth celebrating. If he waited until all was final- ized he would wait until the judgment day.

Finally, he decided to have an annual celebration of all pending and past sales. At least this way, once a year, he and his team had a chance to savor their accomplishments. The people appreciated the chance to celebrate and could then plunge back into the turmoil with more zest. The celebration served as a reminder that despite the continued feeling of going uphill, they were actually making solid progress. The reminder of last year's victories gave them the inspiration to try for next year's successes.

Two classic works on management and motivation are those by Herzberg and McClelland. Although very little of Herzberg was actually used in constructing this chapter, if you haven't read him, you've missed a keystone theorist on the management of motivation. McClelland's book is the model on which much of my chapter is based. Expect more research, authority, exactitude, and information from it than you received here.

Frederick Herzberg, *Work and the Nature of Man* (New York: World, 1971).
David C. McClelland, *Power: The Inner Experience* (New York: Halsted, 1975).

5

Cracking
the stereotype

You work for what you want, not for some greater good. The achieve-ment-oriented manager is the most likely to have his or her desires ap-preciated by the organization. The affiliative manager's intentions for peace and friendship are seldom valued, except in non-task-oriented social agencies. The power-directed manager is often disliked, although the struggle to maintain influence produces extremely beneficial side ef-fects for the organization. Each of these management types is working toward a personal goal and producing the greater good as a by-product.

Your style is the strategy you use to turn your intentions into ac-complishments. For example, all baseball teams hope to win ball games, but each has a different approach to winning. One team bunts, steals, and manages to scratch out its scores. Another builds up an iron-clad defense. A third team counts on its power to put the ball over the fence at the critical moment. Just as each of these approaches identifies the style of a ball club, you have selected a personal style for managing.

AN EXERCISE

The following exercise will give you a hint at your own tendencies in selecting a management style. In answering the following situations, pre-tend that you have only 15 minutes to respond to the situation with your employee. In each situation you are to decide how much time will be given to each of three types of behavior. The point is to determine the amount of emphasis you will place on each behavior. Time is not the only determining factor, but in this case you obviously cannot raise your voice, cry, or use any other techniques to emphasize your point besides taking time. In dividing the 15 minutes in each case, you are not allowed to use up 5 minutes as the amount of time for any segment. In some cases, the example may be close enough to home to recall a similar event. If so, by all means use that event as your basis for dividing the time.

Situation One: Describing the Job
You have just hired a new employee. How much time will you spend:

(a) Telling him what you expect from him on the job.
(b) Asking him what he needs from you on the job.
(c) Discussing the official job description.

Situation Two: The Progress Report
It is the end of the month and you are reviewing with an employee her progress for the month. How much time will you spend:

(a) Giving your feeling on her progress.
(b) Soliciting her feelings on progress.
(c) Comparing actual progress to planned progress as expressed in the official documentation.

Situation Three: The Training Course
You are discussing the possibility of a training course with an employee. How much time will you spend:

(a) Giving your feelings about his attending.
(b) Asking him how he feels about attending.
(c) Discussing the official position of the organization.

Situation Four: Project Review
You are seeking information on a project that an employee has been working on for some time. It is a complicated project. How much time will you spend:

(a) Asking tough, penetrating questions to push the employee to the limit of her understanding.
(b) Asking general questions that let the employee roam about the subject and select important issues as she sees them.
(c) Asking a series of reasonable questions that cover the whole ground at a reasonable depth.

Situation Five: The Transfer
You are about to transfer an employee who cannot, in your opinion, continue to fulfill the responsibilities of his current job. How much time will you spend:

(a) Explaining your feelings on why you need someone else in the postition.
(b) Hearing his feelings about the impending transfer.
(c) Comparing his qualifications to the job description.

By now the three styles are probably beginning to take shape for you. The pattern is consistent from example to example. Answer (a) in all cases reflects the same style. The same holds for answers (b) and (c). The total minutes you spent for (a), (b), and (c) will give you a good idea of the style you tend to use most often—and the one your employees react to in working with you. If you wish to double-check this, you might want to show your answers to some close friends among your peers or your work group. Ask if they think you've done a fair job in picturing yourself.

LABELING THE STEREOTYPES

The answers to the quiz you have just taken correspond to three stereotyped styles: (a) aggressive, (b) supportive, and (c) logical. Picture the aggressive person as tense, a little hunched over, hurrying, and coming toward you with a problem, question, or suggestion. Picture the supportive manager as leaning back in the chair, with all the time in the world, listening to your every word, nodding, agreeing. The logical manager has clipped speech, clear ideas. Neither coming at you nor awaiting your arrival, the strictly logical manager has the passion for life and attendance to emotion of a metronome.

The following section takes a closer look at the way each works in several important aspects.

General Attitude Toward People

Managers who choose an aggressive style start with themselves. Not only "What do I want? What do I need?" but also "What should I do? What are my responsibilities? What are my solutions? What have I done to cause this problem?" The supportive manager focuses on others and asks not only "What should they do? What are their responsibilities?" but also "What are their needs, wants, and desires?" Finally, the manager who chooses a logical style is concerned neither with self nor with others, but with the facts of the case. "What are our responsibilities. What should we do?" The manager with the logical approach avoids personal needs and wants in favor of what is perceived as the demands of the common good, the work group, or the organization as a whole.

The Dominant Emotion

In conjunction with the aggressive manager's chewing-up-the-world style, the dominant emotion is irritation, often outright anger, and only an occasional lapse into something that resembles peace. One business manager reported to his technical counterpart in a team-building session that as they were passing in a hallway the technical manager snapped, "I haven't got time to see you today, I'm much too busy." The business manager hadn't even planned on seeing him, had no reason to see him, and had only intended to make his own way peacefully to the washroom. But he didn't take it personally. He knew that he was dealing with a pre-dominantly aggressive person who was busy realigning the world to more appropriate proportions and experiencing the natural irritation of a person immersed in a monumental task.

The supportive person expresses warmth and love for others. A sense of genuine liking for others is the usual impression, despite the circumstances. This manager is never too busy for your problem, never unwilling to care. Other people and their needs come before the supportive person's business. It is possible for some supportive managers to fake this type of expression for ulterior motives—many genuinely feel it. I once pointed out to such a manager that his kindly approach risked his chances for success in business. He, in turn, pointed out that he was a happy man, no matter what he risked.

The logical person avoids emotion. "Let's not get excited" is the dominant theme. Contract won or contract lost, the logical person plows on, seemingly oblivious to the size and nature of events. One logical manager of my acquaintance said that his wife was tempted to tell him that the baby was dead to see if he would evidence any feeling. His private hunch, which he was clever enough to conceal from her, was that he probably would neither express nor feel much. Obviously, in his case, the logical approach had become not so much a style as a pathology.

Relationship with Employees

The aggressive manager tends to divide the world into two camps: those who are with him, and those who are not. Adversaries are to be attacked, friends are to be defended. As the logical manager is just, so the aggressive manager is loyal. The aggressive manager may fight you in the team, but will stick up for you in public.

The supportive manager maintains a nurturing parental role. "If my kid (employee) did it, it's all right." However, the supportive manager is not likely to fight for an employee with other managers or executives. The supportive manager sees the good on both sides and works toward a compromise. Rather than go to battle for you, this type of manager will seek the end of the battle. The supportive manager is loyal, but does not have the fierce loyalty of the aggressive leader.

The logical manager keeps relationships with employees at a distance. One thing the employee can expect from this type of manager is justice. What the employee deserves, the employee will get.

Here's an experience I once had with a logical manager. As part of an organization development team consulting with the federal government, each of us was assigned a particular client with the management of the agency. Halfway through the year's progress, the management team held a meeting to evaluate the organization development effort and the work of the consultants. Each manager reported to the general meeting on the ways his consultant had helped or hindered the effort. The first manager to speak was the director of the planning office, a person who had a logical approach to management. As he totaled up the benefits provided by his consultant the results were devastating. What was undone, and misdone, was recounted in a calm, unemotional voice—two unmet goals were ticked off for every deed accomplished. I leaned over to my fellow consultant and asked, "Is he mad at you?" "Nope, he's just giving the facts."

I quivered. I happened to know that the facts in my case were not as good as the facts in his case. What was my client about to say? I need not have worried. My client, an aggressive rather than logical manager, praised me to the sky. The facts had nothing to do with it. I was on his team, I was loyal to him, and whatever his concerns about my work, he was not about to show anything but support in a public meeting.

For those of us who need mercy as often as we do justice, dealing with the logical manager can be a frightening experience.

Supportive managers (loyal both to team members and to the entire organization) and logical managers (loyal to the truth) often incite negative feelings in their own teams. "He doesn't stick up for us" or worse, "She lacks backbone." The judgment is harsh but common.

How Do the Stereotypes Motivate?

The aggressive manager drives and leads. Some days he is leading the troops, doing the technical work, pushing himself harder than anyone else, and some days he is stepping on the heels of the slow marchers blistering them into further effort.

The manager who chooses a supportive approach allows employees to be themselves until such time as they see that the work is worth doing. I know one research department where new employees are amazed to discover no one breathing down their backs about what they should or shouldn't do. After a couple of months of deciding whether or not they want to take the responsibility of working hard for their own success, they usually pitch in with both gusto and gratitude for being treated as adults. After all, they did decide originally to be research scientists. The supportive manager of this department has an ace in the hole. The nature of the business is such that within a year if they do not decide to pitch in they will not have generated the money to support their continued research.

The logical manager motivates with reasons. "Here are the rewards if you do this." "Here are the obligations you said you were willing to fulfill." "Here is what our professional code of ethics calls for."

THE NEED FOR FLEXIBILITY

No one style will work all the time. However, if it is not pushed to pathological porportions, one chosen style will probably be somewhat effective in coping with all situations. To obtain the best results, a mixture of styles is required. In the earlier example of baseball teams, the club that can bunt and steal, drive in the home runs, and field an iron-clad defense, depending on the situation, will come out ahead of teams that have mastered only one of these techniques. In the same way, if you are a self-reliant manager you do not rely on one style. You realize that if you have an employee who is a bump on a log, you must decide how you should best approach that person. First you must diagnose why the person is unwilling to move.

Perhaps his past experience has been such that whenever he tries to do something he becomes the object of everyone's anger for having messed up the situation. If you handle the situation aggressively, you will frighten this person even more, and will thus immobilize him. Logic will have little or no effect, since the problem is one of feeling, not of reason. On the other hand, the manager who patiently continues to support this person through a series of small risks, never becomes irritated with his failures, and shows warm appreciation for the successes of the overly sensitive subordinate will have a motivating effect. Even if this person is grossly incompetent, he will do better under this approach than with any other. You will at least have removed his anxiety, even if you both are still left with his lack of skill.

Perhaps your employee is a recalcitrant type who has no desire to do more than the boss demands. This person will play the supportive person for a sucker forever, giving just enough to keep the poor do-gooder satisfied that the therapy is taking effect. Through dominant style and force of will, an aggressive manager has a chance of winning the lazy person's respect and reluctant cooperation—not a tremendous victory for *esprit-de-corps,* but far better than a complete loss. Since the employee already knows the reasons for working, but prefers the rewards without the effort, the use of logic per se would have little impact—unless it is used to lay out job requirements that will be met or else.

Distinguish the logical manager's guillotine from the aggressive manager's ax. The former is never waved and seldom used. It is not employed in anger, but in response to facts. It falls but once. Click. And it's over. The problem is that the logical manager is seldom liked for this strategy. The aggressive manager has at least shown in the midst of fury that he cares. Otherwise why all the fuss? The logical manager's bloodless approach earns a bloodless response. The strictures will be followed, but others will never be converted to the cause.

In another case, a subordinate has felt that his work never got its just reward, and that those who are more appealing or friendlier were always placed at the head of the class by the teacher and given the raise and promotion by the manager. The absolute demonstrated justice shown by the logical manager will have more effect than either an aggressive or supportive strategy here.

Does a person who is about to set up the next quarter's work plan need the aggressive manager's advice, the supportive manager's coaching, or the logical manager's thoughtful explanations? Obviously, the answer will depend on the needs of that particular employee. There is nothing more annoying than getting support and love when all you wanted was someone to tell you you're making the right decision. Unless it is being given the right answer, when all you wanted was some encouragement that you still had time to get on the right track.

You are bound to favor one style of management over another for its appeal to your own disposition. However, there are things you can do to improve on the disposition nature has given you. First, understand your managing disposition, as well as its positive and negative effects. Second, look before you leap. Make a conscious decision about your management style, instead of doing what comes naturally. If you can't always look before you leap, at least try to look before leaping in critical circumstances. Third, if you find you are getting the wrong results from certain kinds of situations or with certain people, try a different approach the next time around.

As a self-reliant manager, rule number one is to adjust your style to the circumstances.

THE IMPACT OF FEAR ON MANAGEMENT STYLE

At the end of the play by the same name, Martha answers the question, "Who's afraid of Virginia Woolf?" saying, "I am George, I am." With these words, she tears down the image of herself she has carefully built over three acts as a tough, sophisticated, demanding woman. At the same moment, those playgoers who have been captured by Edward Albee's drama experience the tottering of their own images and the emerging awareness of their own fears.

More upsetting than the play itself is the audience's typical reaction. How else can you explain the noisy denial that anyone in real life could possibly be like George and Martha, except that it is true? Many people are deeply afraid and are hiding their fright under bluster, or sweetness, or cool detachment.

Fears and the three ways of concealing and coping with them have been identified in *Our Inner Conflicts,* by Karen Horney, a disciple of Sigmund Freud and a major theorist in her own right in the field of clinical psychology. The three pathological styles are the same as the three management styles simply carried to their far and rigid extremes. Aggressiveness becomes bluster when applied inappropriately. Support becomes uncalled-for sweetness. Cool is logic applied when emotion was needed.

According to Horney, the basic fear is being "found out." The frightened person is afraid of being seen by others as less than he has presented himself to be. He may even be afraid to admit to himself that he is only human, can fail as others fail, and make mistakes as others do.

Horney's clinical findings are useful in studying what happens to managers, why they often burn out, become apathetic, or disappear into the woodwork of lush offices in mid-career.

Managers, too, are people, even though their superiors act as if they were not, even though their subordinates like to forget it, and even though they themselves—at least during the working day—try to suppress it. Their peopleness often forces itself out in the last act, with the small ulcer, the early heart attack, or a form of spiritual exhaustion described variously by their younger peers as bitterness, sourness, or laziness.

Managers generally display a marked reluctance to admit that the pathological problems of others can in any way be associated with them. Presumably the clinical case studies of Horney and others were done with laborers, housewives, and movie actors—not with managers. For this reason, the hypothesis that a vast number have given in to fear can neither be proved nor disproved through questionnaires, interviews, or statistics. Most of our war heroes could admit they were afraid. They could admit it because they were not that afraid. The really frightened men were two steps slower getting out of the trenches, blended into the background when volunteers were requested, and were quietly skillful at avoiding the front lines. The really frightened manager is often too afraid to admit it.

It is what the manager does or doesn't do that shows fear—not what he or she does or doesn't admit. Basically the frightened manager demonstrates fear by choosing a set of behavior to respond to situations and hanging onto that management style no matter what the circumstances call for. Since he is unsure of his ability to cope with the actual situation, the manager ignores it and chooses to be warm and friendly, or hostile and attacking, or cold and distant. Without variation. He relies on an artificial approach rather than choosing his own response.

Fear blocks a manager's ability to judge. No longer can he choose whether to do this or that. His view of reality is blocked and distorted. His capacity to think things through is diminished. His willingness to trust himself to choose correct behavior vanishes. He no longer feels that he can rely on himself. He gives up perceptiveness, judgment, and freedom of choice in favor of a subtle form of other-reliance, reliance on a set of stereotyped behaviors.

Here are some damaging behaviors to be expected from the manager who is locked into one way of facing reality.

The supportative style (when it's always warm and loving)
—He never fires or demotes incompetent employees. He either bears with them or transfers them to another department.
—She always smiles; she never fights. Nothing is important enough to cause her to raise her voice, insist, or argue. In stress situations, hope that she is not the only person with the relevant facts and the right answer, because she will not present them adequately.
—He continually weasels to get his own way. This manager is the politician whose undercover deals and tricky subversions of the budget, accompanied with innocent looks and the refusal to openly confront issues, make it difficult for his own manager and peers to find out what is really going on, much less influence it.

The aggressive style (when it's always hostile and attacking)
—His employees have invented a thousand ways to avoid being pushed. They spend the greater part of their work life not on

work, but on defending themselves against his unreasonable attacks.

—Her peers leave her strictly alone. If she is right, she is right. If she
is wrong, why risk telling her? It's her funeral and the mourners
will all be wearing smiles.

—The boss treads carefully. Having this manager for a subordinate
is a little like having a mean Doberman pinscher for a watchdog.
He may discipline employees effectively, but he also scares the
boss.

The logical style (when it's always cold and distant)

—She is a functionary, not an actor. This manager never initiates
anything new or different. She does the job assigned, pushes
papers, fills out reports, makes sure people arrive on time, but
doesn't initiate or rock the boat.

—He doesn't care about anything or anybody except himself, not the
company, the products, the people, or his own management. This
manager would never think to ask the boss seriously, "What do
you need?" He simply doesn't care, as long as position and salary
are assured.

—She is dangerous when panicked. If the pressure is on, watch out.
Expect this manager to blame failure on her peers and undercut
the person she reports to. Much time has been spent making sure
she is not to blame for anything. The case prepared includes
"facts" that show that everyone else is guilty of gross malfeasance.

BREAKING OUT OF THE STEREOTYPE

Fear and its manifestations are not cured by friendly admonitions or
curt warnings. "I think you should be more creative," "Stop bad-
mouthing your peers," "Why don't you put in a little more energy on the
job?" are about as useful as asking a drowning man to calm down and
swim. Similarly, to the extent that you can identify such fear in yourself,
self-exhortations will help but little.

The stereotypes I have described differ only in degree, not in kind,
from you and me. To some extent we are all trapped in a particular style
by our own fear more than we would like. All of us could benefit from
some reduction in the fear we experience.

Harry Stack Sullivan and Kurt Lewin were the first behavioral scientists
to present a forceful case for the impact of the social environment on the
psychological state of individuals. Although a few managers' early train-

ing makes them potential candidates for individual therapy, for most managers a significant difference in the level of fear can be achieved by changing the organizational climate in which they spend their working life.

Making Changes in the Organization

The broad changes in approach are worth promoting in your organization to help reduce the fear experienced by yourself and other managers.

Get your organization to stop rewarding cowardly success and begin rewarding creative failure.

Why promote or even retain the person who simply stays afloat? Such floaters don't get the corporation anywhere, and a pool full of them and their innertubes (fringe benefits, prerogatives, fat expense accounts) makes it extremely difficult for anyone else to swim.

The appraisal and compensation systems may need to be redesigned to reward the person who tries out new ideas, even if he occasionally fails, instead of rewarding those who try the safe route with its limited payoff.

Get your organization to reduce ignorance.

Fear of the unknown has been with us since the days of cave dwellers. If employees don't know what their management is planning, or if management doesn't know what the employees are thinking, everybody is tense and overly cautious. I once observed a management team carefully initiate a series of personnel changes. They went through great pains to ensure that the changes would not upset employees, completely unaware that the employees had desired these very changes for years. The watch words are communicate and listen. Let people know. Provide the forum and atmosphere for pooling opinions. Don't withhold information unless it's absolutely necessary.

Get your organization to give everyone appropriate influence.

One of the reasons managers experience fear is they have so little control over their own destiny or their company's destiny. They feel helplessly swept along by the tide. The company that allows managers genuine influence over corporate direction not only taps a new source of information and advice, but reduces the fear managers experience at being helplessly dependent on the good will and good judgment of their top executives. You can do things aggressively in your own life that will reduce the need to be excessively careful.

Making Changes in Your Lifestyle

Here are some steps you can take to reduce the fear you experience on the job.

Free your wife and children—particularly your wife.

Many managers are paying the price for their family's slavery. If your wife neither works nor does anything creative with her life then she feels, perhaps justly, that you have a duty to provide her with such substitutes for fulfillment as a large home, a second car, finery, and country club membership. Straight confrontations in the business world are tough when a manager knows he may be unable to keep the family going in the style to which it has become accustomed.

Let your family do their own thing. In actual practice it is quite possible that nothing different will happen. A wife who no longer feels bound to the traditional role may choose to stay in it nevertheless. The difference is that it is her choice, and she knows that the whole family may have to go through a tight period if her manager-husband's behavior causes him financial difficulties. The college-bound high school student may still choose not to save for his own education, but he needs to know that his manager-mother is not planning to sacrifice her own integrity to a college fund.

You will experience some immediate costs for this freedom program. Meals may not be on the table. You may have to iron your own shirts. A transfer may not take place because your wife can't find her kind of work in the new area. But the freedom you will feel at having minimized your worries about what happens to the family if you get fired or sidetracked is well worth the price.

Changing deeply entrenched family patterns is, of course, much more easily said than done. If you are the only person in the family who is discontent with the way things are, the task will be extremely difficult. A family counselor may be useful to you as you reorganize the family. If your wife is unused to the newer women's roles she might seek the support of such organizations as University Centers for Women. The YWCA has in some areas taken magnificent steps in assisting women to grow beyond stereotyped roles.

As of now, I know of little that is being done for men to assist them in adjusting to their side of the change. If you think there is no such adjustment, imagine the first time you have to explain to your colleagues that you have to leave the meeting because your wife is working late and you have to pick up the kids from the day-care center before 5:00 P.M. or risk alienating your day-care mother. Or the first time you explain that you would get your wife to quit except she is making more money than you are, and if anyone quits logic demands it be you.

Earn interest—don't pay interest.
If you are heavily in debt you're not likely to risk much else. Of course, there are reasonable levels of debt, which are usefully maintained for tax purposes, but certainly anybody making over $25,000 a year who is desperate for the next paycheck is doing something wrong.

Having debts causes you to move cautiously for fear of getting into trouble. If you have not provided for the trouble, it's smart to stay afraid. You owe your soul to the company store. Any manager should have a savings buffer to keep him financially stable for at least three months.

Set your sights on a bigger view of life.
Join a group that helps you raise your sights above today and tomorrow's work.

If you quake at the thought of your boss's disapproval, you have forgotten that the boss is a mighty small mite on a large globe in an infinite universe. His disapproval won't remove you from the human race. Many managers who have become involved in school boards, community action groups, professional societies, and the like have, through the more democratic processes of these organizations, received the approval and recognition they did not find at work. This improved their self-reliance and, in turn, made them more competent managers.

Develop a network of business friends.
Do things for other people. Be quick to help. You gain at least two benefits. The first is it's fun. You feel good about yourself and your abilities. The second is that in the long run they will help you back. Invest your energy in other people, including your boss. (Or have you forgotten that your boss may need your help too?)

It is important to note that the friends you need will not be made simply by backslapping. Business friends are made by demonstrating over the years your awareness and concern for their needs and your active willingness to do things supportive of them.

When the time comes to say the difficult thing and you take the creative risk, it's relieving to know that the room is full of people who trust your good will, no matter what you are about to say, because you have developed close relationships with all of them.

Learn to live with a little bit of fear.
The manager who cannot tolerate being afraid sets up a risk-free managerial life. But he is also giving away any chance of success. By defini-

tion, success and accomplishment are not immediately within reach. Otherwise everyone would attain them. Success and accomplishment require extra steps beyond those taken by most people, and with those steps comes the risk of failure. Living with those risks is part of a self-reliant manager's life.

Don't try to realize your worst fantasies about what a real confrontation is like.
Everybody, at one time or other, daydreams about really telling the boss off. That polemic blast is not a courageous, fearless act. It is a mistake. There are other gentler, easier, less damaging ways to make your point. Be strategic in your choice of words and place. Enjoy your daydreams, but keep them daydreams. Embarrassing others in public and not leaving ways for others to save face will earn you punishment in the long run.

No one's life is totally free of fear—not even the manager's. As long as you can admit the existence and extent of your fears, these fears can be minimized and managed. A sophisticated manager treats fear as just one more factor in the management problem.

If fear is permitted to run rampant it can bring about a rigid managerial style. You are then blinded to the real demands of the situation, and the inevitable failure will bring about even more fear.

If you continually try to push people, even when it isn't appropriate, you will fail to get what you want. Over time, you will find yourself facing a growing pool of resentment. This will provoke more fear in you, and regrettably more coercive behavior.

If you continue with your logical approach, refusing to respond emotionally to the feelings of others, you will find youself pushed to one side by the majority of people. You will be ignored as a cold fish, too insensitive to be allowed insight into the fears and weaknesses of others. Soon you will find yourself isolated in your own little world of "facts," "truth," and "justice"—a world too unsatisfactorily cold and crystal for most of us to want to join you.

If you are supportive when the situation demands toughness, you will earn the contempt of your employees, and over time find yourself suckered, manipulated, tricked by them, since they no longer respect your will or needs. As fear increases, your next response will be to become even sweeter and continue to blind yourself to the fact that heads should be rolling and you should be rolling them. One manager I know was so stubbornly ignoring the facts of a similar situation that he began to have a recurring dream. In the dream, as he was walking through a woods several people from work ambushed and stabbed him. He was innocent even in the dream, for as he lay dying he was telling them that they could not have stabbed him since they were all his good friends.

An Exercise in Opposite Behavior

Besides working on ways to reduce your fear, there is another approach to increasing the flexibility of your management style. Simply make up your mind to do things differently. Every day for the next two weeks, first thing in the morning, select an event from the calendar and resolve to treat that situation differently than you normally would.

Start, perhaps, with a meeting where you would normally sit, listen, and be agreeable. Be determined to go, and push, question, exhort, and otherwise make an aggressive nuisance of yourself. Perhaps it is an employee interview in which you would normally tell the person everything you think and take little time to listen to his or her opinion. Spend the entire hour listening, taking notes, and asking friendly supportive questions. If you never exhibit a logical style make it a point to look up company policy on matters and do something exactly by the book every day. Keep a diary of the results of this opposite behavior.

Of course, the behavior is no more suited to the situation than your original and more natural behavior. But trying out new behavior in this manner will demonstrate that you can do things in a different and more experimental way without having the world collapse around you. Since we tend to do what we have had experience doing, and do it in the way we did it before, after two weeks of such practice you should have available to you an alternative set of behaviors, a choice of management style with which to face evolving situations.

For a deeper look at the underlying psychology of the three styles discussed in this chapter—aggressive, supportive, and logical—you might want to tackle this classic study.

Karen Horney, *Our Inner Conflicts* (New York: Norton, 1945).

6

Producing quality

Up to this point we have been discussing the underpinnings of self-reliance. In this chapter we move on to the primary purpose of self-reliance—to produce quality products and services. Whether your output involves quality health care, quality doors, quality financial services, or quality computers, the organization that promotes self-reliance has the best chances for providing a quality product. Because of the forces discussed in Chapter 2, other-reliant and isolationist organizations cannot match the quality produced by the self-reliant organization. The military lacks the flexibility, and the country doctor lacks the depth.

In most organizations the decision to produce quality or mediocre products is left to you. You must clarify for yourself whether or not you really want to do a good job, and demand the same from your employees. You can get by with a good deal less. If you avoid making frequent and obvious errors and display the normal human unwillingness to confront the unpleasant and rock the boat, you reduce your chances of being punished for mediocre results. On the other hand, doing excellent work won't necessarily mean huge increases in salary or dramatic leaps on the organization chart.

Why hustle, think lively, treat your situation as important when the repercussions of your own behavior for good or ill are likely to be unimpressive? Why should you care, when no one else does?

The answer is patience. You may not be rewarded immediately for your attention to quality, but others do see it, and over a period of time, slowly and gradually, more things tend to come the way of the person who produces quality than the person who does not. It is often this regard for quality which, over 20 years of service, will make a two- or three-level difference in the organization chart and a 10 or 20 percent difference in pay between two people whose basic skills are quite similar. But as we discussed in the last chapter, 20 years is a long time to wait for a reward. What, if any, are the more immediate rewards for caring about quality?

People in your organization will give you their respect. This will not happen right away, but it will occur long before the pay and position rewards come your way. The effects of being regarded highly by others are pleasant.

Despite these rewards, my experience as a consultant and counselor leads me to believe that the decision to care or not to care is a free one. There are no compelling reasons available for either side of the choice. I have come across mentally retarded busboys who have a firm, almost fanatical commitment to quality, and I have met bored general managers who give minimal attention to decisions that cross their desk.

People care because they choose to care. It is a matter of the will, not of reason. As such, caring defies explanation, for who can explain the unreasonable? How often have you met the object of a good friend's affections, the cause of his or her sleepless nights, the recipient of awestruck praises in absentia, only to wonder how your friend could have come to love that person?

Caring about quality is a case of love. One decides to love quality or one decides not to. It is not reasonable and cannot be. There are those who claim that being in love with anybody or anything is a better state of mind than not being in love, as the lover's special radiance attests. The tradeoff in peace and tranquility that comes in not caring is something the lover will gladly forgo.

Similarly, there are people who dive into their work and delight in doing the best job possible. They claim it is the only way to live, and there is a sparkle to their processes that lends support to their assertion. The person who is not so committed is consistently available for the two-martini lunch, can always assure the spouse of being home in time, and seldom has any cause for shortness of temper.

With the decision not to care comes a corresponding pressure to be either other-reliant or isolated. If you do not care, if you are not in love with your products, you then lack the motivational force to push for your own desires among those who really do care about their work. Inevitably you will either rely on them for direction or isolate yourself in order to avoid being pushed and pulled by their desires. You will be an aimless person treading water among those who have set clear and definite courses.

My bias is, of course, in favor of either caring now or learning to care. Unless you are inspired with that ingredient, the managerial behavior I am promoting will seem empty and without effect.

CARING ABOUT INPUT

Most managers lose the battle for a quality product before they realize the battle has begun. The weariness and the unwillingness to commit that pervade many managers' approach to the effort of producing quality products are caused by their realization that from the spot at which they begin they cannot achieve quality or see results. The battle is lost because of a lack of initial position or sufficient firepower. The manager had best surrender gracefully before the inevitable defeat. One pretends not to care when, if given a chance at winning, a real commitment would be made.

The major difference between British and Japanese motorcycles lies not in craftsmanship but in the factory machinery. The Japanese invested in excellent tools, which is why the Honda and the Yamaha now dominate a market that once belonged to the Triumph. When the Triumph owners gave the British factory worker tools left over from World War II, they should have been prepared for the workmanship to go down and the cost to go up.

In his book *Eupsychian Management* Abraham Maslow recounts some experiments that were run with chickens. The research scientist noted that the healthier chickens always chose the better food. Out of curiosity he began to control the food supply so that there was only one grade. After awhile the healthier chickens came to resemble the average ones in size and strength. But as soon as he stopped controlling the food supply the healthier chickens again chose the better food, and again grew substantially stronger than the average. It's a long way from chickens to people, but in the years since I first read this anecdote nothing has happened to deny its validity, and much has occurred to support it. Certain managers are better because of their ability to discern inferior conditions, materials, employees, and associates and reject them in favor of superior conditions, materials, employees, and associates.

An associate of mine has made an excellent career as a consultant. One of his prime attributes is his inability to tolerate anything less than quality. If his clients are unwilling to allow the optimum time for the meeting, hold it in the most auspicious setting, and make the necessary preparations for it, he will refuse to participate, make do, or create inferior alternatives. If his clients are willing to prepare as he insists, they have guaranteed the success of the meeting before it even takes place.

In order to produce quality, the self-reliant manager first insists on receiving quality. Others will not provide it automatically. Large corporations and agencies always have a number of support services that have quietly gone to sleep because the rest of the organization presumes that they will deliver quality service without being suborned. The print shop doesn't print on time, the people on the switchboard are curt to customers, and the accountant is quicker to highlight your error than to help. Few insist that things be changed for the better. Deprived of that feedback, they gradually slip into providing poor-quality service. Regrettably, many managers who are well aware that they would fare better with more support give in to receiving second-rate assistance in the belief that it is the inevitable price to be paid for belonging to an organization.

If you are accepting poor-quality input, you have your reasons. Take a piece of paper and jot them down now, before you read on. Then let's look at some of the usual reasons for accepting poor quality.

Organization Norms

The word "norm" refers to a rule that governs the behavior of a group of people. For instance, in my family, my father always sat at the head of the table. Although my wife and I run a "liberated" family, I would consider it a major affront if she were to sit at the head of the table, and I would be incensed if the children were even to look at that chair. At our house, without even discussing or suggesting it, that's the way it's done—it is the "norm." So it goes with any group of people. We are quick to form a set of group laws. Unwritten, unspoken, but binding. In organization psychology such laws are also known as norms.

Many organizations have a set of make-do norms. If written, they would read like this: "Doing it on a shoestring is better." "Pain is nice." "Suffering raises profit." An industrial corporation of my acquaintance has its professionals working in semifactory conditions. The computer programmers work in a small space above the explosion test laboratory. On days when tests are being run their calculations are shaken every 15 minutes as a fuse is set off one floor below. Over 100 engineers are practically wedged together in four-person cubicles divided by paper-thin chest-height partitions, while secretaries type inches away. So pervasive is the organization norm that such conditions are conducive to good work that no one ever seriously complains or expects any changes to be made.

Another example involves a colleague of mine who suggested that a rug be laid in her area. Plant engineering replied "We don't do that here." She, being obnoxious (God knows *what* these women in industry will demand next), asked "Why not?" The first response was, "Too expensive to install." She proved that the cost was no more than that of laying linoleum. The next response was, "Too expensive to maintain." She proved that the carpeting was less expensive to maintain. The next objection was, "The top brass will not like people like you having carpeting the same as they have." She checked. The top brass couldn't care less. The final response was the same as the first, "We don't do that here." The norm of suffering was immovable.

Later her gallant strivings made the difference when a director's office was turned into a conference room. In that instance, she got plant engineering to keep the already present carpet rather than rip it out and install linoleum as they had planned. She was able to convince them that the $1,000 it would take to ruin the room was too much to expend in the cause of enforcing the norm, "Ugliness is better."

Professional Norms

The same shoestring psychology that infects many organizations is also endemic to some professions. As a group, social workers tend to accept poor working conditions, poor support, and poor salaries, perhaps because they are in constant contact with the poor. Clearly, an opulent drop-in center for drug addicts in a slum area would be out of place, but there is no reason for the same center to be furnished with second-hand furniture, the professionals paid second-class salaries, and a large part of the clerical work handled by volunteers. The social work profession takes pride in its ability to get good work done in spite of the conditions. On the other hand, consider the quality of work that would be accomplished if the conditions were good.

In response to the argument that they are working with the best resources the community will provide, I offer a counter question. "Would a medical doctor put up with what a social worker endures? And through hard insistence on quality input wouldn't he or she get just what the doctor ordered?"

When professional groups do not feel like professionals they accept subprofessional treatment. The norm for some members of my own profession, human resource development, is to accept the demands and rejections of line management with good grace no matter what consequences such demands and rejections have for their own success or failure. If the boss wants an MBO course that covers the topic in 1 hour, he will get an MBO course that covers everything in 1 hour, despite the professional judgment that it cannot be done and done well in that brief time period.

Middle-Class Norms

Most of our fathers and mothers were, as my father would say, "working stiffs." They instilled in us their concept of our rights. The picture included such things as second or third in line (but not first), a Chevrolet (not a Cadillac), the public golf course (not the exclusive club). Along with that they instilled an approach to working life that said you pretty well tolerate whatever is given to you once you decide to accept a salary. Not caring became a virtue. My father stood on a concrete floor and tested meters, heaving them from one carriage to a test machine to another carriage. With his condition in mind it becomes difficult for me to complain if my secretary turns out smudgy copy. Many professionals break completely free from the limits of their beginnings. But many are still at least partially bound, unwilling to ask for much more than their parents had.

A general manager from middle-class small-town origins considered it a "hangup" to have a private office of any size or comfort. Major economic decisions affecting the well-being of hundreds of employees were made with his staff whispering to one another around his desk because they did not want his secretary on the other side of the partition to overhear their decision making.

The Need for Excuses

Excuses among runners are legendary before a long-distance race. "My calf has been cramping." "I haven't had time to train for this race." "I gotta cold." At the bang of the gun, these three characters will be off like a shot, holding the front positions for the 26 miles of the marathon, and running everyone else into the ground. They were not really crippled, they were just getting their excuses ready.

If the company will not give you the wherewithal to do the job, your excuse is ready. How can anyone expect you to succeed in inferior conditions? The draftsman gave you the drawings late, the marketeer did not set up the appointment, the secretary misspelled three words in the opening sentence, and you still managed to make a sale. Although the sale was not as big as it could have been, under such conditions, do you not still deserve to be congratulated?

Confrontation Is Painful

Most people prefer not to fight. Unless they feel they have a desperate need, they would rather not press others to deliver their due. How often do you wait mildly in a doctor's waiting room because he has double-scheduled? Do you find yourself apologizing to the mechanic for disturbing him when you return your incompletely repaired car for the third time? We allow ourselves to be pushed around, we accept shoddy work or look the other way, because it is the path of least resistance.

A large plant in a small German midwestern town considered confrontation a moral question. The managers were ingrained with the belief that to turn out less than a top-quality product was an immoral act, stealing from the company, so to speak. One would expect moral pressure to ensure that quality products would be passed down the line. However, the person who was most likely to judge the quality of any manager's work was not the manager of that particular unit, but the next manager in the material flow. When the next manager discovered an error he felt that to report it to the manager ahead of him was tantamount to accusing another manager of committing sin. The sanders would sand off huge hunks of waste rather than report the problem upstream. They would as soon accuse the preceding manager of adultery as poor craftsmanship. Although these people carried the issue to an extreme, I am convinced that one of the factors that blocked the willingness to confront poor quality input is the feeling that the other person is in the midst of a deliberate act of not producing quality, rather than that the person is ignorant of the effects of his or her activity.

Reexamine your list of reasons for allowing others to deliver poor-quality work. Are they enough to erode the chances for your own success?

WHAT ARE YOUR RIGHTS?

Nobody gives you rights. History points out that rights are always seized. The United States established its own rights by fighting for them. The civil rights movement and the women's movement attest to the long, hard struggle for equality endured by blacks and women in this country. And the blue-collar worker's rights were established only through the hard-won efforts of the labor unions. The strong do not give to the weak. The strong give only to the strong.

If you want better than second best, you've got to show that you won't accept less than first-rate performance. You *can* establish your rights to quality work as others have if you make it known that less will not do—and keep fighting for your standards.

The following categories are not all-inclusive, but they will give you a clue to analyzing your own situation. To some extent, you are your own Uncle Tom. You have become acculturated to the norm of your group and have not learned to expect anything different. For the black slave a kind and tolerant "massa" was simply enough. For the Black Panther, anything short of full support and opportunity will not be tolerated— "whitey" must give blacks a chance to recover from the bad start they were given. Take a hard look at the following categories and see where you are allowing your organization to shortchange you.

One problem you will face is that there may be a large number of Uncle Toms among your fellow first-line managers. Since they are willing to make do with whatever they are given they will make your task harder. In many of the following areas if you are to cause change with any success you need to acquire the support of your peers. Also you need to make a case to your management for the reasonableness of a shift in their policies and attitudes.

Physical surroundings: Can you pay attention to your work? Is your area unnecessarily dirty? Do you require privacy on occasion, and is it available to you? Do you require a room for conferences, and is it available to you? Are your surroundings gloomy?

Equipment: Does your equipment get in the way of your work? Do you have a calculator available, or do you have to do your own math long-hand? Do you have a dictaphone? Do your people have the right tools, or are they making do? Do they have sufficient space for their jobs?

Support people: Are you trying to be an accountant without knowing how? Are your functions clerical, or are you the manager? Are there departments out there somewhere in the organization whose mission is to help you and whose location you have never seen?

General information: Do you know what is going on? Do you know the future plans of your organization? Has management told you their goals and objectives?

Career development: What plans does your organization have for your future? What are your career opportunities? The potential training? The potential pay raises? The potential new experiences?

Advice and support: Do knowledgeable people, either managers or specialists, regularly sit with you to discuss what you are doing and offer you their opinions and counsel, or are you expected to manage your group alone? When you make decisions, do they join you and stand by you through your successes and failures?

Time: Are people pestering you about things as if they were desperate, when they really aren't? Do they insist that you work late tonight for something they don't need until tomorrow afternoon? Do you and your people have no time to think things through? Are you constantly kept in a state of turmoil? Do you have the time to be a manager, or are you trapped into being an expediter?

Budgetary discretion: How much do you have to say about how resources are used within your area? How tight is the line-item control? If you are allowed no budgetary discretion, then what does it mean to be a manager?

Influence on personnel decisions: Although you cannot expect your every whim to be gratified, how much control do you have over the personnel decisions for your area? Do others ship people in and out as if you had no say? Do you get stuck with poor craftspeople, second-rate technicians? Do you have to accept people who are personally incompatible with your group? Do you have to accept people you don't even like?

This is not an exhaustive list. You can express your rights in all these areas. In fact, you and your work group will function better if you do have control over your situation. But such rights will have to be established through your own efforts; no one will grant them to you.

CARING ABOUT YOURSELF AND CARING ABOUT OTHERS

Your management should want to fill your needs and encourage you to continue to demand further fulfillment.

First, everyone will recognize that machines require oil. The categories listed earlier are simply some of the oil you require if you are to function properly. It is useful to top management to have you define for them what you need rather than asking them to surmise your needs.

Second, people who care about themselves also care about others. The craftsperson who insists on having the right tool will not offend the customer with a shoddy product. The draftsman who insists on the correct drawing materials is the one whose blueprints can be trusted. Caring is an all-inclusive habit. You either care about everything or you care about nothing.

For example, you may consider it an unnecessary demand to insist on cheerfully painted walls in your area. After all, you rationalize, a person can learn to ignore ugly gray walls. But the act of "ignoring" is a task in itself, one that requires a certain amount of misdirected energy. If the issue is simply the color of the walls, the annoyance may be minimal, but if you are expected not only to ignore the walls, but the dirt, and the noise, and the broken spring in the chair, the energy put into "ignoring" becomes a measurable drain on your work effort and state of mind. But what sort of a person would willingly choose to be in the midst of such a mess in the first place? Won't the better craftspeople take out their revenge in small ways on the organization that forces them to tolerate these conditions?

An executive should be delighted to hear a manager reasonably insisting on improved quality support and input. It is a sign that such a manager will demand quality from the unit, and will provide quality service to customers, clients, and other groups within the organization. An essential step, then, toward being the self-reliant manager is to insist on receiving quality before you produce quality. However, your willingness to make demands is based on your image of yourself.

YOU AND YOUR SELF-IMAGE

The way you look at yourself defines the behavior you exhibit to the outside world. Take a moment now and off the top of your head, list ten words you feel describe you. From those ten self-describing words you will be able to predict your behavior. Without seeing them, I have difficulty assisting you in the analysis, but on the basis of other such lists I have seen, allow me to make some general predictions.

If you put "parent" well ahead of "manager," "professional," or "worker," the chances are fairly certain that you are unwilling to risk losing a constant salary for the thrill of some major job accomplishment. If your image of yourself is primarily that of a parent, then I can predict that your behavior will be designed to protect your loved one's livelihood more than to expand the frontiers of your job. Studies involving the people with top jobs in industry indicate that they see themselves as parents and spouses only as the last resort and as businesspeople first. Remember, I am not recommending this stance. I am saying that your behavior will flow from your self-image.

If you have a series of words that describe you as a "nice" guy, you probably have a hard time fighting for your needs and often find yourself stepped on by others.

If you have several words that say you are an important person in your own right, I expect that you will be able to insist on quality input to you and to your group. For example: "smart," "creative," "resourceful." The person who has a positive self-image expects quality; the person who has a low self-image expects and receives the second-rate treatment.

This is a circular phenomenon; after it has begun, it is sometimes hard to define which is the cause and which the effect. A negative self-image causes weak, passive, accepting behavior. People who perceive such behavior in you presume that you have judged yourself correctly and give you second-rate treatment. Upon receiving this treatment, you recognize that the other person has judged you negatively and presume the correctness of that judgment—you then feel even worse about yourself than you did before.

The same cycle can also work the other way. What woman has not made herself beautiful for some occasion and then become even more beautiful after receiving the praises of others? What man has not had occasion after having his physical prowess praised to rise to even greater heights? A friend of mine at age 36 was asked to show his I.D. at a bar by a pretty waitress to prove he was old enough to be served liquor. That night he hit four home runs in a company softball game. This is not necessarily a scientific cause-and-effect situation, but I have my suspicions that her mistaken judgment aided his softball skills.

Christianity had its initial success among the rejects of the first century. Slaves, prostitutes, sailors, were all convinced that they were worthwhile and suddenly they began to act and be saints, bishops, and preachers. Many of the modern self-help psychologies are based on getting the client or reader to alter their self-image. Tape recordings cajole clients to think as if they were millionaires, guaranteeing not all that falsely that if they can think like millionaires they may become millionaires.

So how did those of us who have a less than perfect image of ourselves, those of us who have gotten off on the wrong foot psychologically, how did we get involved in a negative cycle, and why do we stay trapped in a negative cycle?

Our parents, our family, our early surroundings undoubtedly convinced us that we did not deserve what was enjoyed by the rich or the intellectually endowed or the physically attractive. All these things are out of our reach unless we are willing to pay the costs, take the time, and endure the pain of intensive therapy. The price of therapy to bring us around from our clumsy beginnings must be judged against the need. Each person must judge his or her own level of difficulty. The help of a therapist in uncovering the cause of feelings of worthlessness may be of value.

If we are only moderately limping, and only slightly hard on ourselves, a sufficient cure can be brought about by interrupting the negative messages that we encounter daily. When your wife says she cannot take the time to stop what she is doing to discuss your problem, she is saying that she has defined you as less valuable than her projects. You have a choice. You can accept her definition, or you can interfere with it and force her to consciously decide who she considers valuable. My hope is that you will be her choice, and instead of getting a message that says "even your wife doesn't think you count," you will have a message that at least your wife thinks you count.

Right now, the hardness of the chair you are sitting in may be telling your body that it is not important enough for a pad. Interrupt that message, get yourself something comfortable to sit on. Tell yourself you are important.

Take a look at your car. Is that a manager's car? Or is it a rust-encrusted symbol of a failure? How does it feel to drive to work in it? Do you feel like a winner?

Does everyone in the office refer to you as "good old . . ." as in "good old Sam" or "good old Mary"? Do you hear under the superficial message of affection the deeper and deadlier message of contempt? How many times did you play up to their desires and ignore your own in order to deserve the "good old . . ." title?

You are causing the reactions you receive from others. Everybody's wife does not interrupt him. Everybody is not given the hard chair to sit on. Everybody does not drive a dumpy car. Everybody is not called "good old. . . ."

If you and your group are receiving less support than you need, you are signaling others that you are willing to accept less than first place. The self-reliant manager ensures that others get the message—this person is not there to be stepped on.

The risk that goes with this application of self-reliance is that you may give up being liked or even peacefully ignored. During coffee break you will be the SOB they gossip about who rejected the typing three times because of misspellings and smudges. Nobody else ever does that! Or you will be the manager who refused to sand the doors yourself, insisting that they be returned to the saw room to have the original errors corrected. Or you will be the manager who refused to sign the personnel requisitions until you had taken time to study them despite the fact that everyone else had already agreed that they were acceptable. You will not be loved as much but then you will be able to provide excellent quality in turn. Your clients will receive well-put-together letters, your doors will be sanded to specification, and your salary budget will fit your needs.

IMPROVING THE INPUT (AND THEREFORE THE OUTPUT)

SHORT-TERM EXERCISE

Every day, until you get bored with this exercise, realign one minor thing in your work life simply for your own pleasure. Have the office cleaned. Bring a picture from home and hang it up. Get the kind of pens you really like instead of the kind that are standardly supplied. Order a magazine (work-related) that you have always wanted. Work out a way with your secretary to get the typewriter out of your earshot. Get a new desk calendar and get rid of the one of the nubile young ladies from the factory that distresses your sense of feminine dignity.

LONG-TERM EXERCISE

Go back through the categories discussed under What Are Your Rights? The same categories are listed in Figure 2. First select the most critical areas in which you are being short-changed. Set up a long-term action plan to influence the way these categories are being handled by your management. Get support from others. Prepare presentations. Show management the advantages of change. Show them how such a change could have made things better last year. Find out why they do not want the change, and see if you can devise a way to bring about the change while still protecting their needs for control and oversight.

Figure 2. What are your rights? An action plan.

The Area You'd Like to Influence	Degree Present (0-100%)	My Plan for Change
Physical surroundings		
Equipment		
Support people		
General information		
Career development		
Advice and support		
Time		
Budgetary discretion		
Influence on hiring, etc.		
Other		

Here are two books on quality of life, quality of work. Despite its title, the first book is about quality. It bridges the gap between arts, letters, beach bums, and the production-oriented world of technocrats and managers. The second book will tell you how to stick your neck out—within reason—in order to get what you want and need.

Robert M. Pirsig, *Zen and the Art of Motorcycle Maintenance* (New York: Bantam, 1975).
Richard E. Byrd, *A Guide to Personal Risk Taking* (New York: AMA-COM, 1974).

7

Critical habits

I believe that to be a successful self-reliant manager you must develop five supporting habits—decisiveness, understanding, impulse control, friendly suspicion, and integrity.

Virtues or good habits are seldom discussed today. One reason for this is that so many people have lapsed into the helplessness of other-reliance or the impotence of isolationism.

You have no need to be a virtuous person, a person of good habits, if you are waiting for other people to decide your actions. It is much more important that these others who are directing your life be virtuous people. Perhaps this is why we prefer our presidents to be saints as well.

If you decide to spend your life isolated on a beach or in an office cubicle it will make no difference to others whether you are virtuous or not. Your crimes will be victimless and your beneficial acts will have only one recipient, yourself.

However, once you decide to become self-reliant, you begin to make a difference, and your good habits or lack of them will affect your fortunes and the fortunes of others.

You must be *decisive*. A moving person must make constant decisions about where to go next. You must develop the habit of understanding that pierces the clouds blocking a clear perception of what others are saying. Without understanding you will induce unnecessary obstacles to your own progress.

As a self-reliant person you are stronger. With the increased ability to make a difference must come increased judiciousness in using that ability, *impulse control.*

Also, as you grow stronger, more people will seek to use you for their own ends. Sometimes this will be to your own advantage, sometimes not. You must develop the habit of *friendly suspicion.*

Integrity is the unifying virtue. By it you keep yourself a whole person working for your own good and for the good of others in your context.

DECISIVENESS

For the self-reliant person decisiveness is easy, looking at the world from a certain orientation. For those who do not share that orientation, decisiveness is difficult. This orientation has three aspects. It is a present-moment orientation, an experimental orientation, and an imperfect world orientation.

The present-moment orientation

Decisiveness is easy if your actions are directed toward the present and not toward the past and the future. You realize that every moment requires the basic decision to do something or to do nothing. Once that decision is made, the next moment will also require you to make a similar decision, and will provide you the opportunity to remake the previous decision if it needs remaking. Only rarely are we required to make watershed decisions, those that cannot be undone. Many managers treat every decision as if it were crucial.

For example, you are to hire a new employee. A candidate is in your office. If you have a present orientation you have already decided to use this time productively, since this is the only 2 P.M., Thursday, August 5, 1976, you will ever be given. Therefore, you will choose either to hire or not to hire this person, or at least decide not to decide until you have more information or have interviewed more candidates.

If you are not present-moment oriented you may make the basic decision not to use the time productively. Of course, you will never admit what you are doing. Instead you will waste the time with unproductive activity. You may drag out the interview after you have learned all you can. You may fuss over coffee and cigarettes. You may indulge in a rambling discourse about your own needs and desires. If you realize that the only moment available for action is the present moment, and that the choice is between using this moment for something or not using this moment at all, you already have a strong inclination to be decisive.

The experimental orientation

Your decisions will come much more readily if you learn to develop an experimental "Let's try it" orientation. Ideas, daydreams, hypotheses, and plans are all too fuzzy to prove either valid or invalid. Often in the attempt to avoid wasting energy on mistaken projects the energy is wasted on forecasting whether or not the project is assured of success. Why not start the project? If its chances of succeeding are not very good you will know soon enough. You will only want to start those you have hope for in the first place. In the case of large projects that involve major commitments of time, energy, and money, you will not want to start the project itself, but will launch a pilot project first. But you will want to start something.

Consider how many times great inventors built it wrong before they built it right. They didn't talk about it. They experimented and built it. The telephone resulted from endless tinkering with a gadget—a gadget that for a long time did not work. Bell was not as accurate a designer as he was fortunate in his fiddlings with an experimental model.

Penicillin was discovered as the result of a series of laboratory accidents. So also was radium. However, such serendipitous happenings occur only if you have produced something that luck can help. As long as this thing exists only in your head awaiting your decision to create it, nothing good or bad can happen to it. Perhaps the reason so many are reticient with their ideas, parsimonious with their energy, and unwilling to risk putting their prototypes into the forum is that they fear their product will come to a bad end. For the safety they buy the children of their imaginations, they pay the price of the always deferred reward.

The imperfect-world orientation

Since the world is not perfect, don't wait for the perfect answer. Be content with a workable solution Many of the agonies over decision making result from a desire to come to the absolute right answer. Which is the perfect screwdriver to fit that screw? Which is the perfect hammer to hit that nail? Which is the perfect project to solve this problem? In the case of the hammer and the screwdriver we are quickly willing to accept one either slightly too large or slightly too small. In the case of the project, we tend to insist on having it exactly tuned to the problem. The problem often goes away having caused its damage by the time the project is perfected.

Decisiveness, a key supporting habit for the self-reliant manager, is more easily attained when it is understood in terms of its component parts—a passionate interest in using each moment well, a willingness to try things out rather than think and talk them out, and an acceptance of the imperfection of all solutions.

UNDERSTANDING

"He'll never be a good manager. He thinks he knows what's going on." In any field, there is no one quite so frightening as the people who possess the truth. On the one hand that possession contributes immeasurably to their personal strength. They are not swayed by the same doubts and concerns that plague others. On the other hand, their possession of the truth is a chimera, and as they plow through the areas of their ignorance their strength and assurance often have devastating effects.

The manager who presumes to know what is going on and never bothers to ask avoids finding out the important aspects of the situation. Indirectly, such a manager's organization finds ways of shunting the "omniscient" manager into engaging in projects and tasks whose simplicity of goals matches the simplicity of the manager's understanding.

The self-reliant manager depends on personal judgments and perceptions as the basis for action. But joined to that self-reliance is the humble realization that no one can have the whole picture, and that enlisting the aid of others to contribute to his or her understanding is clearly wanted.

Recognize that once you became a manager you were shut out from the friendly, informal communications network of other employees. No longer do they spontaneously tell you the latest gossip. Before you became a manager you couldn't help hearing of the mistakes and errors of other employees. Now that you are in a position of power, only with reluctance will these failures be reported to you. As an employee you heard of the foibles and idiosyncrasies of managers—why they should be avoided and distrusted and their pathologies and quirks. Now you no longer hear about them. Why not? Because now you are the subject of such conversations.

Your peers in management have their own problems. They may have conceived of solutions you need, they may be performing activities you could usefully copy, and they may even have insights into your operations and its problems. But it is unlikely that they will find the time or the inclination to talk with you on their own initiative.

Your own management is overwhelmed with pressures only some of which are known to you. Often the unsolved problems your immediate superior is working on now will become your problems next year. Yet so caught in the turmoil is your manager that the thought of soliciting your help hasn't even come up.

If you want to find out what is going on, you will have to ask.

Allow time. Sit down and talk with people. Talk with them privately, where they do not need to bend what they say, and edit it to fit the lowest common denominator of all those within earshot. It takes time for people to decide what they want to talk about. They are checking your mood, your receptivity, and they are weighing the risks involved in opening up. Do not cut them off prematurely. Allow time! Allow time for your peers and for your manager. They are going through the same testing process as you and your employees in deciding the risks and value of sharing the whole truth.

Ask questions. Let the people you are talking with know that you want to find out what they think. Since it is difficult to pinpoint in advance the areas in which their knowledge could be useful to you, start with more general questions. "How is it going?" "How are we doing?" Then follow their lead and ask more specific questions in the areas they open up in response to the general question. "Things are going pretty good, except for those files." Then ask, "The files are a problem?"

Generally you should give the impression as well as cultivate a genuine interest in wanting to know about anything they want to tell you.

Respect the answers. If they say that they are having a problem filing certain documents, don't make the mistake of saying, "That's no problem." If they think it's a problem, treat it as a problem and help them solve it. They may even be testing to see if you are willing to listen to another more difficult problem they would like to discuss. Certainly they are testing generally to see if after all this effort in asking them to chat, you intend to value what they say.

If your manager says, "I have some financial problems," the right answer is, "How can I help?" If a peer suggests a new course of action for you and your group don't say, "We did that before and it didn't work," but "We tried something like that before. Let me describe what we did and what happened. Maybe you can tell me how to change it for a better result."

IMPULSE CONTROL

The six million dollar man has to be careful when swatting flies with his atomic-powered arm. He may take out the entire building along with the offending insect. Similarly once you become a manager, the power involved in the role should force you to reconsider the way you respond to your impulses. If you feel anger toward an employee you may like to tell him off. Since you have a right to live your own life, do tell him off. But decide when and where you will let him have it, and whether shouting will be necessary to get your point across. Remember that what you do and say is amplified by your role. Your statements are atomic-powered and need to be appropriately modulated.

The bright and competent enjoy spontaneity, since it makes them look good. Unfortunately not everyone can be very bright and very competent. As a consultant for one company I often heard a particular group of engineers referred to with less-than-gentle Anglo-Saxon epithets. Translated into management vocabulary, they were being called hostile, abrasive, and punitive people. In actually working with the group, I found them to be charming, friendly, and above all else extremely intelligent and frank. Candor and spontaneity were their watchwords. However, when one would say to the other: "That's a dumb idea!" the resulting argument, no matter which way resolved, would prove the technical competence of both. The level at which they were debating proved their expertise. However, when they interacted with other groups, the challenge, "You dummy," often proved just that. The challenged person was a comparative dummy and made to look like one in front of colleagues.

One of the reasons you were selected to be manager is that someone judged you to be more knowledgeable and sharper than your peers. Make sure that your skill is not making your own people feel second rate. Check your impulses to make sure that what you are about to do is tailored to closing the gap between your understanding of the situation and the understanding of the person you are talking to. Be certain that you are not about to emphasize that gap to their embarrassment.

FRIENDLY SUSPICION

"Things are seldom what they seem." Many an enthusiastic and well-intentioned manager has been wrecked on the shoals located behind the fog of other people's smiling intentions.

The person who is offering you a new plan for success probably hopes it will be the basis for their own promotion a year from now. The peer who is offering to cooperate on a venture may be in desperate need of your assistance to save his or her group from disaster. The vendor who is offering to buy your lunch may plan to convince you to buy his or her consulting service. Everyone works from their own needs. Even you must admit that pure altruism is seldom your own motivation.

There are a number of responses to these seductions. You can be seduced and end up putting your energies into fulfilling other people's dreams. Or you can retreat, leave them alone, and watch them fail from the safety of the distance. Or you can decide when it is to your benefit to be seduced. Then enjoy and profit from the seduction. Perhaps the consulting service will improve your product, and the lunch is free. Perhaps the cooperative venture will be the salvation of both of your groups. Perhaps the new plan merits the promotion of its designer. Most helping hands are being offered because the helper sees profit for self as well as for you. Yet many helping hands will genuinely help. Although every free gift comes with a hidden price, the price may be worth paying.

INTEGRITY

Thomas Aquinas, a medieval monk and theologian, said that through their sin in the garden of paradise Adam and Eve lost the virtue of "integrity," after which came the collapse of everything else. Scholars of modern scripture are fairly unanimous in saying that the Adam and Eve story was designed by Hebrew storytellers to explain their condition. They found that humans were not at peace with one another, with nature, or within themselves. The story explains this lack of peace by Man's disobedience to God. As we ignored our relationship to God so our relationships to other people and nature broke down. Even the calm relationship between body and mind became the relationship between an embittered servant and a weak-willed master.

Whatever your religious upbringing or present beliefs, you must admit that the Hebrew storyteller has accurately portrayed the human condition. What Thomas Aquinas has concluded is that each of these phenomena is not isolated but related. Peace and wholeness cannot be maintained by a person who is stridently angry with others. The converse is also true. People who are at harmony with others and with themselves are said, by Aquinas, to possess the virtue of integrity. Not fragmented, they are at one with their environment.

There are many organizational and societal roles in which integrity is not necessary for success—technician, secretary, entrepreneur, laborer, marketeer, to name a few. In these positions it is useful to have integrity, but it is not essential. For managers integrity is necessary for success.

The task of a manager is to take care of the context in which he or she works. By defined organizational role the manager is to have caring relationships with the work groups in the organization. Rensis Likert, the classic theorist in organizational behavior, uses an oddly cold title for this role when he describes the manager as the linking pin between the people in the unit and the total organization. Back to the spiritual front, Thomas Aquinas warns that no one can take on that role who is not first at peace with themselves.

How do you achieve that peace? If it were easily done, more would have accomplished it. First, you must know your own needs; second, you must have satisfied them to a level where they no longer bother you. For instance, if you have a need for power, and either do not recognize it or are unable to fill that need you will be too distracted to pay attention to the needs of others, either in your group or elsewhere in the organization. Just as when you are broke and your family is hungry the worries of other people will not interest you, if you are in need of praise, you will not address real issues but say only the words that will gain you applause.

Integrity cannot be achieved through either intellectual understanding or an act of the will. It can only be achieved by being good to yourself. This is true of the successful manager who has what he or she wants. With that fulfillment comes personal peace. And with that peace comes the ability to care about others.

DO YOU COME ACROSS AS A SELF-RELIANT MANAGER?

Have the following questionnaire duplicated. Obtain the assistance of someone from your personnel department or someone in your organization who is in a position to be trusted and yet far enough removed from your daily activity not to continue to exert influence over your destiny. Ideally, your organization should make such assistance available under the title of a management specialist, organization development specialist, career development counselor, or training analyst.

Have that person administer this questionnaire anonymously to a selected group of those who work with you—employees, peers, interfacing department members, and management. Obtain a large enough sample to ensure some accuracy in the results, and to ensure that confidentiality can be maintained. It should be impossible for you to pick out which individual scored you either positively or negatively.

Ask the administering person to clarify to everyone the ground rules, including that of anonymity, and then provide you with the following: (1) your average score on each item, (2) the extreme score at both ends of each item, and (3) the average difference from the extreme. The advantage to receiving the latter two pieces of information is that you can see the variety of impressions from different people. Clarify to everyone that you will never see the original questionnaire they filled out but only a compilation.

You may feel it desirable to discuss your results with others. If so, warn people at the initiation of the project that you will be following up. A simple trick to get more information about yourself, and yet not put people on the spot, is to ask: "Why do you think that *people* gave me this score on the questionnaire?" (Asking: "How do *you* feel about me on this

item?" could cause discomfort and squirming answers.) You will probably be hearing the respondents' own feelings in answer to both queries,
but the former phrasing permits a little more comfortability and obscurity
to the reply. This technique will work for any type of sensitive information
that will be more easily given in an anonymous setting. Perhaps you
would like to add some questions to this form before having it distributed.
Or if this one turns out to be successful, you will do something similar in
the future.

The first five questions refer to those aspects of being a self-reliant
manager that were discussed in this chapter. The other questions refer to
earlier chapters. Refer to them if you need to refresh your memory on
the values behind the questions.

A SURVEY ON SELECTED MANAGERIAL CHARACTERISTICS

In connection with a book he/she is studying, [your name] has asked
me to conduct a survey. The purpose of the survey is to give him/her
more information as to how he/she is seen by others. The information
you give here will not be kept by anyone in my department. He/she will
not see your completed form but only a compilation of the data. Your
response will be one of [more than 15]. Please respond honestly and
quickly. Use the enclosed envelope for a confidential return.

Answer questions 1–5 by placing a check in the box that most describes your opinion. The caret is placed at the perfect balance point of
the scale.

1. How decisive is (s)he?

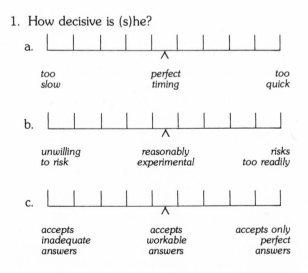

a.
    too   perfect   too
    slow   timing   quick

b.
    unwilling   reasonably   risks
    to risk   experimental   too readily

c.
    accepts   accepts   accepts only
    inadequate   workable   perfect
    answers   answers   answers

2. How understanding does (s)he tend to be of your opinion?

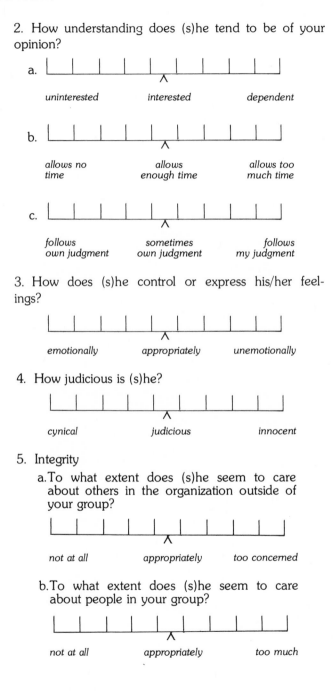

a.

uninterested   interested   dependent

b.

allows no   allows   allows too
time   enough time   much time

c.

follows   sometimes   follows
own judgment   own judgment   my judgment

3. How does (s)he control or express his/her feelings?

emotionally   appropriately   unemotionally

4. How judicious is (s)he?

cynical   judicious   innocent

5. Integrity

a. To what extent does (s)he seem to care about others in the organization outside of your group?

not at all   appropriately   too concerned

b. To what extent does (s)he seem to care about people in your group?

not at all   appropriately   too much

c.To what extent does (s)he seem to be at peace with self?

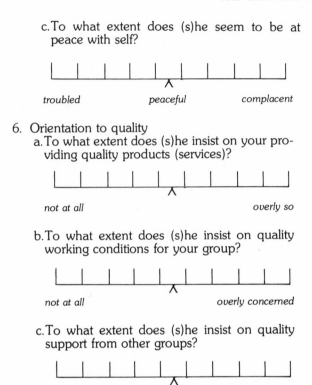

troubled   peaceful   complacent

6. Orientation to quality
   a.To what extent does (s)he insist on your pro-viding quality products (services)?

not at all   overly so

   b.To what extent does (s)he insist on quality working conditions for your group?

not at all   overly concerned

   c.To what extent does (s)he insist on quality support from other groups?

not at all   overly concerned

7. Management style. After each letter circle the one word that most describes your manager, or the word you most associate with him/her. Choose a word in each instance even if it is simply the least inaccurate of the three.
   a. *aggressive, supportive, logical*
   b. *tough, warm, cool*
   c. *determined, friendly, just*
   d. *fierce, sweet, distant*
   e. *battler, seducer, debater*

8. Motivation. Same directions as (7).
   a. *achievement, friendship, power*
   b. *accomplishments, relationships, politics*
   c. *work unit, group, kingdom*
   d. *expert, leader, boss*
   e. *work, love, influence*

9. Self-Reliance. After each letter divide ten points among the three options provided on the basis of the frequency with which you see this behavior in your manager.

a.	Waits for others to make decisions	_____	Makes decisions with others	_____	Makes own decisions	_____
b.	Blames others for failure	_____	Shares blame for failure	_____	Blames self for failure	_____
c.	Depends on others' judgment	_____	Listens, but makes own judgment	_____	Does not listen to others	_____
d.	Moves only with others' permission	_____	Moves with regard for others	_____	No regard for others	_____
e.	Asks for, but does not get, help	_____	Asks for, and gets, help	_____	Does not ask for help	_____

PART II

DEVELOPING
SELF-RELIANT
EMPLOYEES

You waste energy (yours and theirs) if you allow your employees to be overly dependent on you. This section tells you why it is useful to encourage self-reliance among your employees and gives strategies and tactics for improving employee self-reliance.

8

The self-reliant manager's philosophy

This is an age in which it is considered fitting to respond only to the feelings of the moment, look for the short-term rewards, and avoid the painful consequences of adhering to principles. A defense for a philosophy is needed. Certainly, schools no longer overwhelm their students with an appeal to develop an ethic, a sense of right order, a set of guidelines for conduct. Businessmen seldom find their principles blocking their behavior. The government agencies of the early 1970s showed a frightening willingness to compromise their morals in favor of executive whim. Even that citadel of honor, West Point, has shown signs of serious deterioration.

Not so very long ago our absolutes were too pure, our norms too rigid, and our values too black and white. People were to stay married until death. Those who did not were bad people. Good businessmen told the truth, even if it made them the prey to the malicious sharks who would use it against them. Wars were fought in which we knew who was good and who was evil. Suddenly, partially through the disaster of Vietnam, but also through more complicated social forces, we have become aware that the absolutes do not hold. Sometimes marriages are best dissolved. Sometimes a small lie is wiser and less wicked than the truth. Incredulously, a second world war radio play had Ivan (the Russian soldier) asking Hank (the American soldier) how some crazy people could think that after this war America and Russia could become enemies.

Values in a world of viable alternatives are much harder to obtain and formulate than they are in a world of absolutes. For that reason, many people have given up fashioning their own philosophies or deciding on consistent courses of action and unifying principles for their lives. The choices have become too multiple, the situations too complex, the right answers too shrouded. In the absence of a ready answer, many people have decided to settle for no answer at all.

What is it worth to have a philosophy of management? Why take the time to work through a "why" for the way you do things? Why not solve problems pragmatically rather than think things through in terms of a greater context? Here are two reasons.

Doing what comes naturally doesn't always work. Human beings instinctively avoid pain and seek pleasure. So did the dinosaur. However, the distinctive quality that makes us flourish, while the dinosaur is extinct, is our ability to decide to accept short run pain in favor of a long-run betterment of our situation. Such thinking brings us to the dentist's chair, a solution not likely to have occurred to the dinosaur. If I will do such and so I will receive a reward far out of proportion to the pain I am now experiencing. In some instances having a thought-out philosophy is taken too far, and pleasure is always deferred, never enjoyed. For instance, the reward of being designated a Ph.D. often does not seem at all commensurate with the pain of attaining it. On the other hand, the pleasure of lying on a beach does not appear all that valuable if it doesn't lead to anything. Even Big Sur must get boring in time.

A political figure of my acquaintance was given control of a metropolitan agency. He removed the professional manager on the grounds that "management is simply doing what comes naturally." Since for him "doing what comes naturally" is being a political person, everyone leaves his office assured of his complete support and concern. Only now, after three years, are they beginning to realize that in his efforts to avoid pain he is giving in to everyone, and his agency sits on the brink of disintegration. A manager must operate from some set of principles more compelling than the expediency of the moment or the organization will be driven on the rocks as he follows whatever wind seems favorable for that day.

There are a number of things a good manager must do that will bring no immediate reward. Who enjoys taking on recalcitrant employees to discuss defects and inadequacies? Is it not much less painful to simply let them go their own way? Who enjoys watching another person clumsily doing the tasks the manager could do with ease and skill? Or developing a detailed defense of the budget?

I am not suggesting that you develop a philosophy in which you deliberately seek suffering, but that you create one that directs your actions so that sometimes you take short-run pain as a means to avoid even greater pain in the long run, or as a means to capture even greater pleasures. Doing what comes naturally as a manager can get you into trouble just as doing what comes naturally can hurt a brain surgeon. You must have a "why" for your actions.

Consistent behavior frees others. Inconsistent people are charming, delightful, and hard to work with. Since their actions cannot be predicted, no one else knows where to move. An improvisational dancer makes an annoying dancing partner. Although these persons may be graceful as individuals, you will find it difficult to stay off their feet.

The manager who one day tolerates lateness only to explode about it the next, confuses employees. What does the boss want? Employees feel they have to make a choice between playing everything safely or barging ahead and expecting to pay the consequences. After a short period with a manager whose behavior is inconsistent, most employees willingly accept even the most hard-willed of bosses. Better a confining consistency than a demoralizing ambush.

Consistency is not achieved naturally, but as a result of a philosophy. Emotions slip and slide for a variety of reasons, ranging from your spouse's disposition to finding someone else in the treasured manager's parking spot. No matter what slings or arrows have assaulted the manager, a philosophy remains as a consistent guide to behavior.

CONVENTIONAL PHILOSOPHIES TOWARD WORK

Here are a variety of philosophies that have been employed as the organizing principle of work. For each, I point out the assumptions behind the philosophy, its guiding principle, the resulting managerial behaviors, its benefits, and its drawbacks as an approach to management.

A. Blue-Collar Management

Blue-collar management is, as the term implies, that style of management that is designed for and most fits common laborer jobs. It also fits employees whose thinking matches that of the common laborer. The assumptions that must hold true in order for this style to be successful are (1) the task must be simple; (2) the workers must expect low rewards from the work itself; and (3) the workers must not be upwardly mobile.

The guiding principle is that management can expect to receive a fair day's work for a fair day's pay. The definition of "fair" has been worked out between management and the union over a period of time both formally and informally. Generally, any particular manager and any particular employee will have a sense for how much work is required. Seldom does it approach the strenuous level. The manager tells people what to do and checks to see that they do it. The manager ensures that people are being treated equally and tries to limit disputes among them and between them and the company.

For the situations in which blue-collar management evolved, this style of management is excellent. Its long tradition makes it acceptable both to employees and to managers. A more enlightened approach to management in such situations must be undertaken with great caution. Blue-collar management is the result of years of struggle between the union and the company. Change will awaken suspicion from all employees as to management interests. Union officials will be concerned about the undermining of their power base, not only for the protection of their own jobs, but for the protection of workers. As any old-time employee is willing to point out, management may say it is altruistic now. But before unions its behavior was much less generous than it promises to be now, if only the yoke of the bargaining table were removed.

On the other hand, compared to other styles of management, this style produces only minimal productivity, and if any of the preceding assumptions do not hold true, blue-collar management will not fill the needs of either the task, the employee, or the manager.

B. Scientific Management

This approach to management recognizes the increasing complexity of the task and judges that the employees do not want to stretch themselves, or cannot stretch themselves, to grasp and respond to these complexities. The guiding principle behind scientific management is to organize the work so that the people cannot interfere with it. Complex tasks are broken into simple components and each component assigned to an individual. The thinking required of employees is minimal. The manager, with sophisticated staff assistance, decides on the way work flows in his or her area, and then with the complex task simplified, settles into the same style as the blue-collar manager. The stock example of this approach is the auto assembly line. Since, in the manager's judgment, laborers cannot be expected to grasp the intricacies of car assembly, each laborer is given a simple task, such as the installation of a fender, or even the tightening of several bolts.

The style has the same advantages and drawbacks as its predecessor, blue-collar management. However, since the simplified task that results from this style is often even less taxing than that faced by the blue-collar laborer, it is even less motivating. The blue-collar job, though apparently simple, holds more complexity than the scientifically managed job of the assembly line. For instance, a blue-collar laborer installing gas services to homes has many options in the basic task of digging holes in the ground. The blue-collar worker chooses which equipment to use, the shape and position of the holes, the speed of work, the time for coffee. He or she often works with the pipe, installs valves, and occasionally drives equipment. These choices may not seem many, but they are unavailable to the assembly-line worker. Morale is so poor in some auto assembly plants that use scientific management principles, that it is measured not by employee attitude surveys, but by the level of deliberate sabotage.

Management in one Detroit factory was convinced of the basic ignorance of their predominantly black laborers because of their continual failure to catch errors in the assembly process. One continually repeated mistake was that whenever the assembly process brought a truck motor and a passenger vehicle to the assembly point, the ignorant laborer plunked the motor into the vehicle, even if the motor had to be installed backwards. Management was unaware that out in the yard, with minimal supervision, good conditions, and a relaxed atmosphere was another group of laborers whose job it was to reassemble the incorrect installations for 10 percent more pay. The man inside knew that the more mistakes he made, the more brothers had better jobs, and the more likely it became that he too would one day enjoy the superior conditions of the yard. The point is that personal boredom is likely to bring on clever but counterproductive gamesmanship when tasks are oversimplified. On the other hand, there are times when scientific management can be advisedly applied as there are instances when the work is much too complex for one person's understanding. At those times, defining and delineating the limits of the job provides the clarity needed for the employee to function.

C. Laissez Faire

The "leave 'em alone" approach has been used to manage the professional employee as specialization has made the existence of the "professional team" essential. The style works with some success for the professional who knows what to do and will do his or her best, without cajoling, interfering, or exercising control. The manager—or "administrator"— provides the physical conditions and resources for the work to continue. Usually, both because of dedication and training, professionals do adequate work if left alone to manage themselves. However, compared to their potential if they were required to interact, search for new possibilities together, find new ways to organize work, find new ways to be cost-effective, they do not do well at all. The continuance of a laissez faire style of management presumes the willingness of society to allow itself the luxury of ten doctors doing a task that could be handled more capably and economically by two doctors, three medical corps people, two social workers, two nurses, and one manager. These people would talk to each other, divide the work, discuss the cases, work out efficiencies, plan the future, and otherwise control not only themselves but each other.

D. The Human Relations Strategy

The human relations approach is heavily used among professionals. The strategy is simple, and as far as it goes, excellent. A major reason why professionals are unwilling to work closely with others is their lack of competence in forming interpersonal relationships and in communicating with others. The human relations manager focuses on improving these relationships, patterns, and communication. The problem of overdistance and overisolation may thus be solved, or at least minimized, as well. The manager who uses this approach relies heavily on a third-party consultant to train the group to relate better to one another.

The strength of this strategy is that it does help people work through the softer, kinder, more trusting aspects of the human condition, aspects that must be part of the professional's relationship with others.

But human relations training tends to avoid touching two areas: the realities of work and the tougher emotions.

The realities of work

I was once asked to work with a group of research scientists. "They have interpersonal issues which they refuse to confront and solve," was their manager's diagnosis of their problem. He was partially right. As he said, they were angry, and they didn't want to talk about it. What the manager failed to see was that their attitude was only a result, not the underlying problem. They were unsuccessful in landing contracts. Their group was financially impoverished. A number of them were about to be laid off. Under that kind of pressure every minor irritation became the cause of a major falling out.

The pure human relations approach would have had them air their negative feelings about each other, to their further detriment. A sensible practitioner admits that the sensitivity group has its limitations, which is why it cannot serve as a total approach to management.

Realities other than the marketplace lie outside its scope. For instance, responsible T group trainers do whatever possible to prevent the really sick person from entering their T groups. Borderline sick people (the neurotic, the impoverished ego) cannot afford to lower their defenses further.

They risk damage to their already fragile personality structure. The really sick (the psychopath, the hysteric) are dangerous to the others in the group. Since they are unaware of and uncaring about the feelings of others, they may manage to destructively open the problems of others. However, in organizations the group is whoever belongs to that department or section. Sometimes candor must be limited and effectiveness sacrificed for the continued emotional balance and career potential of individual members.

The "tougher" emotions

I once offered to teach social workers who were managing small agencies how to get in touch with their emotions. My potential client and I went ring-around-the-rosy, with her insisting that social workers already know how to do that and I insisting that they did not. Finally, the cause of our disparity hit me.

By emotions she meant empathy, follow-feeling, trust, kindness, and love. And I meant the worry about the agency's financial condition that will drive you to produce proposals and seek support urgently. I also meant anger with employees who are wasting that money without producing, which will lead to a confrontation. These are perfectly valid emotions that require expression if a manager is to manage well.

The human relations group not only ignores feelings that have to do with power and control, but even tries to eradicate them from participants. Managers who refuse to respond to such feelings are setting the stage for their own defeat, since these emotions exist to move the person who has them to prompt, vigorous, and necessary action.

E. Rational Management

There has been a recent move toward a rational approach to management, witness the Program Planning and Budgeting System (PPBS) of the federal government and the Management-by-Objectives (MBO) approach of private industry. These approaches support the movement toward developing a professional worker by involving the professional in planning goals. Many of these processes allow the manager the freedom to choose the right means to their ends, which is essential to being a professional.

The new management system has a two-pronged effect—it aids in the development of professionals by providing a mechanism for allowing them the necessary autonomy and influence on organization decisions, as well as providing a mechanism for limiting and controlling the behavior of the professional for the good of the organization. It involves the joint preparation of a written plan by manager and employee or manager and work group.

Again, as with the human relations approach, if they are part of a limited strategy pursued for limited ends, these rational approaches are useful. However, when they are undertaken with evangelical fervor as the ultimate panacea, they can lead to disastrous oversights. A guiding assumption—and an erroneous one when so applied—is that work is pursued for rational ends alone. "Rational" and "real" are seen as synonymous. So too are "emotional" and "unreal."

Two examples illustrate this point. A large federal agency was formed to coordinate the work of nine former separate bureaus. Two new systems were installed—PPBS and OPS (operational planning system). Yet neither one improved the collaborative effort. Despite endless meetings and acrimonious arguments, each of the nine bureaus continued to go its own way. What had happened? The nine bureaus had each formed and maintained a separate identity for 10 to 20 years prior to the existence of the umbrella agency. No matter how reasonable the cause, nor how rational the mechanism, they were not likely to surrender this identity. So the rational systems ground on. Those who were dedicated to the rational approach could never understand the reason for the system's inadequacies because they did not take into account the blind, highly emotional loyalty individuals had to their original, separate bureaus.

The general manager of a major complex of a large wood-processing company was informed that management was dissatisfied with the level at which he was achieving his objectives. He was puzzled because until that moment he had felt fairly successful, if not outstandingly so. His immediate superior gave him a set of nine objectives to hit within six months or he was out. Within three months he had those objectives accomplished.

Next he learned that a member of top corporate management considered the first nine objectives quite inadequate. This executive had a set of 20 targets to be hit by the close of the fiscal year. If they were not, again, the word was "out!" The general manager gulped once or twice but then proceeded to fulfill these new objectives. The typical MBO case history—with intent to demonstrate the need for rational thinking in business—would have him promoted, honored, or in receipt of a raise.

In fact, none of the above resulted. He was given a lateral transfer. His management was faced with a dilemma. They had already decided that he was not hard-driving enough to continue to fill the general manager job long before they gave him his first set of objectives. The objectives had been designed to prove they were right. Although he (in a sense) had proved otherwise by hitting the objectives on target, they were still convinced he lacked the emotional characteristics necessary for the job. He had not passed the management "sniffing" test. Since he now held the best bottom-line position in the corporation, they could no longer punish him, so they had to move him laterally.

There is an important bottom line to this case. They were probably right. The general manager was a gentle person who preferred to avoid conflict, hated to push others, did not naturally enjoy the power plays of management. Emotionally it had cost him to bring about the one-year turnaround. If he had had a choice it was indeed questionable if he would have wanted the struggle and turmoil of that general manager position. But so committed were his employers to a rational approach to management that they could not even discuss their observations of his emotional style. They could not admit to themselves or to him that he did not pass the "sniffing" test. They could not even admit that such a test existed. They could not say that even though he hit the objectives they intuitively knew he didn't belong in that job.

Rational management can have an excellent impact on an organization, but only if it is not used as if it were the entire answer. Emotions, characteristics, traits, and feelings are also a part of the management equation. To be effective, rational management must be used in conjunction with strategies and approaches that emphasize the emotional side of the human animal.

F. Organization Development Management

One of the unfortunate assumptions of a manager gun-ho on organization development philosophy is that people are both rational and emotional. One of the major responsibilities of the manager is thought to involve the application of both rational and emotional techniques to develop a sound social system oriented toward work. Such a manager will use the special techniques for developing interpersonal awareness combined with the rational planning technologies to contract with employees for the performance of work.

The manager's purpose is to instill a sense of trust among group members, improve their ability to communicate within the group, and clarify the goals as well as get total commitment to them.

The guiding principle is to emphasize and develop those norms that are likely to increase cooperation and team-oriented behavior. The manager makes abundant use of off-site retreats, team-oriented management systems, and third-party consultants to facilitate interpersonal communication.

I have seen excellent results. This approach has demonstrated an ability to develop strength, collaboration, and genuine caring, particularly in the long term, in organizations that must solve complex problems.

Now for the negative side of OD. In an effort to develop a sense of well-being, individual managers become too dependent on the program and on the installing manager. Thus, they do not learn to take their own risks, and end up using the program to achieve their own ends. When the boss in charge of installing the program is transferred, all action usually comes to a halt. Why? The subordinate managers, all decked out in their collaborative and team-oriented garb, have gained no more strength to identify and struggle for their "rights" than they had before. Which brings us back to the mistaken assumption we alluded to earlier that the installing manager can simply say, "Be free and strong," and voilà—free and strong subordinate managers. The OD approach may teach subordinate managers to have an air of self-confidence, but at the first thundercloud that crosses the boss's face that pseudo-freedom often disappears.

G. Self-Reliant Management

The manager who follows a philosophy of self-reliance uses as the guiding principle to so manage the situation and the people within it that over time all the group members become increasingly able to rely on their own judgment in making decisions, selecting behaviors, planning approaches. Self-reliant management is the ultimate response to the rapid acceleration of the forces described in Chapter 2.

Just as self-reliant managers have learned to manage the quality of their inputs, learned to reduce and cope with their own fears and to develop a flexible approach to others, they also work to ensure that their employees cope with their fears, develop flexible approaches, and manage the quality of their own inputs. The self-motivating manager attempts to teach employees to tap their own motivational resources, to be decisive, understanding, and mature.

It is quite a different approach to management. Instead of simply reducing the reason for fear, you will help others cope with their own fears. Instead of dealing with other groups for them, you will allow them to deal with other groups themselves. Instead of motivating them, you will allow them to follow their own motivations. Instead of defending their budgets, you will allow them to defend their own.

This philosophy will allow you to pick and choose among strategies derived from the other six philosophies as the situation demands and yet have an ordering principle, that of enhancing the self-reliance of individuals. For the new person on the job who needs time to get oriented, give him direct blue-collar orders for awhile until he can set his own directions. Are people too confused about the limits of their jobs to take independent action? Have a scientific management analysis made (with group input) to define the roles more clearly. But in all instances, the "why" of what you are doing remains clear. You are doing whatever is necessary to increase their self-reliance.

Here are two examples of this different approach. Most career-development programs assist employees in discovering how their management values them, what reasonable career opportunities are next in store for them, and what training their management is willing to provide them. An internal ombudsman in a corporation installed a quite different self-reliant-oriented career-development program. In the course of a two-day workshop he helped employees identify what they wanted to do next, what training or assistance they would need to get there, and how they would go about getting that training or assistance. He made no promises for management. If they wanted to become staff engineers, that was their business. Nobody said that they could or couldn't. They could invest their own energy, take their own risks, and taste either their own success or failure.

On the other hand, management required nothing of them as a result of the workshop. Some chose to seek opportunities outside of the company. They left with everyone's blessing. In this instance, management had come to an understanding that having two self-reliant employees functioning within the company was worth the loss of one self-reliant employee who decided to work somewhere else.

A similar program was designed and used by two training staff members in the same corporation as an EEO program. Many management-oriented equal opportunity programs contain far more promise than delivery. These women encouraged participants in their worshops to realize that there was little or no motivation for white male managers to assist any minority up the ladder. The participants were encouraged to rely on themselves—not their managers—and were given an understanding of the law and optional strategies for coercing change from reluctant chauvinists. Their program's success is not measured in praise but in promotions and salary increases. Although at times management wonders at the wisdom of encouraging such self-reliant vipers within its bosom, whenever the federal inspectors arrive to check on EEO compliance, the managers thank this course for the self-reliant minorities who are quickly and vigorously swinging their own way up the promotional ladder.

IDENTIFYING YOUR MANAGEMENT PHILOSOPHY

You may not have thought out your own management philosophy. However, based on the actual behavior you and your organization exhibit, you can deduce the philosophy you actually tend to implement even if it is not carefully articulated. The following questionnaire indicates the behavior consequent on each philosophy in response to six common organizational issues. In answering each question put a number 3 by the most likely response, 2 by the second most likely, and 1 by the third most likely. To score simply add the numbers next to each of the seven letters. The highest number indicates the dominant philosophy of your organization. (Most organizations are run with a mixture of philosophies.) Each letter corresponds to the same letter in the preceding text, for example: A = blue-collar management, B = self-reliant management. (You may also learn more about the management philosophies by studying the questions.)

QUESTIONNAIRE ON DOMINANT MANAGEMENT PHILOSOPHY

1. Who makes the decisions about what people are to do on a given day?
    _____ A. The boss tells people what to do.
    _____ B. The job is already defined by the job description. Further direction is seldom necessary.
    _____ C. Employees decide what to do on their own.
    _____ D. Employees usually decide with concern for the needs of others.
    _____ E. Employees decide by referring to the contract made with management.
    _____ F. Employees decide based on earlier team agreements.
    _____ G. Either employee, or team, or boss may decide, depending on the needs of the moment.
2. Are feelings valued?
    _____ A. Depends on the individual manager's own desire to pay attention to feelings.
    _____ B. Feelings have little to do with work; we rely on job descriptions.
    _____ C. People do not have enough contact to be aware of the feelings of others.
    _____ D. Feelings are of prime importance.
    _____ E. Feelings have little to do with work; we rely on rational agreements.
    _____ F. Management encourages the expression of feelings.

_____ G. Feelings are important, but everyone is expected to stick up for their own.

3. Who sets the broad organizational goals?

_____ A. Our boss—who has to listen to his/her boss on the subject.

_____ B. Outside experts have defined our unit's function.

_____ C. There are no broad goals as far as I know. That's management's problem.

_____ D. Broad goals emerge from the combined needs of employees.

_____ E. Broad goals result from a series of individual contract negotiations.

_____ F. Broad goals are set by the team based on both organizational and personal needs.

_____ G. Broad goals are the result of myriad arguments, seductions, power plays. Sometimes done individually, sometimes in team meetings.

4. Who possesses critical information?

_____ A. The boss. Employees know little.

_____ B. The staff experts. Line management and employees do what the experts say is best.

_____ C. People know own job better than anybody, but they know little else.

_____ D. Everybody knows everything. Critical or not.

_____ E. The appropriate information is passed to the proper people.

_____ F. The team members constantly review what is happening in each other's areas.

_____ G. Everyone is responsible for passing on what they think is important and for requesting what they need.

5. What best describes your organization?

_____ A. Monarchy—rule by the boss.

_____ B. Rule by experts.

_____ C. Chaos—rule by nobody.

_____ D. Family—rule by love.

_____ E. Rule by reason.

_____ F. Team—rule by consensus.

_____ G. Anarchy—rule by everybody.

6. What is the organization's slogan?

_____ A. Do what you are told.

_____ B. Fulfill your job description.

_____ C. Don't interfere.

_____ D. Like each other.
_____ E. Plan.
_____ F. Collaborate.
_____ G. Be responsible for yourself.

A series of informal, rambling notes from the journal of the father of
self-actualization theory made during his tenure of observation at a
California electronics plant will serve as a gentle potboiler for your
thinking:

Abraham H. Maslow, *Eupsychian Management* (Homewood, Ill.:
Dorsey, 1965).

9

Self-reliance
through MBO

There are many purposes for having a management by objectives (MBO) system. In this chapter we are looking at the management by objectives system only as a vehicle for fostering employee self-reliance. We hold in abeyance its other purposes, such as a method for demonstrating success, for top management to keep track of the working echelons, and for predicting costs.

Perhaps you are already working with an MBO system. Use what I am about to say as a new perspective to your existing system. After reading this, you may want to fine-tune that system. If you do not have an operating system, don't be overawed by the terms "management system" and MBO. A management system is any formal method for organizing people to accomplish work, and as such it can be very simple indeed. MBO is a management system whereby managers and employees come to an agreement over the results to be accomplished within a given period and use this agreement as their target and measure.

One of the most spectacularly successful MBO systems I have seen was designed and run by a man who had not finished high school. First, he described each person's job to each assembly-line employee. Then he came to an agreement with them as to what would be a reasonable output to expect from them at their position for that week taking into account such conditions as the quality of the material, the trustworthiness of the machine, the employee's expectations of cooperation from the maintenance department and from other employees. He wrote the agreed-to output on a piece of paper and placed it beside a counter on the machine. As the week progressed, both he and the employee knew how well they were proceeding. Based on the results of that week he and the employee again came to an agreement for the next week, and discussed ways to limit the problems of last week. In effect, they had a home-grown MBO system but, because of its simplicity, it would never have occurred to them to describe it as such.

MBO will help you improve your employees' self-reliance by (1) reducing the impact of your person on their daily decisions and (2) making free choices more possible for them.

How do your employees know they have done well? Do they rely on you or on some other member of management telling them so? Do they know what resources are available to them—time, money, assistance—to accomplish tasks, or must they go to you or some other member of management on a daily basis to find out? The more such questions are answered affirmatively, the less equipped they are to take a self-reliant stance. How can they be expected to move or decide or judge when they have no idea what impact such a change will have on the resources? How can they take their own chances when the touchstone of their success is your approval?

One way is to implement an MBO system to ensure that these questions are answered before the employee has to make a decision.

1. Hold a series of meetings with your employees, either on an individual or team basis. Ask each employee to come to the meeting with a draft of the specific end results he or she feels you have a right to expect of them for a given period of time. Also have them bring a list of the resources they need to get the job done.

2. Prepare a similar draft for each employee.

3. Compare the drafts. Look for similarities and differences. Try to understand each other's different points of view.

4. Come to an agreement on what the two of you will expect for that period. How much time you allot to this discussion depends on the complexity of the task and the nature of your relationship with the employee. The more complex the task, the more time you will need. Two hours to plan six months' work will be ample only for simple jobs. Plan on 4 to 8 hours for professional employees. The more your people trust and respect you, the more you will have the openness necessary for a realistic and efficient discussion. The less they like you, the more they will find it necessary to beat around the bush.

5. Particularly if the period is long (4 months to a year), schedule

monthly or quarterly progress checks, during which you meet with the employee, see how things are coming along, and find out if your help is needed. If the expected results look like they will come out either too high or too low, alter the contract. Before you make any changes be sure both of you understand the factors that have made a difference in the attainability of the objective.

6. At the end of the period discuss the degree of accomplishment and the employees' strengths and weaknesses as exhibited in pursuing these objectives. Define what can or should be done differently for the next year.

The more you and the employee can cast your statements of expected results to make them specific and measurable, the more certain you can both be of the reality of your agreement. Avoid cloudy generalities. "I will greet customers pleasantly," will do better as, "Instead of last year's 20 complaints about me from customers, this year you will receive no more than five." "I will straighten up the files," should be replaced by a statement that clarifies what those straight files will look like. "I will get us more customers," will be clearer if the number of customers and the initial dollar volume of their business are also stated, along with the cost of this new bonanza.

If you have been involved in an MBO program, the foregoing is simple. You have probably gone far beyond this. But could it be that you have gone too far? Often, in an attempt to assure the success of the system's objectives, the MBO experts become overly dependent on multiplying forms and distinctions. They encourage their manager clients to be similarly dependent. If you and your employees are already having a hard time agreeing on anything, you certainly won't get them to agree to using ten instead of one. The extra paper will give you more things to be distracted with while avoiding the question. If you and your employees do not want to be clear with one another, no amount of instructions on how to write objectives will bring it about. On the other hand, if you really want to communicate with each other, minimal hints and low-key instruction will do the trick.

A subtle type of other-reliance inherent in using official forms is the dependency you have on what someone else has had the cleverness to print up for you. I learned a similar tactic during the course of running sensitivity exercises with engineers in an ordnance-producing corporation. If I said, "Go to your team rooms and discuss your feelings about each other's behavior," I encountered resistance and anger. People wanted to know, in a very self-reliant way, why I thought this exercise would be good for them, as they did not see its value. On the other

hand, if I were to say, "The manual says go to your team rooms and
. . . etc." everyone would trudge off unquestioningly. If the manual said
it, how could it fail to help? (Of course I wrote the manual.)

If you have not taken part in an MBO program, start out with something as simple as I have described here. After a couple of cycles, you
and your employees will want to add fillips, curlicues, and even some essential hardware, but what to add will become clear later. If you already
have a complicated system in your organization that is not working, go
back to the basics, or as near to them as organization norms and politics
will allow. Then begin to rebuild, incorporating only those parts of the official system you and your people see as necessary. Here are some
pointers.

1. You and your employees must tailor the MBO system to fit the
needs and problems of your own organization. If you do not, you risk
overdependence on the system, rather than recognizing its limitations
and relying on your own and each other's competence.

2. The training process must be considered just as important as the
training content. Be wary of sending your people as individuals (rather
than as a group) to MBO training courses.

3. Arrange to conduct an evaluation at the end of each cycle. You and
your employees can then use the result of that evaluation to replan the
next cycle. In the process you will ensure that everybody agrees with the
methodology used.

This gives you some idea of the guidelines. Now let's see how they
work in practice.

TAILORING THE SYSTEM

Here are some examples of how *not* to do it:

A large federal agency's central office pressed for the total application
of its MBO system in all its regional offices. One stipulation the central office made was that work objectives had to be set, despite the fact that
regional employees had already clarified their objectives using a different
system months before. Another part of the central office's plan called for
setting career-development objectives. The majority of senior (GS 13 and
above) employees couldn't see that this would be of any use in the catch-
as-catch-can world of government promotions. The regional offices du-
tifully—but unenthusiastically—went through the MBO motions, but basically what they got out of it was the conviction that management was not
making very much of an attempt to understand them.

When a large Minneapolis-based industrial corporation's training department was about to launch an MBO system in an engineering area,

the chief engineer asked the training department's manager if they would like to hear about the work-planning method he had been using. The training department had not bothered to ask him if he had such a system, apparently presuming that without their help he had never even heard of planning. Now that permission was granted, he outlined a sophisticated approach to management—a 1974 Lincoln Continental, compared with the Model T of the training department. Thus he rescued the training department from a failure that would have damaged their credibility, and made it possible for their staff to be of real use in helping them with aspects other than work-planning, such as career development, training, and long-range resource development.

An example of failure to integrate MBO activities may be found in the experience of a large engineering, production-oriented division of a major corporation. During a period of economic downturn and change in top management, an MBO approach was used to clarify the end results expected from each individual. But the training and implementing process was carried out without suggesting any diagnostic or problem-solving interventions—this in a climate of job insecurity, fear of negative appraisals, and uncertainty about management attitudes. Trust was the major issue, and of course the MBO process by itself could do little to engender more trust. Five years later the engineers organized a professional association and among their first demands was the removal of the MBO system.

Now let's look at a how-to illustration:

In a medium-size service company, the behavioral scientist who headed the MBO program met first with the president to ascertain his goals for the system and then with a task force that represented all levels of management. The first step for the task force was to diagnose the present state of the organization in terms of those variables that could be influenced by and have influence on MBO. In this case, the conceptual model for the diagnosis was Likert's four systems of management: (1) authoritarian, (2) benevolent authoritarian, (3) consultative, and (4) participative. The conclusion reached by the task force was that the company wavered between System 2 and System 3 and that both management and employees had the need and the motivation to warrant an MBO approach that would solidify System 3 through the company. (The nature of the business and the personal styles of management, it was decided, precluded System 4—as ideal as that system might appear viewed in the abstract.)

The task-force members then set more specific objectives for the program; selected from among the alternative strategies proposed by the behavioral scientist for their objectives; developed the basic outline for training, including who was to be trained and when; and supervised the writing of a descriptive manual. Before any major step was taken, however, the president met with the task force to confirm that the proposed system was congruent with his values and objectives.

This sequence shifted the emphasis from the textbook approach to one based on the situation at hand as well as the real needs. For example, no career-development program was implemented. The president's policy was to pay well and promote regularly and innovatively but, in his personal value system, training for the next job was primarily the employees' responsibility. Had the proposed MBO system suggested any other course, he would not have gone along with it, and employees trusting the words of the MBO manual would have been disillusioned by the president's values as expressed in the company training budget.

Very little needed to be done about sorting out basic job responsibilities, since job descriptions had been written previously and there were detailed manuals describing all functions for most areas. Furthermore, the company concentrated on hiring highly motivated people of above-average intelligence and capability. These people disposed of routine obligations quickly; their interest lay in the challenge of the more difficult, the stretching, the stepping stone to advancement. For these reasons, their MBO program concentrated on "performance" objectives. By coincidence, employees had just received bonuses based on their year-old profit-sharing plan. Corporate objectives were described in relationship to the profit-sharing plan, so that individual employees could anticipate the dollar reward to them for succeeding in hitting the profit and cost objectives of the company for the next fiscal year.

A second area of emphasis involved setting "development" objectives to increase responsiveness to the company's strained capacity to deliver service and coordinate functions. The company had grown rapidly and needed more coordination, interdepartmental meetings, cross-department training, and joint problem solving.

Since the task force judged the employees to be almost completely ignorant of the corporation's objectives, MBO was used to help corporate officers develop clear statements of their objectives. Seminars were run for all employees. Employees were informed of company directions to give them a sense of top management's priorities when they met to establish their own objectives.

The company had a comprehensive budgeting/profit-planning system. The task force recommended that it neither be supplanted nor diminished by MBO, but that MBO support and further it. For example, performance objectives were geared to a corporate objective "to increase profits beyond plan by 10 percent and to cut costs below plan by 10 percent." Every department then set similar, but more specific, objectives related to that one.

The people in this corporation were asked, "What do you want? What do you need? What is happening now?" As a result, the company now has a tactical system designed for and by the people who work for it, based on the general MBO strategy.

To provide you with a picture of the situation you and your group are designing your own system for, fill in your responses to the following questions.

CREATING AN MBO SYSTEM

Place an N for "now" in the box that is most indicative of the present reality, and an L for "later" to indicate desired change.

1. What is our general management style?

permissive   *dictatorial*

2. To what extent are our jobs defined?

fuzzily   *rigidly*

3. To what extent do we have a sense of belonging?

little loyalty   *very clubby*

4. Do we agree on what we are trying to accomplish?

no: *yes:*
chaos,   *lockstep*
conflict   *agreement*

5. Do we control people's activity?

do what they want   *tightly controlled*

6. Do we communicate with each other?

| | | | | | | | | | |

no, secretive,   gabby,
private   no secrets, no privacy

7. What are our economic conditions?

| | | | | | | | | | |

lean and   fat and
hungry   lazy

8. Job security?

| | | | | | | | | | |

uptight   ultrasafe

9. Competitiveness among individuals?

| | | | | | | | | | |

all buddies   cutthroat

10. Competitiveness among departments?

| | | | | | | | | | |

all buddies   cutthroat

11. To what extent are we held accountable?

| | | | | | | | | | |

not at all   unreasonably so

12. Are we function oriented or results oriented?

| | | | | | | | | | |

completely   completely results
function oriented   oriented

13. What has been your organization's experience with previous changes in management systems? List specific problems.

_____
_____
_____

14. Is it possible to go up in this organization?

|___|___|___|___|___|___|___|___|___|

everyone is   hardly learned
stuck where   one job before
they are   promoted

15. Are people's skills being developed?

|___|___|___|___|___|___|___|___|___|

do-it-yourself   academy organization

16. Are we proactive or reactive?

|___|___|___|___|___|___|___|___|___|

completely   completely
reactive   proactive

Look over the span differences between your nows (N) and laters (L). How far apart are they? Take this factor into account as you design your system, and use it to bridge the gap. Here are a number of examples of how to do that.

Is your company in a period of economic downturn? Encourage all employees to come up with cost-saving objectives. Are you in a period of economic upturn? Take this opportunity to have employees identify various end results for their professional improvement or for the improvement of the organization's ability to respond to situations. This may be just the time to begin the extensive training courses or team-building sessions you've been putting off, or the time to make capital expenditures.

You may be extremely permissive and want to tighten up. Schedule more regular reviews. Or you may be extremely dictatorial and do not like it. Try spacing meetings far apart, and arrange to leave people alone as they pursue their objectives.

If you are a private person and wish to change, hold team-objective review sessions. Or if you are private and prefer it that way, make sure a private place is designated for individual reviews and objective-setting sessions.

MBO TRAINING

The training process defines the management process even more than the training content does. In most organizations MBO training is a lecture-oriented course to which individuals are sent at different times. One naive assumption behind this approach is that the same words mean the same things to different people. Even allowing for discussion periods, managers separated from their peers have small chance of clarifying their perceptions. For instance, Sam asks the instructor, "You mean I should use this system to push my employees harder?" The instructor, impressed by Sam's white hair, lumpy jowls, and well-chewed cigar, thinks he has an authoritarian tiger on his hands and quickly disclaims the interpretation, using words like freedom, autonomy, and bottom−up employee influence. His peers, knowing Sam for the softy he really is, would have chimed in, "Yes! You are too easygoing—your employees want and need more direction."

A second naive assumption is that if the training uses objectives from a different world—the one more familiar to the instructor—the trainees will be able to extrapolate to their own work. Courses on MBO abound with examples that reflect the training department's own objectives. Most instructors dread the trainee who asks for specific help in objectifying his fuzzy world. But this needn't be so. One company used the MBO training process to initiate and define the management process in the following well-planned disciplined way:

The company ran one-day training sessions for its various departments, three to four work units at a time. During the sessions the groups wrote team objectives for the next year and received criticism and suggestions from other work units both on the writing techniques and the actual usefulness of the objectives. After these training sessions, work teams were able to set objectives with relative ease, referring to the models that were set during the training sessions. The advice other work teams had given them definitely broadened the scope of their objectives setting.

Your work-unit members should sit down with the instructor and explore MBO, practice with real objectives, describe opportunities and alternative solutions, and even rejigger the official system so it fits them a little better.

If you cannot afford an instructor, or if your company or organization does not agree to supply one, at least arrange that any book to be used as the theoretical basis of the system is studied and discussed by your work group as a whole. Even through reading, different people can often end up with the same differences of perception that occur during a training session.

EVALUATION

MBO is a technique for guiding a process. However, long after the process has stopped, the technique continues to exist. Periodic participant evaluation can help assure viability of the process.

The large federal agency used as an example earlier adopted an evaluation procedure that first surveyed 25 percent of each department through a questionnaire, and then brought the sample population together in small groups to explain the meaning of the questionnaire results. The explanations were also recorded for the benefit of line management and of the department that was responsible for redesigning the system.

One regional commissioner discovered that 40 percent of his sample group had never participated in an MBO session, despite the fact that his assistants had all reported the process as completed. Furthermore, the process had broken down for a number of reasons, among which was the attitude that feigned compliance was less energy-consuming than arguing for system improvements. As in this case, shrewd employees may be trying to decide if it is worth their time and energy to inform you of the deficiencies in "your" management systems. If they believe you are resistant to hearing their opinions, their alternative is to go through the motions quietly and quickly. Less fuss, less muss, and fewer ulcers for them. Unfortunately for you, as they sidestep the system, you are no longer able to accomplish what you set out for.

Those responsible for the design of the MBO program found that they had been trying to meet two incompatible needs at once—an informal setting for supervisor–employee work relationship clarification for a formal tie to agency objectives. Thus, the evaluation procedure produced the information necessary for corrective action.

Frequently, you are unaware that your behavior doesn't jibe with the MBO principles you espouse. The open feedback provided through periodic evaluation helps keep you honest with yourself. Otherwise, your employees may subvert their own goals, because their cynicism and distrust of management make them reject as coercive any management system, and reject as opportunistic any MBO consultant or personnel department specialist. They then create what they expect—a legalistic but dishonest system. Promised, then implemented, evaluation can do more for your managerial credibility and an effective system than can any number of speeches about the need for cooperation.

The evaluation needn't be complex. Ask the same person who assisted you with the questionnaire for exploring your managerial characteristics to come back and help you with the following questionnaire. Use the same ground rules, but this time promise the group that the anonymous results will be used as the opening discussion for changing the system.

SAMPLE QUESTIONNAIRE

1. Overall, how do you rate the effectiveness of the system?

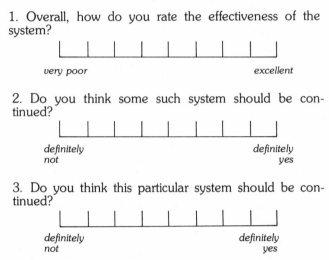

very poor   excellent

2. Do you think some such system should be continued?

definitely   definitely
not   yes

3. Do you think this particular system should be continued?

definitely   definitely
not   yes

4. What do you like most about the system? (Can use more than one item.)

5. What do you like least? (Can use more than one item.)

6. What additions do you recommend? (Can use more than one item.)

These questions should give you a good start on the conversation, which will enable you and your people to redesign and improve your system.

Here's the recap.

You have probably become immersed in the details of how to install an MBO system. Let's step back and remember that your purpose is to enable your employees to take a more self-reliant stance. The methods and process outlined here assist the employee to be self-reliant by:

—Freeing the employee from the need for your daily direction.
—Giving the employee a forum for influencing results expected and resources allocated.
—Allowing the employee to influence the system itself by participating in its design and evaluation.

Your MBO system need not be complicated. As a matter of fact, the simpler the better. The important thing is to establish a method for contracting for end results. And then use that contract as the focal point for your conversations.

The contents of the contract and the frequency of its discussion should be decided based on a previous diagnosis of organizational needs. The whole system should be evaluated at least yearly to ascertain whether or not it is meeting the needs for which it was created.

MBO is not a panacea. Its evangelists often expect more from it than it can deliver. But if you use it realistically it can assist you in providing some of the essential conditions of employee self-reliance.

Two indispensable works on MBO: From Drucker you will learn more about how to think with a results orientation. From Odiorne you will learn more about a practical system for implementing such an orientation.

Peter F. Drucker, *Managing for Results* (New York: Harper & Row, 1964).
George S. Odiorne, *Management by Objectives* (A system of managerial leadership) (New York: Pitman, 1965).

10

Establishing
self-reliant employee
relationships

If employees are to be self-reliant, they must have strong relationships with other employees. If they lack such relationships, their capacity will be so weakened that they will either falter into isolationism or seek refuge as other-reliant people.

The isolationist makes the mistake of thinking that he or she can get along without other people. The isolationist blocks out the real—often negative—effects of this stance both intellectually and emotionally. Furthermore, by avoiding healthy interaction with others—new blood, as it were—the isolationist tends to produce anemic products. Only rare genius works best cut off from the influence of others. It takes a very unique temperament to use isolation to advantage. Whatever may be said for the virtues of this stance in such fields as the arts or pure research, work produced in the majority of fields is impoverished compared to work created through the willingness to share ideas, accept suggestions, and be influenced by contradictory opinions.

The other-reliant person avoids strong relationships with others for the anonymity of the crowd. The other-reliant employee uses the pretense of relationships with you and the other employees to cover up for passivity.

As a manager, you can greatly improve the functioning of your group by promoting objectives to foil both these stances. In opposition to the isolationist's style, you press for getting one individual to relate to another. To counter the other-reliant person's habit, you stress the need for individual responsibility, effort, and accountability.

Although a good team effort makes it difficult to distinguish the output of one person from that of another, you are still able to hold all members individually responsible for that output. After several joint projects, you will know who is consistently involved in team failures, and who is consistently involved in team successes.

Hockey teams evaluate their players and cope with the same phenomenon by giving all the players on the ice a point whenever a goal is scored by the entire team. They subtract a point from every player who is on the ice when the team is scored against. They recognize the team effort, of course, but every team member is accountable individually for what occurs on the ice.

Many managers get so carried away with their zeal for the new ideal of teamsmanship, they forget that the team depends on the strength of its individuals. Zero plus zero still equals zero. On the other hand, in a good team relationship one plus one can equal far more than two. The stronger the individuals, the stronger the potential for unusually productive relationships.

Why take the time to develop intragroup relationships? How do you diagnose the present state of relationships in your group? What can you do to influence the state of the relationships in your group? These questions are discussed below. We then move on to the other side of the issue: What needs are met by continuing to emphasize the distinctness of individuals? What kinds of strategies will maintain that distinctness without sacrificing close ties with other team members?

FOSTERING RELATIONSHIPS

What Are the Reasons?

Reduce their dependency on you.

Have you noticed how few managers are graded highly by their own employees? Managers usually fail on one level or another, especially in the eyes of their employees. "He isn't fair." "She never gives me a pat on the back." "I never get any advice from her." "He doesn't seem to care if I come to work or not." "She never greets us as we come in the door."

Underlying all these complaints and accusations is the assumption that the manager should somehow be different. The manager is expected to meet each person's needs for fairness despite differing viewpoints as to what is fair.

In one plant the constant complaint was that the general manager, who was responsible for 900 employees, failed to walk through the plant and say "hello" to everyone he met. When he decided to show his good intentions and do just that, many were disappointed that he did not know their names, and were even more disappointed when he could not give them advice on how to run their machines. He retreated to his office quickly. After that experience only rarely, and for a definite purpose, did he reappear in the plant.

All these needs are legitimate. Nevertheless, it is neither equitable nor possible to have the manager fill them all or fill them always. Someone else can say, "Good going. That's excellent work," or "Good morning."

One simple, selfish reason why you should help your employees develop their relationships with one another is to assure that you do not fall into the trap of filling everyone's needs or being condemned for failing to do so.

Improve intragroup communications.

Too many managers try to improve communications without working on relationships, not realizing that the two issues are inseparable. People communicate with people they like. If your people have been encouraged to like one another, they will relate to one another.

I have had client teams in which the level of friendly communication was practically nonexistent—in order to communicate with the team, I had to call each person individually or have an announcement made at the once-a-week team meeting. Other than that, they never saw each other. They claimed they were too busy. However, they did find time to eat lunch with someone—never a fellow team member. They did go to the theatre with someone—never a fellow team member. If your group members develop genuine relationships, you will be amazed at the odd circumstances under which they will be found discussing business. I once attended a party put on by two close business associates. About midnight they both disappeared. Their wives, with annoyance and yet a certain exasperated understanding, sent me to search them out. "The boys are talking business again." Partway to the bar, alongside the band, there were "the boys" working on next month's sales strategy.

No number of show-and-tell sessions, or memos distributed "for your information," or new communication policies can take the place of genuine liking among team members.

Increase input to each individual.

As we said in an earlier chapter, the quality of output is directly related to the quality of the input. A work unit made up of close relationships draws on the multiple contacts and the specialized skills of others in the group.

In one of the more successful advanced development engineering teams I know of, key sales are the result of pooled information gained from trips by various team members throughout the United States. The information is shared at a level that is more intensive and useful than a simple presentation of facts could be, as each member of the team is deeply committed to the success of the others, understands their projects and skills, and bears the intentions of one good friend for another. Instead of giving cut-and-dried presentations of the major events of the trip, the returned traveler will stop in at a neighboring office and say, "I've found a new contact for you. His name is John Doe, in Dallas. This is what he does. I explained your technical history, and since he seemed interested, I have already promised him that you will call later today."

Even if your group's contacts are not as far flung as theirs, there certainly must be times when you wished the team member who had the right information would think of sharing it before disaster struck. "I hear Rudy is irritated that you haven't returned form 28 yet," or even, "I heard a rumor over coffee that the big boss doesn't think you run a tight ship out here." Only people who have close personal ties share information of this quality and intensity.

People gain from using one another's specialized skills. Even when everyone in a group is supposedly trained in the same profession, either because of differences in aptitude or differences in experience, some quickly become extremely capable in one corner of the business while others find their special niche. Much can be gained if your team members help train each other, acting as specialists consulting with each other. In the catch-as-catch-can organizational world such assistance is more likely to come as the result of friendly opportunism than as the result of your planning.

Lend personal support.

In my youth, the Saturday matinee at the local theatre often featured the cowboy who stood alone, without assistance from anyone, against the town bully and his gang of gunslinging rascals. Ever since, I have sought that hero in real life through corporate corridors, academic halls, the church hierarchy, and government bureaucracy. On the rare occasions when I thought I had found this person, I also discovered the band of comrades who encouraged him: "You're doing fine. We're on your side." Jimmy Carter may have appeared to stand alone against the Democratic establishment in the 1976 primary drive, but he had a number of talented close friends who were right there with him, assuring him that he had a chance. As a matter of fact, they told him to run for President.

So convinced am I that no one can stand completely alone and be successful that I have suggested to more than one manager that he either withdraw from his lone stance, or withdraw from the organization—unless he was willing to risk martyrdom.

Without personal support, people are, if not immobilized, at least greatly hindered. For that reason, your group will seek such support from you, their manager. But if you try to be their only source of such help, your energy is drained and your employees become overreliant on you. I have known work groups that couldn't handle the boss's anger or rejection—they were afraid to disagree, because they might lose the support of their only source. There is a certain pleasure in being your group's guru because of the power in being the center and sustainer of everyone else. However, this type of guru centrality breeds weak, dependent employees.

Push and control.

"Have you got that report done yet?" "Have you considered approaching Jones on this?" "Will you prepare a slick presentation to convince Applewood that the only course of action is our course of action?" "Dadburn it Jerry, that is second-rate work. I want you to do it over." Although statements such as these are annoying at the moment they are delivered, they can also save the person being addressed and perhaps the entire team from catastrophe. Do these statements have to come from the boss? If the employees have close working relationships, if they are friends, they can exercise push and control among themselves. If they aren't friends, they won't dare say anything even resembling this to another employee.

"You're so crusty I'm not sure we should let you interact with anyone outside our own team, except under controlled circumstances." I heard that statement said by one friend to another in a tightly knit work setting. In this case the speaker was the employee, and the chagrined but accepting listener was the boss.

Create a rich emotional climate.

There is an old story of the Mexican American, a naturalized citizen for some years, who was explaining life in the United States to his cousin who had just moved across the border. "Americans are very nice people. However, they get very upset if you mention to them that they are dead."

Compared to the warmth and affection, joy and sorrow, rage and rejection of the emotional climate in Mexico, the average cocktail party seems like a gathering of zombies. How much more morbid is the stilted, sterile posturing of organizational meetings. We are, as organization members, far too willing to accept an emotionally impoverished climate, where we focus too much on our heads and deny our hearts.

I consulted to a team that was having difficulty dealing with its feelings about work. Finally, one member said, "I don't believe I have any feelings at all about work." I could not believe it. I even accused him of deliberately kidding me. Everyone has feelings, all the time, I assured him. "Well," he said, "is boredom a feeling?" Certainly! "Then I have a feeling about work."

There is a corporate advantage to being "alive"—the organization will be richer if there is a better emotional climate. "Unencumbered" by emotions, zombies may be efficient, but to surmount challenges you must have employees who can rise emotionally to the challenge. The Minnesota Vikings have made a career of winning enough games to get into the playoffs with technical efficiency, but they lose in the crucial playoffs because the other team comes in on an emotional high and blows them off the field. The methodical plodder more often plods *by* the right answer instead of *into* it, while the alert and vigorous searcher finds the right answer in half the time at half the cost.

One manager cut beyond these reasons in explaining a significant financial outlay to improve the relationships in his 40-person work group. "Look," he said, "I work ten-hour days, I am always here for part of Saturday, and I am often here on Sunday. I spend more of my life with these people than I do with my own family. Is it so unreasonable that I prefer to like them?"

The cost may be high, but. . . .
Why don't managers leap at the opportunity to improve their intragroup relationships? One reason is the costs are high and must be known before you enter any such program. Many of the best methods for improving such relationships cost a lot of money and time.

The greatest cost is the personal pain of such closeness. Misunderstandings have to be reexplored. Old fears have to be erased. Past feelings of anger and irritation do come up. For every step people take toward one another, they may encounter some element in the other person's makeup that they find distressing. Although it is for the ultimate good of their relationships, and for the ultimate good of the work group as a whole, like most medicine, the effort is not always pleasant.

You, as a manager, are more likely to discover your areas of inadequacy, or the areas in which they see you as inadequate, than will any other employee. In the past, you may have been separated from honest feedback in your position as manager. Now, as you attempt to improve relationships, the dam breaks or is lowered and you are struck with the flood of their past feelings. They may have been unreasonably dependent on you without your seeing it. Before they are able to look to one another to fill their needs they look to you. They demand greater interest of you, your advice, and that you meet them at the door and say, "Good morning." This phase takes time and a lot of patience.

Meetings and training events designed to improve relationships run to two and three days. There are usually consulting costs, which seem large in themselves, until they are compared to salaried time spent on the development project. If you decide to improve the group's internal relationships, there will be times when you wonder if the game is worth the candle. You know that the end result of such a project will be a group of employees who are more competent, interdependent, and self-reliant. But the road itself is long and rocky.

How Do You Know If Your Group Has a Problem?

I was employed by a large corporation as the internal organization development specialist. During a period of about two years almost every first-line manager in one major division attended a five-day workshop on team behavior. At the workshop, they were put on a team with other managers they either didn't know or knew only slightly. These teams took on a series of competitive game assignments, and after each assignment they did a study of their own team's strengths and weaknesses to complete the assignment. Personally, I had great reservations about the impact the course would have on the way things were done within the corporation, despite the trainees' high evaluations of the course and sometimes rhapsodical reports on what it had meant to them as individuals. I could see how they might have gained personally from the experience, but the division itself wasn't making concomitant job changes to match the new level of understanding of the managers.

After a break of three years, I met some of the people who had taken those courses in the context of their work within the division. Their management teams were now in many ways being run in accordance with the principles learned in the course. These managers reported that what they had learned was not how to create a team, but what a team was. Before being part of that experimental team, most of them had not known what team work could be like, what an in-depth relationship among producers could mean to the quality and quantity of production, or the relief and ease that clarity and candor of communication could bring to formerly distorted perceptions.

As one manager put it, "I didn't know how I was going to do it, but after experiencing team behavior in the workshop, I knew I was no longer going to be able to survive without experiencing it with my own team members." On the other hand, in another setting, when I suggested to a government manager that his team was in disarray, he disagreed. "My team's together. I make them meet every Tuesday morning." To him the ideal team behavior was a once-a-week meeting. He sought no more and he received no more.

The following questions are designed to help you discern if your group is really working together, even close to the ideal. These questions will be of particular help if you have not had the experience of working with a free-flowing team.

The questions are intended for you alone, not for a public questionnaire. Do a little detective work. Do you really have a team of self-reliant individuals working closely together? Do you have a crowd of other-directed zombies doing exactly what they are told, or do you have a group of isolationists, each a kingdom unto him or herself?

QUESTIONS TO ASK ABOUT TEAMWORK IN YOUR GROUP

1. What percentage of time does each person spend communicating (writing memos, giving or listening to reports, attending meetings)?

0%   100%

2. Who communicates? Are one or two people generally the center of all communication while others are on the periphery?

two   all
communicate   communicate

3. Is anyone left completely out of the channels of communication?

several   nobody

4. How much can any one person on the team tell you about what the other people on the team are doing?

| | | | | | | | | |

nobody
knows

everybody
knows

5. If you say something to one person, how long does it take for everyone to know it?

| | | | | | | | | |

never

immediately

6. When someone is out of the office how many people have a fairly clear notion of where that person has gone and what he or she is doing?

| | | | | | | | | |

nobody

everybody

7. Do you see people arguing—even fighting—in a spirit of equanimity?

| | | | | | | | | |

never

constantly

8. Do people depend on one another?

| | | | | | | | | |

never

always

9. Do they tell you that someone else is working on a portion of their assignment or that they are working on part of what has been assigned to someone else?

| | | | | | | | | |

never

always

10. Do they refer to each other's ideas?

| | | | | | | | | |

never

always

11. Do they choose to work on joint projects?

never   always

12. Do they share credit or blame?

never   always

13. Do they seek each other's advice?

never   always

14. Do they hide behind facades, or are they vulnerable to one another?

facades   vulnerable

15. Do they confess openly to their own errors?

never   always

16. Are they willing to admit ignorance?

never   always

17. Do they readily seek help, or are they trying to portray cool competence at all times?

cool
competence   readily
                                         seek help

18. Are they willing to confront one another openly?

never   always

19. Are they willing to explore their differences, or do they try as quickly as possible to cover them up?

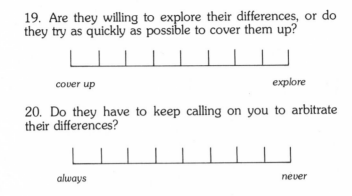

cover up   explore

20. Do they have to keep calling on you to arbitrate their differences?

always   never

What Can You Do About It?

In the next two chapters I will discuss the approach to handling common managerial functions in terms of a general approach to developing self-reliant employees. Much of what is said is designed to promote intragroup relationships. Prior to making major decisions, you must ask yourself what impact a given act will have on the relationships among your people. Will it improve or hinder the way they work with one another? Here are some directions that are aimed at improving relationships.

Use project teams.

Why divide a task into two or three separate parts and assign it to separate individuals? Why not assign the whole task to a project team and allow them to subdivide the tasks? Why manage every team yourself? Why not allow one of the employees the excitement of directing the traffic?

One corporation opens every proposal effort by bringing together everyone who may be involved in the work if the proposal is accepted. They spend two to three days of intensive discussion together, no interruptions allowed. They outline as a group, subdivide writing tasks, separate to write, and come back together to criticize one another's work. Not only does this process provide winning proposals, but it also supplies a depth of knowledge into one another that could never be gained by studying a batch of résumés. Many long, productive, and profitable relationships have been launched when one member of a proposal team heard another answer a question to which the first had thought there was no answer.

Encourage peer coaching and peer review.

The president of a service corporation has initiated the closed-door policy of management to encourage self-reliance. He says that when he had the open-door policy everybody spent time in his office getting his advice on how to do their job better, or just finding out what might be the answer to a complex problem. They also returned to seek his approval when the project was completed. One day it occurred to him that after he had spent an entire day with customers, and had therefore been unavailable to his own executives, he should then have had twice as many and twice as desperate visitors at his door. Actually he had no more and no less.

His secretary explained the phenomenon: "When they can't get you, they talk to each other. When they can get you, they talk to you." At that point he decided to close the door more often, lower their reliance on him, and force them to rely more on one another.

Just as this company president did, you probably have certain peculiar insights to transfer to employees in the course of coaching them on projects. But so do other employees. In order to make the best use of employee capacity and to foster relationships among employees, why not recommend that they use each other as coaches in certain instances? "Have Harry show you how to operate the forklift. Harry, make sure that Sam, here, understands the safety regulations. One month from now I want you to certify that he is qualified to run this Hyster with no further assistance from you." "I think Marge knows more about the application of hydraulics to medical technology than anyone else in the group. Take your project down to her and tell her I've asked her to help you out of this log-jam."

This in no way conflicts with your reviews of their performance, particularly over the long haul. You represent the organization to your own work group; your people gain a different perspective from having their performance reviewed by one another on particular tasks. Such reviews are best kept informal and private.

Look at the physical setup.

Some meeting rooms resemble tunnels. People cannot interact well when they have to wait between statements for the echo to die out. It certainly doesn't help not even to be able to see the face of the person on the same side of the table as you, but eight down the row. Both circumstances make it nigh impossible to carry on a decent discussion, let alone a creative argument.

Are you stacking the cards against team interaction by the way your physical plant is set up? One group of lawyers traded places with their secretaries. All the secretaries spent many hours banging away on noisy typewriters; their work required a minimum of conversation and they were mildly annoyed at the next secretary whose typewriter was sounding a different note and a different rhythm. Meanwhile, the lawyers were running back and forth between each other's offices, asking questions, seeking advice, and relying on each other's help.

They put the secretaries in the private offices where they could concentrate. They put the lawyers back to back in the center of the office where they could confer simply by rotating their swivel chairs. They set aside a couple of offices for private conferences. This resulted in a workspace that fit the needs of the people concerned, although its unorthodoxy required continual explanation to those who visited it.

Analyze your physical layout. If people want to relate to each another, where might they do it?

I conducted a study for the managers of two engineering groups that were often at war. Sometimes when they ran joint projects, they succeeded. Other times the projects failed. Was there any common denominator for success?

Yes. Whenever the engineers moved their offices into the same area, the project succeeded. Whenever they did not, the project failed. Will one flight of stairs between groups reduce the interaction between them? Substantially!

Consider how many conversations begin because you just bumped into each other in the hallway, and then consider how many ideas you probably did not share because you would have to leave your work for a substantial period of time simply to see the person you would like to chat with.

Allow time for interaction.

People cannot interact when every moment is tracked and every second accounted for. It takes time to have a conversation.

Have you noticed that most of us usually start quite aways away from the topic we would really like to discuss, and then gently, in gradual swirls, drift over to the real, sensitive, troublesome topic? Some managers, of course, attempt to make a virtue of getting right to the point. I have found that they either pick points that are not all that deep, penetrating, or potentially problematic, or they continually leave behind them dismayed, irritated receivers of their terse messages.

One general manager who likes to get to the point always calls immediately and tells his employees to quit doing anything he hears about that he doesn't like. No beating around the bush for him. Of course, by now everyone has learned to avoid telling him anything that may get any of their friends a preemptory phonecall. His insistence on efficient communication is causing the loss of all communication. He has to learn to take his time and explore situations with employees, or they will continue to sidestep his rude interventions in their business by being silent.

The opening gyrations are designed to get the lay of the land, find out the risks of opening the topic, assuage potential damage to the other person's feelings, and perhaps even gather the courage to tell the truth. If you don't allow time for this to happen, you may be cutting off important communication.

Examine the mix in your group.

Some people are natural isolates. Some professions attract groups of natural isolates. If no one in your group enjoys being with people, they will probably never come together. Try to staff your area with an eye toward making sure there is at least one person in your group who tends to gather people together around the watercooler.

A consulting associate of mine was hired by the new president of a company to assist him in promoting team behavior among the executives. After a year of minimal headway, in the course of a team meeting, my friend administered an inventory that reported people's predilections for interacting with others. According to the inventory, the new president enjoyed such interaction more than average people do. Down to a person, the executives did not enjoy being with other people. When the inventory results were shared, everyone felt the relief of insight. The president found another company instead of continuing to swim against the stream.

What about training courses?

Most people have never had a good course in how to relate to other people, although such training now exists. We have tended to think that this most delicate of functions is learned naturally, whereas we have invested billions of dollars in teaching the subtleties of various forms of athletic endeavor.

There is such a person as a natural communicator, one who learned the better ways of interacting almost from mother's knee. There is also the natural athlete, gifted by heredity and environment with an early jump on the rest of us less adroit animals. However, just as I do not have to foresake the basketball court just because I was not born 6'7'', so I don't need to fumble continually in my dealings with other people. There are interpersonal skills that can be learned.

Among the reasons that such courses are not patronized more is the misguided zeal of returnees who describe the course as if it were a religious experience. Don't allow yourself to be repelled by such an over-statement of the course's benefits. If a person has never really been able to understand other people or to come across to them, you must forgive that person a certain rapture in the experience of breakthrough. The interpersonal training session has not introduced a person to a new and different form of reality, but it can seem that way.

The American Management Associations, National Training Labora-tories, and a host of other groups hold courses in interpersonal skills. Perhaps you and your employees can gain from them.

Hire a consultant.

Again, being self-reliant does not mean going it alone. A third person who is not enmeshed in the daily routine and the politics of your group can be useful to you in deciphering your group's needs for improved relationships. After an initial analysis such a consultant can also assist you in working out various meeting formats and designs that will contribute to deepening the relationships among your team members.

Many organizations have begun to provide internal staff people to as-sist their managers. If you belong to such an organization you will find them listed as organization development specialists, and less often as management specialists.

One caveat. Find out through an exploratory interview if the consultant is really there to help you or to give you trouble. Good consultants are very manager oriented and are not looking for the chance to compete with you for the respect of your employees. A good consultant wants to make your group better, but not at your expense. Nevertheless, many are still working through their own feelings of dependency and counter-dependency. Such consultants privately enjoy seeing the boss come up with egg on his or her face. Here are some cues to watch for:

—Does the consultant want center stage, or does the consultant work with you on ways to maintain leadership of the group?
—Does the consultant care about your concern that the project may go awry?
—Does the consultant lay all the cards on the table and let you make the decisions or encourage you to forge ahead blindly relying on his or her mystical process to make things come out well?

There are both kinds of consultant. Make sure you get the right one. For example, one corporate management group has such unpleasant contacts with consultants that they refer to them with macabre humor as "insultants." According to this group's experience, consultants exist to plague the managers and point out their errors. They make a paying profession out of insulting others.

If your organization does not have consultants, and if your budget won't allow you to use one from outside your organization, consider establishing a consulting relationship with another manager you respect. Both of you can chat with members of each other's group. Presuming that you can avoid being gleeful about discovering the other person's errors, and defensive about their discovery of yours, you will be able to offer each other different perspectives on each other's situations.

FOSTERING INDIVIDUALITY

Why the Need?

Although most American organizations are concerned with the individual to a fault, a new phenomenon is emerging. The very real gains to be received from an emphasis on relationships, an emphasis on communication, and an emphasis on teams, have so enamored many, that "groupiness" has become the order of the day, even when "groupiness" is not appropriate.

When I approached one internal development officer in a corporation with my stock in trade, teambuilding, she wailed, "We don't need more teams or better teams. Everybody around here spends all their time relating to one another. We need someone who will shut their office door and do some work." "All we do around here is attend meetings" is becoming the increasing complaint of craftspeople enmeshed in team-oriented organizations.

Even the schools put an early emphasis on getting along well with others, social skillfulness, and sharing toys and materials. I take a perverse delight in my son's insistence on not only having his own toys, but the neighbor's toys, in the face of the mounting social pressure to become a placid, friendly, and nonacquisitive group member.

Although various strategies that emphasize how to improve relationships will allow your employees to become more self-reliant, overdoing these same strategies without countering approaches that emphasize individual responsibility will overbalance the situation. The basic mistake is to think there is a spectrum from high group orientation to high individual orientation and that you must choose a spot on the spectrum for your group. On the contrary, you can do many things to promote group behavior and individual responsibility at the same time. The two are not incompatible.

Too little orientation toward individuals, and you lose the sense of who is responsible for what.

"If I sink my teeth into this will I be duplicating someone else's effort?" "How many people do I have to check with before I can begin?" or even, "Who was supposed to inform our customers we would be a day late in delivery?"

Too little orientation toward individuals, and you lose the sense of having accomplished anything.

As the task is merrily spun from hand to hand, the individual producer loses a sense of ownership for the product. Instead of planning to use federal funds to assist nursing homes, the bureaucrat has some input into those plans. Translated this means, "She attended a lot of meetings on the subject and isn't too sure what happened to her ideas." Not a satisfying or motivating way to do business, at least not for the achievement or power motivated.

Too little orientation toward individuals, and everyone begins to look and sound like everyone else.

You can't have relationships unless there is someone else to relate to. The more people are encouraged to relate to one another, the more they begin to share the same values, strategies, and approaches. Continual discussion rubs off the edges and brings about eventual agreement.

To some extent, that is precisely one of the advantages to working on relationships. Instead of having a group in which everyone thinks differently, they now think similarly enough to be able to work together toward a common product. But if they think too much alike, there is little to be gained by their conversing, and they cease to give one another fresh ideas or challenge one another's habitual practices. No longer does the conflict of their opinion create unusual opportunities. They all become intellectual hostages of each other.

What Are the Strategies?

You undoubtedly know these strategies. Ten years ago they were the only approaches to management. To maintain the uniqueness and strength of the individuals within your group you do not need to try anything new. Just don't throw out everything old as you increase your concern for the relationships within your group. You should still insist on each person having defined individual objectives as well as team objectives. Even though you hold the team responsible for completion of a task, each individual on that team should also be held responsible. When you hold appraisals, hold them with individuals as well as with teams. Before meetings, insist that people have their homework done or reschedule the meeting. After meetings, insist that individuals have tasks to do, or if not, challenge the usefulness of further meetings.

11

Management methods that promote self-reliance

How do you handle hiring, planning, organizing, controlling, evaluating, and disciplining in your group? Here are some specific questions on the way your unit works. Note in some detail who does what and in what order it is done, covering the formal steps and the informal steps. You might like to add a few of your own, for example, how people get fired. Under question 1 (hiring) you might begin with: I notify the personnel office that I have an opening. I also notify my own manager. My manager decides whether or not the position is to be filled. The personnel office checks with him (or her) and then circulates a description of the job, and so forth, within the company.

How are people hired for your group?
How are plans made for next quarter's or next year's activities?
How are people organized for the activities of the day or week?
How do you ensure that plans are followed?
How are employees disciplined?
How are people's competencies evaluated?

If your goal is to have self-reliant employees, you have to rely on them. If you, your management, or some other unit in your organization is doing all the management work, you remove from your people the opportunity to be self-reliant. Your employees will become other-reliant expecting the work to be done for them. Or your employees will become isolationists. They will hold management tasks in contempt and pursue their own technical work without understanding the needs of the whole work unit.

In order to manage your group, whom do you rely on? Yourself? Your employees? Your management? An outside group? Use the matrix (Figure 3) to find out. First go back through your answers to the six questions listed above. Put a check in the top half of the appropriate box of the matrix for each time you rely on one of the four groups in column 1 to accomplish one of the six tasks. No fair adding at this point to your description of the way things are done. If you didn't notice that someone did something the first time around, it probably isn't too important to you. Next, multiply the number of checks by the value given at the bottom of the column, and put that figure in the bottom half of each box. Then add each subtotal across. For instance, if under Initiates Process/Employees you placed two checks in the top in the box, you would multiply that by the value given at the bottom of the chart, 3 points, for a total of 6. This will give you a good idea of who is relied on most to perform management tasks.

The values are arbitrary. If you think they should be different, feel free to change them. There is no perfect, or even average, score for each of the categories on the matrix. As you examine the scores, how does your situation appear to you?

Is your group overreliant on people outside your group for decisions and direction? If so, to be a self-reliant manager, you must begin the arduous task of winning back the responsibilities they have appropriated.

Do your employees get adequately involved in the decision-making process? Are they self-reliant, or do they rely on you, your management, or on other groups to make their decisions for them? If their score isn't even close to yours, the personnel department's, or your management's, your employees are in the impoverished position of allowing their destiny to be decided by someone else.

It is often difficult to convince those outside your group to exert less influence on decisions that affect your group. The request to "Leave that to us," stands a good chance of being ignored by management. For reasons of their own, perhaps a distrust of you or your abilities, they want things to stay the way they are. Such groups as personnel and accounting, which encourage sameness in order to maintain order throughout the organization, tend to be wary of innovation.

However, it should not be difficult to convince those within your group to try to have *more* influence in the decision-making process. Since this is

Figure 3. Whom do you rely on to perform most management tasks?

Management Tasks

Who Is in Charge?	Initiates Process	Provides Info	Provides Alternatives	Discusses Decision	Makes Decision	Communicates Decision	Totals
Employees							
You							
Your management							
Outside person/group							
Point value:	3	1	2	3	4	2	

not a zero-sum game, your having more influence does not mean that others will have less. For instance, perhaps in the hiring decision example used above, the decision to fill or not fill the position is not up to you, but is your manager's decision. It will probably be difficult to get your boss to relinquish that decision to your group. But will it be difficult to get your group to develop a detailed rationale for filling the position? Will it be difficult to get some members of your group to accompany you to present that rationale to your manager?

Perhaps your personnel department has a copy of the job description and a run-down on the characteristics of the type of person to fill it. Personnel is unlikely to give up that role. Yet the personnel officer in charge of the search may prove extremely open to assistance from your group in developing an informal set of characteristics more tightly in line with this year's requirements. That personnel officer is well aware that ultimately he or she will be judged by how well satisfied you are with the people who parade through your office. On the other hand, your consideration for the rules and goals by which the personnel officer is bound will help you in obtaining his or her cooperation.

Some examples of how to approach various functions to enhance employee self-reliance are discussed below. They are not a compendium on how to handle each of the functions. Much of the good advice contained in management manuals, handbooks, and textbooks still holds. Rather than define how you should handle these management tasks for you, my intention is to indicate how you can adjust existing successful management practices so that they will also improve the capacity of your people to take responsibility for their own actions as well as the shape and direction of their own group.

Managers in some organizations may find the methods suggested here to be far in advance of the capability of their organization to use them. On the other hand, for some organizations the time for these methods may be overdue. Look again at the diagnostic test at the end of Chapter 2. It will serve as an indicator of how ready your organization is for these methods. If in your estimation they are ready, apply these methods as they are given. But if you are likely to meet with resistance, modify as necessary. Don't overwhelm your employees with more opportunity for self-reliance than they can handle, or than other organizational factors demand.

Although there are faster ways to do things than with the techniques indicated here, employee growth—not task speed—will be your objective. The time you take with these procedures will be given back tenfold if you succeed in developing self-reliant employees.

HIRING

Deciding whom you need

If your employees are to learn self-reliance they must have influence on whoever enters their group. Ordinarily the manager is held responsible for the capacity of new staff members to be of genuine assistance to the group. If not the manager, then some outside department, or even an external temporary board, performs this function. However, in most groups, it will be the people's productivity, future, and environment that are most affected by the new employee. Let them have a hand in deciding who that employee will be.

The first step is to announce a meeting at which you and your group will prepare a profile of the person you need both to fill in for group deficiencies and yet be compatible with others in the group. Although you will never find the perfect person to fit this profile, it is important to nail down a picture of who you really want at this early stage to help you and your group to avoid hiring the first attractive hunk of flesh or bit of fluff that meets your eye.

The questions you need to answer as a group should cover all sides and aspects of the person and leave out nothing that is important to you or to your group. Some of the qualifications may be difficult to explain to others. For example, a female manager of my acquaintance couldn't stand people who were not well groomed. One of her criteria for working with her was attractiveness. Although many a potential candidate for her group may have been disappointed at not being hired on that criterion, if they had been hired, these candidates would have experienced a subtle rejection both from her and her group. Everyone gained in the long run from her ability to state her personal requirements even though they were neither rational nor particularly fair.

Another group established pathological honesty as their criterion for hiring. On a personality inventory, every person in the group scored as either "honest" or "pathologically honest." They would tell the truth, no matter what the circumstances, and no matter what the consequences. If Joe's wife asked if they saw Joe at the bar last night, they would readily share the true information, secure in the justice of what they said, unmindful of the consequences for Joe and his marriage. Under similar circumstances, they would expect Joe to do the same. I pointed out to them that they tended to be extreme on the question, even a little "crazy." I suggested that they relax their standards. However, since their group ran a county tax assessment and collection department, they decided that pathological honesty had to remain a criterion for membership in their group.

Here are some questions you can ask your group to get them started in thinking about the profile of the new member. What technical skills are required to perform in this group? How exactly can we state them? Are there technical skills that this group does not now possess which we need to have in the person of this new member? What are they? Do we need someone with skills from other areas besides the basic skills of our technology? A trainer? A marketeer? An accountant? What personal characteristics are required? The ability to work alone without support? The ability to work constantly with others, continually responding to their demands and needs? The ability to take the initiative? The ability to take orders without question? What level of skill is required? What educational background and what credentials are necessary?

Starting with an accurate profile will save you trouble in the long run, although it will cost you time here and now. Be particularly cautious about overstating your needs in this profile, or of hiring someone more competent than the profile requires. It's tempting, but disastrous. The federal government over the last few years has started as secretaries many bright, college-educated women. They do not make good secretaries for more than six months because they get bored with the job and start putting more energy into getting out of it. So also will the master in electrical engineering who is willing to take a job as a draftsperson, or the architect who is willing to lay bricks, if they are doing this because they have no choice.

One warning as you get your group involved in the hiring process: Since groups tend to be self-protective, they need confrontation. Have some people from outside your group review the final product to ensure that your group hasn't eliminated the real person they need in favor of someone they will not find personally or professionally dangerous. One group of my acquaintance either asks for someone with a doctorate in their field or for a beginning practitioner. They have B.A.'s, and for the most part learned the trade within their own company. If a Ph.D. outshines them, they will not suffer by comparison since they cannot be expected to compare favorably to a person of such status and salary. On the other hand, a beginning practitioner cannot outshine them. However, they carefully rule out hiring another practitioner with credentials similar to their own, for that person might make their work look weak in comparison, arriving with different insights and techniques.

Allow the candidate to be self-reliant

Most organizations give the candidate a step-by-step description of the job, and allow little room for self-reliance or initiative. Often candidates are judged on their ability to answer questions posed by others in the organization, when the real task the candidate will perform involves formulating the right questions, not answering them.

One county government uses such a technique for hiring even at the director level. Placidly ignoring the fact that the last time most of these candidates will receive clear directions and questions is during the hiring interviews, they even cut off as suspect and unfortunate any efforts the candidate makes to move independently. "I cannot see you—you are a candidate for a job," the county personnel director informed one person who wished to explore the possibility of his skills and the job matching.

I suggest that you give potential candidates a copy of your organization chart. Encourage them to contact whoever they wish in order to understand your needs and sell themselves, especially if self-reliance is the expected mode of operation within your group. If they are helpless in hunting down a job, they will be helpless later in carrying it out.

Use multiple interviews

If your group is small enough, allow everyone to be involved in the interviewing process. If the group is too large for that, then allow the group to select their own representatives as the interviewers. Five or six are a great plenty. I suggest that you use individual interviews, or at the most two or three interviewers at a time. The candidate experiences enough pressure without having to face six people at once. In the course of the one-to-one interview, each candidate can become known at a more intimate level.

On the other hand, for one group I know, stress during the interview was a highly desired factor. Every group member was repeatedly put in the position of explaining to doubting candidates the technical excellence of the group's latest product. This group had candidates meet with the entire group and sell the group on the merits of one of the candidate's own designs. Although the questions asked at the end of the interview were not deliberately hostile, they weren't friendly either. Candidates who passed this acid test without wavering were then invited to come back for a series of friendlier conversations about their job-related needs and desires.

Get group input to your decision

If you try to achieve total consensus before you hire someone, you will probably hire no one. There is always someone who doesn't want to hire a given candidate. Sometimes the battle is really between people who are already on your staff. "If Mary likes him, Sam does not want him." Reserve the final decision for yourself. Weigh the support and resistance to any given candidate along with your own feelings. Make your own decision. Test your decision with the group. Listen to their response. Be very slow to go against the will of the majority. Consider what problem must exist if you and your group differ widely on a candidate. Nor should you be quick to disregard the opinions of the minority, even if it is a minority of one. Allow time to hear and understand their arguments. Sometimes their insights will aid or turn around your decision. But, in the last analysis *you* decide.

PLANNING

The better manuals on planning always emphasize that the plan that appears on paper is only as valuable as the agreements of the people who have developed them. Plans so often fail to be executed because only a few people were involved.

The vice-president of marketing got the president of his company to demand that the accounting department develop a new expense system for salespeople. Since the accountants were not involved in the decision, you can expect either no product, a slipshod product, or a misinformed product. What will motivate the accountants to work on this when there are other more pressing products awaiting their energies? Why do a good job in response to what appears to be an arbitrary whim? And if these two blocks are surmounted, what are the chances of meeting the salespeople's needs accurately when they have never been involved in discussing these needs. Look at planning not as a method for writing something down on paper, but as a method for getting heads together on problems and opportunities. Look at it as a chance to force people to influence one another on how to use their time and energy.

The federal government is classic in producing plans designed by one person to be carried out by another. Many of these plans are not only not implemented, they aren't read.

While temporarily filling in for the agency planning director, a friend of mine received an irate call from the agency's EEO officer. "Who's in charge of objective 28b? They haven't done a thing on it all year." She was flustered and had to admit she did not know but would look it up. Later in the day with feigned meekness and great private joy she called him back to inform him that according to the planning documents *he* was in charge of objective 28b.

But then how was he supposed to know? He had not been present when the objective was discussed and written. Easily enough, he had forgotten the curt memo from the planning director informing him of his new responsibility.

On the other hand, one firm never managed to get to the final draft on any of its quarterly plans, yet as a product of the conversation in which they attempted to develop their plans, much of the planned-for work was completed. For instance, although at one planning meeting the group did not decide that they wanted Henry to produce a particular new design, Henry felt that he had enough support to attempt a draft of that design on his own. At the next planning meeting, Henry showed the draft, and at that time not only did the group officially plan to have him finish it, but three members of the group committed themselves to joining him on the project. Along with a definite rise in the level of accomplishment, group involvement in planning will bring about a corresponding drop in the neatness of the plans themselves.

If you already have a formal planning process in your organization, increase your employees' ability to exercise their own judgment, to be responsible for the use of their own time and energy, and in short, to be self-reliant, by bringing them into the planning process. If your organization does not have a formal planning process, or if it does not customarily encourage planning for work units in your area or at your level, set up your own simple process.

ORGANIZING

One reason employees can't be self-reliant is they are kept in the dark about what needs to be done. All they are given to understand is that small parcel of work that has been doled out to them. Even if they see what may be potential catastrophe, they don't know if they should solve it or if someone else should. They don't even know if it really is a catastrophe. Perhaps it is the next step in your plans for the day. People who don't know what is going on are immobilized. They are justly afraid that if they do what they think needs doing, they may contribute to the failure of some carefully wrought scheme of their manager or their peers. If they move anyway, they risk being known as a bull in the china shop. They will probably knock over some project or other in blind ignorance.

A weekly organization session can shed light on otherwise unillumi-nated areas. A summer camp used a simple yet practical system that could be installed usefully in groups that ranged from librarians to engineers to bank examiners. At the start of the week, they held a staff meeting. The director started out with a list of items he felt needed to be done; then others chimed in and added items to the list. Everyone was involved in a discussion of priorities from this list. After priorities were assigned, people volunteered for various tasks based on their skills and availabilities. The only rule was that first-priority tasks generally had to be volunteered for before later priority tasks. As soon as people could no longer commit their time with certainty, the bidding for jobs was closed. The complete list of tasks with the names of the volunteers was left posted.

The advantages to employee self-reliance in this camp situation were many. First, employees knew their priorities and had decided that they had the time to do the task. Second, employees knew what other people were to do. They could safely ignore certain areas as they went their daily rounds secure in the knowledge that someone else had already volunteered to cope with those situations. Third, if extra time turned up, they could still return to the posted list and sign up for another job, thereby removing that one from the list of concerns for others. At the end of the week, the success of the project was reviewed for that week.

CONTROLLING

Many managers spend much of their time making sure that other people are doing their jobs. The self-reliant approach to managing takes care of that problem. Instead of telling others what to do, they now had the time to plan the long-range directions for the group and organize the work better. For example, in the summer camp mentioned earlier, no one tracked employees from the start of the week to its end. The employees had agreed to do their jobs and knew that they were to be held accountable at the end of the week. They controlled their own work.

But let's not kid ourselves. People always need to be nudged. Few of us are so thoroughly involved in our work that we do not try to avoid it on many occasions. Having someone around who will remind us that we are slipping is valuable. Although employees will hold one another accountable, you must, because of your position in the group, do more than anyone else.

However, if you find you are spending a major portion of your time running around "reminding" others of their errors, there is a good chance that you have failed to provide the conditions whereby they can take on a self-reliant stance.

If they are not controlling themselves, apparently they do not see the importance of the task. Have they truly been involved in its planning? Did they genuinely assent to doing things that way?

DISCIPLINING

Many of the techniques involved in fostering self-reliance are open to employee manipulation, connivance, malingering, and other such strategies. Most employees will respond well to the opportunity to choose and plan their own work. Some, however, will use that as an opportunity to duck work and to volunteer for the easiest, as well as the fewest, assignments. Ideally, peers will exert pressure for change. But if they do not, they will resent your allowing anyone to get away with subverting the purposes of the self-reliant approach. You must do something to get things back on course. You are the court of last resort who ensures that if self-discipline and peer discipline both fail, some discipline will remain.

The first step in handling any discipline problem should be an attempt to understand the nature of the problem. Often, laziness or ignorance can drive you to reach much too quickly, in your irritation, for some bludgeon to drive recalcitrant employees to do your will. Check with the employees. Do they realize they are behaving this way? Ask them what is happening, why they are behaving the way they are. There is more than a slight chance that your considerate attention to their problem may serve as cure. They may also tell you the source of their difficulty. Perhaps they feel overwhelmed by a poorly understood job. Perhaps they do not feel accepted by the group they work with. Perhaps the job is so unchallenging they aren't motivated to do it. Perhaps they have personal problems outside the job. After they have identified the problem, ask them to help you work out a solution—above all, don't solve it for them. That ready-made solution will keep them reliant on you for further solutions.

Get them to ask for help on the poorly understood job. Have them identify, if they can, the person most likely to possess the needed knowledge and the appropriate teaching skills. Have them suggest ways they can influence group members to let them into the informal conversations, chatter, and friendships. Let them identify methods for broadening the job content to their satisfaction.

Beating on people is seldom of much value. Studies show that most people do not respond well to what is termed "negative reinforcement." They will play a complicated game with you. First, they will conceal what they are doing. Then, they will find sneaky ways to obstruct the work of others. Finally, they will do only enough to avoid your wrath, but not enough to give you or anyone else any pleasure. This tends to set up generally negative, distrustful attitudes. If you succeed in being so frighteningly forceful that your employees do not dare play games with you, you will have raised their anxiety to the point where they will have difficulty getting their work done. As I pointed out in Chapter 5, fear has negative effects on people's behavior. Even beyond the subtle stylistic problems discussed in that chapter, fear and anxiety cause people to make mistakes.

A much better approach is to appeal to the people's sense of self-worth. Praise their strengths. Give them responsibility. Most foot-draggers will brighten up and pick up their tasks when it is clear to them that you see them as a valuable or potentially valuable member of the team and offer them the opportunity to realize that potential. Remember how your fourth-grade teacher always put the mischievous students in charge of cleaning the erasers? Docility often comes with responsibility. This will not happen, automatically, but it will require sincere effort on your part. Don't give up the effort the first time your attempts go unappreciated.

There are always some team members who do not even respond to repeated attempts at getting them involved in sharing responsibility. One company has experimented with simply telling such people that they are not working at a level worthy of their own skills and abilities. The company sends them home for a day to think it over, and the company pays their salary while they are thinking. However, if they do not return to work up to their ability, the company fires them. Employees at that firm have reported that they had never considered before that they were betraying themselves by holding back on their efforts. Although only a few were actually fired, many changed their ways.

A self-reliant manager must do something that has a similar effect, sending a clear message to employees: "I have set up an approach to management that allows you to be self-reliant. It will not work if you are not self-reliant. You must control yourself. You must discipline yourself. If I find that I must discipline you or control you, the chances are good that you do not belong in my group. And I will find a way to get you out of here."

Too many managers are predicating their management style on the lowest common denominator of employee. "I have 20 employees who do not need watching, but Harry requires constant watching, so I constantly watch all 21 employees." There is an alternative. Get rid of Harry. After he has bounced around from group to group even old Harry may get the point—that Harry is in charge of Harry and has to do a better job of it.

I once challenged a group of managers on the amount of documentation they required in their performance appraisal process. They responded by saying that civil service required that amount of documentation to fire a nonperformer. I asked them how many out of 100 employees they might want to remove in that manner. The answer was, "One in a hundred." Still, the manager was forced to be involved in mountains of unnecessary paper about the 99 docile employees for the sake of that one who might prove intractable.

For the record, I do not feel that my incisive question solved their problem. They were working within the federal civil service system, a system established to protect employees from arbitrary punitive acts. This system is certainly both useful and necessary. Unfortunately, it often makes the practice of reasonable management impossible. When I left this group, they still planned to document everyone as thoroughly as before. Regrettably, I know no better solution, until such time as the civil service requirements are redesigned, to allow for employee protection and reasonable control, guidance, and discipline efforts from managers. Private-sector managers needn't feel smug at not having to contend with these bureaucratic restraints. Laws are already being written and enforced that will require you to document your decision to fire people who come under some minority class. I predict that these are but the first of many government restrictions on what you will be allowed to do with your own workers.

The ultimate discipline is the esprit de corps of a successful group. If your work unit radiates happiness and success, group members will hold the line on one another and on themselves in subtle ways. Many an island has been taken over by the marines because of the conviction of the members of the corps that marines can do no less than succeed against impossible odds simply because they are marines. Successful work units have a way of demanding quality work from one another without relying on the constant goading of a manager who represents the company interests.

EVALUATING PERSONNEL

There are a number of reasons for evaluating personnel and a corresponding variety in approaches. You could be evaluating for the sake of the company's promotional system, or in order to inform employees of your opinions as the manager, or to increase the employee's capacity and ability to plan his or her own future.

Evaluating for the sake of the promotional system has led to evaluation approaches that leave the employee completely out of the loop. If you wish to transmit accurately to the files or the computer your judgment on an employee, do not invite the employee to be part of the process. Studies done during the mid-1930s show that managers consistently fail to report their true feelings if they know that their employees will see their reports. Most managers will forsake the purity of the system to ensure that they won't have to control a hostile employee for the next year.

Decide who is competent to take whose place and who should be trained to fill which slot and you simply have more excuses to make. Hurt feelings will have to be assuaged when the time for change comes and the realities of organizational life dictate that the person "in line for the job" be bypassed for someone more competent, someone with special skills, or someone the boss likes.

The basic problem in comprehensive company-oriented workforce training, development, promotion, and appraisals is that no one is really willing to take the training and promotion of anyone else seriously unless the chips are down. Before the slot is open, the workforce system is seen as another personnel rain dance, to be completed pro forma. When the slot is open, the personnel system becomes an obstruction on the way to finding the right candidate.

The person whose training and promotion most people are willing to take seriously is their own. Rather than construct an evaluation system, which is the first step in getting everyone to try to help everyone else, a more effective method is an evaluation system that gets each person to rely on self to seek professional improvement, promotions, and pay increases.

A federal agency has experimented with such a self-appraisal method. At the conclusion of the evaluation, both the employees' self-evaluation and the manager's comments on that evaluation go to the central file. Employees who don't think the manager is giving them a square deal can appeal to a special board set up for that purpose. The manager is bound to conduct the appraisal, but the training sessions are held with the managers and their employees. The employees are thoroughly instructed in their rights under the system and are told that they have the self-reliant obligation to remind the manager of these rights if the manager slipped. They are guaranteed the support of the agency in defending these rights.

The appraisal itself started with the employees' self-evaluation. To construct the self-evaluation, employees examined their MBO contracts, noting where objectives had been achieved and where they had not. They noted factors that influenced success and those that influenced failure. Among those factors, employees highlighted those factors that indicated their personal strengths and weaknesses.

Managers made comments on the evaluations. There was no demand that they give their complete opinion. Basically, the manager was seen as a coach to help the employee to a more complete self-evaluation. The guiding principle was the belief that employees will change only on those issues where they see the need for change. Sometimes during the course of the conversation employees will be open to new insights from the manager, and sometimes not. At the end of the evaluation, it is only the employees' self-opinion that will make a difference in their growth.

Here is an example. As he studied his objectives, one employee noted that whenever the outcome was entirely up to him he accomplished the objective superlatively. On the other hand, whenever he had to involve others they failed to provide him input on time. During the interview with his manager, he dismissed his inability to get them to produce as part of their civil service employee laziness. The manager let that pass for the moment and instead asked the employee to explain what there was about him that caused such superlative results when he worked alone. The employee found it difficult to express these characteristics.

"Oh, I'm fairly bright."

"How bright?" asked the manager.

"Well, I have a fairly high IQ."

"How high?" insisted the manager.

"Oh, somewhere in the neighborhood of 160."

Bit by bit other strengths were drawn out: "unusually creative," "expansive vocabularly," "quickness of insight," "extremely competent with words."

Then the manager asked: "How do you think the average person feels, turning work in to you?"

More question than reply, the hesitant answer was "Scared?"

The manager said, "Well, I can't speak for them, but I know that it makes me nervous to ask you to review my work. I think you should try to find out how they feel. Maybe they miss deadlines because they are afraid to put their work under your microscope."

Here is an example of how *not* to do it. A gifted technician and staff scientist was bypassed for the management role in the organization, which was created to take advantage of his own marketing and technical work. He was informed carefully and in detail by his management of those characteristics and blindspots they felt were now blocking him from being a successful manager. They insisted that he spend at least two years working under another manager, learning from that manager, and attending a plethora of management training courses.

The staff scientist disagreed violently and openly with his management's judgment. When it became evident that he had lost the battle, he begrudgingly agreed to go through the motions. Two years and many dollars later he was promoted to manager as they promised, only a little worse for the wear and stubbornly no wiser than before. He never agreed with the evaluation, and was never able to gain from the prescription. Although we might like to pretend to be more malleable than that, most of us share that same stubborn streak. Not that we will not agree sometimes with the deftly noted error, but if we do not agree, neither tide nor person is going to change us.

Evaluation should include self-evaluation. Encourage your people to confide their strengths and weaknesses. Encourage them to define their developmental needs. Ask them to point out to you what career steps they would like to take. Then, by all means, attempt to influence them. Feel free to disagree. Be prepared to argue and fight if it seems appropriate, if they can argue with you and still listen. Don't club them over the head with disagreement or take advantage of their vulnerability in the interview to drive home your pet peeves. If you wish them to remain self-reliant, recognize that at the end of the interview it is their opinion of themselves that will make the difference, not your opinion of them.

AN EXERCISE

The theme of this chapter is employee involvement, whenever feasible or possible. Employees will never become self-reliant unless you rely on them to take a hand in shaping their own destiny and that of their work group. If in answering the opening quiz you found that they are left out of most management decisions, try this. Take a look at the upcoming month. What management function are you about to perform during that period that would benefit you by their input and benefit them through their participation? Invite them to join you in working on it. Give them ample warning and facts to prepare. Tell them this is an experiment and that you are interested in seeing how things work out when you make decisions this way instead of your usual way. Clarify the management prerogatives you intend to maintain so they won't be disappointed at the end of the process.

Try this experiment three or four times before you make any definitive judgment as to its value. If you have never done anything like this before, it will take a few repetitions for both you and your employees to become skillful at it and for you to see the positive effects of their increased self-reliance.

LOSING CONTROL

You may object to giving employees this much to say about the functions of management, feeling that if you do, others will think you have lost control of your unit. But you can make this effort pay off for you, your group, and your organization. As you invite employees to take on management functions, bear these three principles in mind.

You can give privileges to employees without diminishing your own.

You can say to employees, "You are now going to have a great deal to say about the next person we hire," without relinquishing your privilege of the final say. They can be given free rein to organize their own work week, with the full understanding that one or two miserable tasks will have to be taken on if they can't be avoided.

You can only use these approaches with a healthy group.

If everybody is against you and management, the principles advocated in this chapter just won't work. There has to be basic mutual trust and respect before an attempt can be made to increase self-reliance. Why should you want them to be self-reliant if they are against you? On the other hand, if your employees are on your side, why not increase their opportunities for self-reliance? Helping them will put them in a better position to help you instead of causing you trouble.

Control is a mirage.

You don't have things that much under control anyway. If you're afraid that teaching your group to be self-reliant will give them the power to cut the ground from under you, remember: they could do it almost as well before, if that were their plan. You are already dependent on their good will as you manage your group. Why not acknowledge the fact? It's hard to admit, even to yourself, that you can't get your group to budge an inch more than it wants to.

Our prison system is an excellent example of the difficulty of getting people to do what they do not want to do. We certainly aren't very successful at it. We succeed in keeping most prisoners in prison. But we can't keep drugs and weapons out. And people in prisons manage to commit murder behind prison walls. We rehabilitate only a small percentage of the prison population. No matter how restrictive prison managers are, no matter how sophisticated the confining barriers, prisoners prove daily that control is, indeed, a mirage.

12

New models
of behavior

The last three chapters promote the planned approach to management as a means to achieving employee self-reliance. There is yet another way that will give you the same impact, one that is far more subtle, powerful, and difficult to control. That way is your daily on-the-job behavior.

Planned techniques allow you the luxury of thinking through your approach. They give you time. On the minus side, your employees may feel that everything you do is based on strategy, rather than your deeply felt stance toward them as employees and toward the practice of management. This by no means invalidates the use of these practices, but it does temper their impact.

It is what you do in the unguarded moment that is the true test of how you feel toward them. For example, although your group will appreciate and value the lengthy meetings you hold to get their input for next year's plans, they will appreciate it even more if they can disagree with you in the hallways. That makes you accessible and genuinely interested.

The managerial behavior most likely to engender employee self-reliance cannot be programmed. Earnest dedication will produce spontaneity in the way you work with your group. And you will be more believable.

MAKING DEMANDS OF YOUR GROUP

The clearest signal you can give an employee of your doubts about that person's strength, skill, and competence is your own unwillingness to make demands of them. Any obvious easiness, gentleness, softness implies the inability of the other person to respond adequately to the full demand, which is being so diluted. When you have indicated to them that you are unable to rely on them, how can you then expect them to rely on themselves?

Some managers consider the undemanding stance either an act of kindness or an enlightened approach to getting the most from employees. Although it is true that a level of demand may be so high that everyone gives up trying to satisfy it, there is also a level of demand that is so low that it not only fails to motivate, it even insults.

Demand quality and production

Although quality and production are obvious demands, I feel I must discuss them briefly lest my own behavioral science approach to the management of people obscure my deepest belief in the essential validity of the old-line manager's dictum: "Demand a fair day's work for a fair day's pay."

Turn back all work that does not match the level of quality you have a right to expect from your group. If you don't criticize slipshod performance, you send your group the message that that's all you expect of them anyway. This message will further drag down their ability to do good work. Tolerance for below-standard work has a debilitating effect on employee self-regard.

Do not stand for laziness. Deadlines should not be allowed to slip without sufficient reason, and they should not be missed often. Commitments were made to be met, not avoided or explained away. Your group will respond to real expectancies by delivering.

The call for quality and production should be transmitted daily through your facial expressions and behavioral cues, not simply through stated goals and objectives. The time comes for someone to turn in a relatively easy assignment, and they claim they did not even have time to start it. Do you look surprised? If not, they think you didn't expect them to be able to do it.

A key member of your staff announces that she will be unable to attend a critical meeting with management because she decided to take a vacation day to stay home and catch up on the housework. Do you look annoyed? Do you grunt? Do you look hurt? Do you even swear a little? If not, you indicate that she really isn't that critical and that, in your judgment, she is more necessary to wifely tasks than to professional tasks. On the other hand, if you spontaneously complain, "How the heck do you expect me to get through that meeting without you?" she will get a clear message of her importance to you and the task.

Demand support

Managers can't do it all alone. Think of the proverbial Western sheriff, or even the daring Sir Lancelot. People have always demanded heroism from their leaders. Against the odds and against the very people they are trying to lead, managers are expected to single-handedly solve dragon-size problems and subdue mangy cutthroats in other divisions. You have a right to help.

I remain mystified at the behavior of that lone sheriff who does battle as other able-bodied people cower at a distance. My advice is: "Turn in your badge and find a new town where you can get a little cooperation." Why does Sir Lancelot insist on killing the dragon alone? If everybody really wanted the dragon dead, wouldn't they be out there tossing a few spears and getting off an arrow on their own?

There is no reason for you to be the sole defender of your operation, unless you expect no better from your people. I am afraid Sir Lancelot thought of himself as the only man with enough skill, fortitude, daring, and moxie to come within miles of the dragon. He wasn't disappointed when no one else showed up, because he did not think they were capable of doing battle. Fundamentally, the sheriff feels the same, or he would refuse to fight without company. When the knight and the sheriff are done, what's left are not only dead villains and a conquering hero, but helpless bystanders as well.

"I can't do this without your help," is not an admission of your weakness as much as a promulgation of the other person's strength. One of my favorite true stories is the defeat of the Jesse James gang at Northfield, Minnesota. No single hero took on the gang against the odds with blazing six-guns. I am not sure the sheriff was even involved. Instead, the whole town exploded! Shopkeepers, butchers, barbers, druggists, and barkeeps annihilated the gang as they left the bank.

Your whole work unit should be involved in a group effort. Information should be freely given to you on the state of clients, the feelings of management, and the developments in civil service. Whatever the potential sources of such information in your organization, your people should be passing it on to you to ensure that their boss does not get into trouble. Your group should be pointing out problems long before they have developed into potential calamities. They are capable not only of identifying the problems, but of working out the solutions. They should sometimes offer to take some of the load of management off your back, by letting you know, "I know how to do that."

I am not recommending that you demand such support for your sake alone, although it will certainly lighten your load. You should do it for the sake of your employees. Employees can learn about their own strength when you recognize it in them. "If the boss relies on me so heavily, I must be the sort of person who can be counted on." True, it's easier to appreciate an employee's capability when it isn't kept hidden under a bushel. But even when it is, it's worth digging for. Very little gold is found on the surface.

Demand group loyalty

Many units fall apart as a result of gossip and backbiting among group members and with people outside the group itself. The strain of working closely with people you have bitterly denounced behind their backs has a corrosive effect on the quality of service and product your group is able to give.

Many managers chalk it up to human frailty. They may even exacerbate the problem by allowing individuals to complain to them privately about other group members.

The psychodynamics of the situation are that everyone involved assumes they are too fragile or sensitive for a sustained conflict on the subject. Angry feelings do not go away. They must be dissipated somewhere. People who are unwilling to fight cleanly need some form of ventilation for their pent-up emotions. Since spouses are only willing to listen to so much complaining, "tit-for-tat" discussion groups are soon formed. "If you will agree with me while I complain about my group, I'll sympathize with you as you belly-ache about yours."

If you tolerate this as part of the human condition, you too assume that the feelings of the people involved are too sensitive for more straight-forward and open disagreements. But if you demand that conflicts be worked out face to face, you show that people—your own included—are basically strong and capable. You reduce the negative impact on the group's image, free them of suppressed interpersonal hostilities, and demonstrate that you feel they are strong enough to handle confrontation.

Demand answers

Many of us were trained to sidestep the truth. Almost automatically we duck responses to direct questions. Most of us have grown up believing that giving direct answers can get us in trouble. Why is it that when asked, "When will you have this report ready?" we prefer such ambiguous answers as: "Soon," or, "In awhile," to the clear, determinate: "One hour from now," or the equally clear: "By 6:00." If we said "6:00" and couldn't deliver by then, we would have to confess either an error in judgment or a flagging of energy.

"Which office do you want?" "Oh, any old one will do," is not an answer but the opening of a long and manipulative campaign to get the corner office. We choose the manipulative route over the straightforward one because we don't have enough self-confidence to make a case for getting what we really want. If you make it clear that you want only straight answers, you will convince your employees that you have faith in their basic competence to cope with reality. Time and experience will demonstrate that they have that strength. The best way, of course, to start getting straight answers is to start giving them. If you are willing to show an openness by the way you express yourself, so will they. They will learn that the truth needn't be intimidating.

WHICH BEHAVIORS TO SUPPRESS

Your attitude toward self-reliance is demonstrated not only by what you do, but by what you do not do. The father who gives the keys to his teenage son without detailed directions on how to keep the car intact says to his son that he assumes that he already has that understanding. The mother who hovers over her daughter in social situations, on the other hand, says clearly that she expects her daughter to commit a faux pas. If she wishes to transmit that she values her daughter's social skills, she had best suppress the behavior of hovering.

Mothers are ready objects of ridicule on this subject, but I have seen more hovering managers in my consulting career than I have seen hovering mothers in my social life. Here are some typical behaviors, hovering and otherwise, that should be avoided.

Tracking mickey mouse issues

In some situations, coming to work on time is critical, and it must be tracked and insisted on by the manager. If the library opens at noon, someone has to be there to open it before the customers decide to call the mayor for the keys. If the production line is to run, the laborer in stall three must be there, or the others won't be able to start. However, in many situations five minutes does not mean a great deal one way or the other. I remember being greatly annoyed at a member of a work group who consistently arrived 15 minutes to a half-hour late every morning. I couldn't understand how he dared waste the company's money that way. Then I noticed that after arriving exactly on time, I always spent the first hour of the morning drinking coffee and finding ways to avoid work. He actually began working a good half-hour before I did.

Try to allow people their own working cadence, and do not interfere with it by insisting on meticulous observance of rules and policies that make no difference. What seems essential to some of us may be arbitrary to others. And what is arbitrary in one situation is essential in others.

A friend of mine owns two businesses. In the service company he is both president and chairman of the board, and in the production company he is only chairman. He was greeted one day by the president of the second company with the message that the operating staff had decided suits and ties were unnecessary. They preferred neatness, but not formality, from their officers. In the future, he did not have to arrive looking as svelte as he had in the past. He appreciated the chance to relax and started buying and wearing leisure suits to work. But back at the service company he was confronted by the vice-president of sales. "My people are disturbed. They don't like bringing potential customers in here and having them meet the president of the company, who is not even wearing a tie. They don't like the impression of informality you give." He decided to honor both dress codes depending on which company he was visiting. In the one clothing was crucial, and in the other it was not.

If you are unsure whether or not your wishes on similar issues are important, invite your group to discuss the matter with you. After all sides of the issue have been aired, even if the same policy is still followed everyone will follow it because they understand it.

A disagreement between a personnel director and his staff on leaving the job early was ironed out this way. The director came to the understanding that his people regularly gave the company extra time it needed to get the job done. They saw this as a professional duty, but they felt they had a right to take a few minutes back when they had nothing to do but wait for quitting time to come. The group realized that their boss was getting a lot of flack from other directors on failing to hold the line because his people were seen slipping out early. They compromised: when employees were taking compensatory time, they were to take it in large enough chunks not to be seen leaving close to the end of the day. This solution made it possible for the director to avoid criticism from his peers, without having to maintain an inconvenient, unnecessary standard that was annoying to his own staff.

Giving instant solutions

One of the reasons you were selected as manager was for your superior technical skill in your profession. Most managers do, although there is disagreement among management experts as to whether that skill helps or hinders the fulfillment of management tasks. You are often aware of the answer to a problem, can identify an opportunity, and so forth, long before the employee who is handling the matter. At times the issue may be so critical that you have to intervene, but beware of constantly giving instantaneous solutions. Every time you do it, you once again impress your employees with their ignorance, weakness, or lack of skill.

When you let them work the situation through, not only do they learn how to solve such problems, but they also see that they are capable of handling them without being bailed out by the boss. If waiting for them to bumble into the correct solution will be too time-consuming, learn to ask the question, or drop the hint that helps them direct their thinking. "Have you thought of checking this out with Mary?" "Have you tested this yet to see if the presumed properties are actually present?" These hints may be broad, but they are much better than saying, "Mary will fry your hide and refuse to approve the procedure unless you see her immediately," or "It's behaving that way because there is nitrate in it."

The achievement-oriented manager, in particular, needs to hold back on the instant solution. Of course, things will get done so much more quickly if you just go around and tell people the right answers. In the short run that is. In the long run, you will find that you are the only person still actively seeking answers. Everyone else in your group is waiting for you to arrive with the right one. After rapidly and smoothly bringing old Cessna 73 Sierra into a crosswind landing during a small gale my flight instructor turned to me and asked, "Now do you see how it's done?" What I saw was that he was an incomparably brilliant pilot while I was a dummy who could never hope to even come close to his abilities.

Embarrassing people

Even when they deserve it, do not embarrass people. If you are angry, tell them off in private. Servile people respond to being publicly chewed out by becoming even more obsequious. "Shy" and "sly" are often the same characteristic—such people will then seek devious ways to pay you back. Self-reliant people, whatever the mistakes they may have made, will not let you get away with embarrassing them in public. They will either openly turn the tables and show you to be wrong, or they will openly tell you where to put your job. Either way, the public reprimand will gain you nothing and risk much.

Being your employees' friend

It is regrettable, but the role of manager makes it very difficult to have friends among the people you manage. This problem is brought by an imbalance in the relationship. Give-and-take friendship occurs among equals, and at least on the level of power you are no longer equals. The choices available to you are to continue to seek your friendships in the work group, but to do so with care, or to seek new friendships outside the work group and not foster them within the group.

Although this may seem harsh, my own preference is definitely for the latter strategy. It consumes less time and energy on the job. It also means that when you are with friends away from the job, you are really away from it. You duck certain issues handily by avoiding close friendships in your work group: What happens to the new group member who you personally cannot like, but is perfectly adequate to the job? Who gets fired when you have a reduction in force? Are they coming to your party because they like you, or because you are the boss? Why did they laugh at your joke? Were you really that funny? How do you tell your best friend you will have to mention her tardiness in her service rating?

Why tie yourself down with these relationships? From the employees' point of view, they do need you less as a friend, than as a shrewd, impartial manager. Friends they can get. They have only one manager. I am not saying you have to be cold and distant. Nor that you should not have warm feelings and strong relationships. I am questioning the wisdom of having the close, intimate, mutually disclosing deep bond of friendship. This, to my mind, is only possible when you hold equal sway over each others' lives, not when one of you can fire the other.

One company president of my acquaintance was so adept, that one employee he had fired asked him to perform an important function at his wedding. He fired another who asked him to help patch up his marriage. In both situations the compassionate president had to live with the obvious fact that if he really wanted to be friendly and make the wedding a happier moment he could give him back his job. In the other instance, the marriage might be helped if the ex-employee were returned to his rather substantial income.

This manager found himself under severe conflicting pressure because the two employees involved were also close friends. Because of this situation, what would have been under any other circumstances a difficult act was now an heroic act.

Think of the confusion you bring to your employee. How often will the employee rely on your friendship to solve work-related problems rather than rely on his or her own talents, abilities, and skills?

Perhaps you prefer these ties with employees and are willing to pay the price and live an emotionally complex life. It can be done. Distinctions can be made: "As your friend, I am sorry you are losing this job, but as your employer I am firing you." Although rationally I can understand such a sentence, emotionally I am unable to. Perhaps my advice here speaks only to my own limitations. But even if you are emotionally capable of making these subtle distinctions, watch out—some of your employees are like me and do not understand. If you fire me, don't invite me to your birthday party. My vindictiveness will not stop at 5:00 P.M. I'll hate you while I'm eating your cake. So will my wife. And my kids will beat up on your kids.

Although it should go without saying that having love affairs with members of your staff, particularly covert extramarital affairs, is asking for trouble, it needs to be said. I never cease to be amazed at the manner in which sexually active managers remain oblivious to the effects they are having. Some people are gossiping. Others are morally outraged. Some are competing for the boss's affections. Still others are working out devious ways to punish the object of the boss's affection. Everybody is holding their cards close to the vest. If you want to play this game you do not need a book on self-reliant management—what you need is a book on wild-animal training. Instead of a work group you have an emotional zoo.

GIVING SUPPORT

Self-reliance usually isn't learned by being tossed into the deep end of the pool with no further support. The outcome of such a sudden entrance into work life is either drowning, or at best learning to survive with the dogpaddle. Shallow water, support, and advice are required to train strong swimmers. Even after the swimmer is strong and the employee has learned the ropes some support is still necessary from the coach and from the manager.

Share information

Some managers hold onto information the way misers clutch money. Information is only of value when it is either being used or being passed on to others. Why hang on to it, guard it, treasure it, nurse it, but not bestow it? First of all, there is the sly, secret pleasure of being the only one to know. While others grope, you sit securely knowing. Second, in some corporations and agencies, knowledge is the key to status.

After working with the federal government for some time I realized that fully half the managers who used the acronyms MBO and OD did not know what they stood for. They did know that these letters represented a new program that anyone who was anybody knew about, and they certainly were not going to confess both ignorance and a lack of status at the same time. Third, there is the simple difficulty of taking the effort to pass on things which may or may not turn out to be important. Fourth, you may assume that what you know everyone else already knows.

On the other hand, there is no more stiffling cause of other-reliance than the lack of information. Why did the employee initiate a new program that was already in effect in another section? He didn't know it was being done, but now that he has been bitten by this experience he is less likely to take the initiative again. Why didn't your people seek the help of the new labor relations professional at corporate headquarters? They did not know he was there. Why did Harry inform three important customers in different corners of the nation that they would be visited during March? Didn't he know the travel budget was already nearly drained in mid-February? You guessed it. The budget and actual are kept at the bottom of your desk drawer. He had no idea that he was pledging you to a disaster.

The real danger is not in the initial slip based on the lack of information. This you can remedy. What cannot be altered is the long-range erosion of your people's confidence in themselves and their base of information. They begin to play safe, and neither you nor they notice the effects of it. They are not excited about work. They are not creative. They cannot be self-reliant.

Give them a broader perspective

Most employees readily—even eagerly—lose track of the complex nature of the entire management situation. Most employees enjoy the technical side of the work and abhor the financial, sales, and political side of the enterprise. Librarians prefer to work with books and information. They will quickly forget that someone has to stay in contact with the members of the city council or there will be no library, or a vastly curtailed library. Selling gizmos does not appeal to most research scientists. Even making salable gizmos does not excite them. Inventing and creating is their love. Sales is hopefully someone else's problem. The craftsman insists that if he had new equipment he could make better doors, contentedly ignoring the fact that the stockholders are already receiving a minimal return on their investment.

Have it their way, and most employees would be quite happy to leave the problem of perspective to you. They like what they do, and you are the manager, aren't you? In that sense the problem is yours, since others are unlikely to worry about it spontaneously.

However, it is in your self-interest and theirs to make sure they worry about it. You cannot compensate for the errors they will make, because they lack perspective. They cannot function self-reliantly, remain unaware of perspective, and count on you to pick up the pieces. For them to remain ignorant of the entire situation with all its complex forces and rely on you for day-to-day direction is both ineffective and clumsy. It allows your people the unfair privilege of grumbling about your decisions because they do not understand them. They do not know why you refused to press for the capital expenditure or why you turned down their work plan to invent the greatest gizmo ever invented, or why you insisted that the reference room librarian stay an hour late so that the mayor's wife could inspect the new information retrieval system. They must know and understand the total picture. They have to respond to the forces that impinge on you.

Allow them more visibility

One federal agency I've consulted with uses the following system to prepare documents for publication to the industry it governs. First, a staff person does all the leg work and prepares a draft document, sometimes the size of a small book. The work involved can take three to six months. The document is then turned over to the boss, who reviews and revises it. That version goes to the next immediate superior, who repeats the procedure. Finally, the document is turned over to the governing board, which does the final editing touches and then, in its own name, publishes the document. The original staff person receives no credit for the document except from his or her boss. The others do not even know who originated the document.

This system is quite demoralizing. Saints alone work hard without credit. Most of us work with one eye on the product and the other on our careers and the effect of the product on our careers.

If you don't allow your people to be seen around the organization and for their work to be acknowledged as their own, they are completely dependent on you for their career progress. They also rely on interpretations of their work through what others think of you. If the agency director does not appreciate you how will he respond to your endorsement of them? Even if he does like you and does respond favorably to your endorsement of them, they will still have to prove themselves to him anyway. It's like double jeopardy.

But if you make sure their work is seen and known throughout the organization they will stand or fall on their own merits. They will know that any judgments are being made about them personally, not about you as a manager or them as members of an anonymous group.

Making a partnership in tough situations

Sometimes the job is more than the person should be expected to handle. In that case, instead of withdrawing the job from them, lend them yourself, or lend them some senior person who can assist when the going gets rough. Let the person carry enough of the weight to provide a learning experience.

The first presentation to the board of directors? Help him get it lined up and be there to intercede with the smooth answer when he needs time to get unflustered. And stand back when he has the situation well in hand. First time operating a back hoe? Have a senior operator join him for a half-day. It will lessen frustration and save on the equipment. Sinking does not teach you how to swim; it teaches you to stay away from the water. Failure does not teach a worker to be self-reliant, but to avoid working.

Sharing a vision

Although this will be taken up much more fully in a later chapter on defining success it also deserves mention as a managerial function. People in work groups tend to only see their small corner of the total task and lose the vision of the whole, if they ever had it. As the old story goes, they think of themselves as bricklayers and forget that the grand design is to build a cathedral. Through a variety of means it is your job as manager to keep the grand design in front of them. The best way to do that is to bring them into the designing process. But, as I say, this will be covered in Part IV.

OBSTACLES YOU CAN REMOVE

First, do not remove all the obstacles, even if you can. Chewing meat develops teeth. If you take care of everything, your employees will never grow up. On the other hand, if you take care of nothing, they may never have a chance to grow up. Here are some of the times I think you must intervene in order to give your employees enough room to exercise self-reliance.

General-to-general contacts

Some managers feel it is beneath their dignity to work directly with people who have less status than they within the organization. Some may be willing to cross status lines, but they fall back on their status to win their points, crown their arguments, and have their own way. In their dealings with this type, employees need your help. Do not, in the name of self-reliance, send them into losing battles. The neighboring general may have to be taken on by you and not by them.

However, in your routine work within the organization, try to do what you can to lower the 'general'' syndrome. It is an awkward way to do business, suited more to the pomp and circumstance of ceremonial organizations than to organizations designed to accomplish work.

Unreasonable pressures

To some extent, your people have to learn how to get unreasonable pressure off their back without your help. But there are times when only you can do it, either because you possess the power, or because you have the perspective to see the unreasonableness of the pressure. If someone from the governor's office sends a memo to one of your employees demanding an immediate detailed analysis of spending patterns among nursing homes, most likely your employee will try to deliver, no matter what the cost. You are probably more used to such harassment and are in a better place to push back, find the real need, curtail the project to within reasonable limits, and expand the time frame to more human dimensions. Even the strongest running-back requires blockers. Often even the most self-reliant employees will require that you "run interference" to give them the protection they need to get the job done.

Confusion on details

I once participated in an experimental learning design with a group of 30 experts on organization development. Our task was, within a period of five days, to organize ourselves to prepare a group paper on a certain designated style of organization. We were in a retreat setting, and each of us possessed a great deal of knowledge about the type of organization in question. All of us also possessed infinite confidence in our ability to work with other people in high stress situations.

At the end of the experiment, we turned in a partially completed, haphazard, ragtailed document. Our organization had not jelled despite our most skilled democratic efforts.

My learning from the experience? Thirty people cannot organize themselves, even if they are expert, and even if all the time in the world is available. Every work group needs a boss to eliminate the confusion.

In most situations, as we abundantly proved in that situation, there are almost unlimited alternative methods for approaching any task and for organizing. Eventually someone must decide which will be used. Everyone else can then go back to work and stop wasting their energy on which of the good solutions is the best. Not that you as boss will come to a better solution than the members of the group. It's just that you will come to a quicker solution, one that eliminates unending confusion, hassle, power politics, and argument. Although such a decision should not come so early that it shuts off team involvement in planning and managing, it should come at the point where the team in your judgment has done all a team can.

AN EXERCISE

If you are interested in discovering whether or not your employees feel your behavior is the type I say will foster their self-reliance, use the following questionnaire. Distribute it to them with whatever mechanism seems appropriate. I assume that you have already used previous questionnaires with them and know how much anonymity and subtlety is required to obtain their honest response.

If you are not interested in using the questionnaire that way, consider using it for yourself. Again, although a planned program will do much to foster self-reliance among your people, your informal, almost unconscious ways of operating count far more in how your group judges you.

QUIZ ON BEHAVIOR THAT PROMOTES SELF-RELIANCE

SD = Strongly Disagree   D = Disagree   A = Agree
SA = Strongly Agree

1. I demand quality and production from you.
   SD   D   A   SA
2. Often I depend on you to save my neck.
   SD   D   A   SA
3. I insist on group loyalty.
   SD   D   A   SA
4. I demand answers, and will not let you off the hook with slipshod responses.
   SD   D   A   SA
5. I pay attention to every minute detail.
   SD   D   A   SA
6. I come to you with solutions before you want my help.
   SD   D   A   SA
7. I embarrass you.
   SD   D   A   SA

8. My personal relationships with employees interfere with work.

    SD   D   A   SA

9. I pass on appropriate information always.

    SD   D   A   SA

10. I help you see the broad perspective of our situation.

    SD   D   A   SA

11. I assist you to become visible to others in the organization.

    SD   D   A   SA

12. I see to it that you do not have to tackle extremely difficult situations alone.

    SD   D   A   SA

13. I "run interference" for you with other managers when necessary.

    SD   D   A   SA

14. I "run interference" for you when others are trying to put unreasonable pressures on you.

    SD   D   A   SA

15. I eliminate confusion by taking a descisive stance when we are unable to achieve group agreement.

    SD   D   A   SA

PART III

THE SELF-RELIANT GROUP

Most groups wish that their management and other units in the organization would value them more highly, treat them more kindly, and frustrate them less often. Your group can produce such behavior in others, but only if it stops wishing and starts doing.

13

Destroying
debilitating myths

Being a self-reliant person and managing a self-reliant group does not guarantee success. It simply puts you in contention for it. The world is still out there, almost eager to frustrate your aims.

The popular analogy between an organization and a jungle is accurate, if you understand jungles. Jungles are frightening only to those of us who have spent our lives in civilization. To those who inhabit the jungle—both human being and beast—its terrors are extremely limited and its beauties many. Those who live there know what to fear—they know when they are in danger and they know what to avoid.

Think of the problems an African from a primitive tribe would have on a visit to one of our cities. Just as we stay on the sidewalk to reduce our chances of being struck by an automobile, that African avoids watering places at nightfall to reduce the chances of being eaten by a leopard. We could hardly arrange to move out of the city every time we hear that someone has been hit by a car; similarly, the jungle dweller doesn't clear out of the jungle whenever someone has made a meal for a leopard.

Organizations are jungles. Moreover, the harsh realities of organization life are obscured by a number of ill-founded beliefs. Smoke screens have been put up by people within the organization whose reaction to potential disaster is to deny its existence. They are jungle dwellers who have decided that leopards do not exist. They are city people who deny the reality of cars. In order to survive in such a state of unreality, they huddle together in a mindless clump hoping that the problems they ignore will be taken elsewhere.

Because you are a self-reliant manager, your group is in motion. You must identify the problem areas of organization life. Look at them coldly and realistically and then deal with them. The first step to *seeing* is to set aside the myths. In this chapter we'll look at a number of dangerous myths typically heard in many organizations.

You can depend on the organization.

No matter what you have done for the organization, you can't really depend on it. A lifetime of scurrying for safety under the wings of either the corporation or civil service may be rewarded. On the other hand, it may not be rewarded.

During the aerospace and defense cutback in the early 1970s one weapons manufacturer faced with unfavorable economic conditions was able to predict the size and nature of its personnel reductions six months in advance. Although by contract they were only required to give two weeks' notice for layoff, this corporation tried to ease the pain of severance by informing those professional employees who would be laid off two months in advance. Management reasoned that this would give employees ample time to seek alternative sources of income, begin to tighten their belts, and utilize in-company services, such as secretarial help, editorial and printing assistance, and the job-search capability of the personnel department.

They needn't have bothered. Even when informed by the company itself that they should not depend on it beyond a designated time, most professional people were so conditioned that they weren't able to grasp that their dream of a permanent source of income was coming to an end.

When the personnel department did not find themselves flooded by calls for assistance, they began inquiring of soon-to-be-terminated professionals: "Didn't they want help?" "No, I'm sure that conditions will change by my termination time. I've been with the company for years, and I don't think it will let me down now."

Before tight times were over, the company "let down" more than 1,000 professional people. Whose fault was it? Who in the corporate hierarchy had ever said: "We will never have a layoff"? The myth that the corporation could be depended on was invented by people who refused to face the fact that corporate allegiance was not going to provide them universal safety.

Karl Marx called religion the "opiate of the masses" because religionists propagated the myth that if people lived with their present miseries they would receive a greater reward in the future. There is a new "opiate of the worker": "If you patiently suffer the indignities of organization life, the organization will take care of you until the day you die." Don't count on it.

Around here it doesn't make any difference who you know or what you're like. We reward accomplishment.

Most organizations reward accomplishment, but they also reward you for who you know and what you're like. If a manager is surveying a list of candidates for promotion and knows one and not the others, isn't it reasonable to expect that the one who is known is most likely to be selected?

Since he values his own method for getting things done, a manager will select as a candidate for promotion the person who resembles him, all other things being equal. That is why management groups have a tendency to look homogeneous over a period of time, as "birds of a feather flock together."

This myth was created to get employees to focus on accomplishment, a much more productive goal from the point of view of the organization. But if you expect to go up the ladder, you had best put more than a little energy into getting known and into mirroring the organization's image of the successful person. Otherwise you'll be regularly, even systematically, bypassed in favor of those who have expended energy in that direction.

No one will tell you that you were bypassed because they didn't know you, or because they didn't like "the cut of your jib." The myth must be maintained at all costs. You will be told you were passed over for promotion because someone else had accomplished even more.

Your group may not pay attention to such political issues as "getting known," "being seen," and "manipulating your own image." But it then risks being stymied in its efforts toward achieving success both by those who do not understand its goals and purposes and by those who don't like to see the accepted modes of behavior contradicted.

The myth that goal accomplishment is all that counts is often passed along by those who lack social skill of the deeper order, such as the capacity to understand the needs of other people and to make lasting friendships, and the willingness to establish and maintain personal loyalties. Since a strictly accomplishment-oriented work world is the only world in which such persons can succeed, they prefer to see only that aspect of their organization's life and regard everything else as unhealthy politics and beneath their dignity.

One of my most interesting, and yet strangest, clients was so interpersonally ineffective that it was his policy to send subordinates to discuss issues with other department heads rather than risk putting his own foot into it. It should come as no surprise that the monument he left behind to his agency was an appraisal system that did not permit evaluation of personal impact. I have nothing but admiration for the man. How many students are smart enough to gain the power to redesign report cards so that the subjects they are failing do not appear? Unfortunately, in real life, if your failures don't show up on the report card, they will show up in the memory of the offended person. If you can't be flunked, you can at least be blocked or tripped.

The organization isn't going to buy my soul.

That will depend. How successful do you want to be? How thoroughly does your group want to be professionals? To that extent, the organization will buy a piece, even a substantial chunk, of your soul.

The voyageurs had a campfire song that said: "*Vive la compagnie!*" which literally translated means: "Long live the company!" Of course, they were referring to the immediate company, the twenty or so strong men who had just conquered another 20 or 30 miles of river, forest, and swamp. However, as they became enmeshed in the trying and difficult task of transporting furs out of the wilderness, they ended up giving more than a fair share of labor to the greater company which had hired them. In the struggle and their desire to succeed, they gave a bit of their soul, and on occasion even their lives.

On the whole, hourly wage earners aren't expected to do much more than show up, spend the time, and perform minimal functions. Creativity, involvement, and going the extra mile aren't expected, although even at the hourly wage level such efforts are often made. Professionals are expected to have a higher willingness to give to the success of their organizations.

Real professionals do have such a willingness. Perhaps their loyalty is to the job or the client or, as with the voyageurs, their loyalty is to others in the immediate *compagnie,* rather than the broader organization. Whatever the motive, if the job isn't complete, they stay late and finish it. When the answer can't be found on Friday, they take it home and work it out on Saturday. When the budget is cut, they invent a way to provide the same service for less cost. And it is they, not some mythical company, who expect the same of others. It is they who intend to and will buy your soul if you hope to be a member of the *compagnie.* Your group can't be successful unless it is willing to put out extra effort. Others are already doing that, and these others will expect it of your group as well.

The myth that the company has no right to your soul was invented by those lazy employees who hope to put in only seven hours a day and be successful as well. The company certainly can't demand that you give your soul, but it will reward those who do far more than it will reward those who do not.

There is a thing or person called The Corporation.
Corporations are legal fictions. The term conveniently masks the fact that somewhere there are a few people who are making decisions for others. This is also true of such phrases as "the government," "the state," and "the agency." None of these exists in and of itself. Such terms are seldom used to mean the total will of all individuals within the legal fiction. They usually designate a few people and serve as protective coloration to prevent these people from having to deal with the objections—even the wrath—of the many. Some examples will make this clear.

"It is corporate policy that grade 10's can't have doors to their offices." Translated, this reads that Sam, Joe, and Harry up in plant engineering decided that they could be heroes with their boss if they cut the costs of hanging all those doors. So they made a policy to get rid of your door.

"The state of Minnesota will not permit reimbursements to social workers for visiting the housing projects when the social workers' clients are capable of coming to the downtown offices." The State, in this case, is old Harvey Witherspoon who holds his job only because his brother-in-law is commissioner of administration. Harvey wouldn't know a social worker if he saw one. Harvey doesn't understand social work. On the other hand, if social workers think Harvey is really the state of Minnesota they are either going to have to dip into their own pocketbooks for travel money or miss contacting many people who need their services but feel uncomfortable downtown.

Harvey himself could be intimidated into doing the right thing if someone has the sense to search him out and confront him with the negative impact of his policy. And I found that after I recovered my door from the storage room and rehung it myself, "the corporation" not only didn't complain, it didn't even notice. If you allow yourself to be convinced that organizations exist as if they are people, you will soon be subdued into the helplessness of other-reliance. The concept of organizations may be hard to handle, but people will respond.

***Corporate objectives, if accomplished, will benefit
everyone in the corporation.***
Corporate objectives are not the objectives of all the people in the corporation. These objectives are designed by the top executives of the corporation in order to reward the stockholders. In the case of public agencies, they were designed to meet the needs of the political party in power,

and in the case of volunteer agencies they were designed to bring the most money possible to bear on the organization's cause or service.

Unswerving allegiance to and pursuit of corporate objectives can result in your demise. Does it say: "Cut cost"? Don't forget, you're a cost. Does it say: "Emphasize product"? Don't forget, you're a service. Does it say: "Find new fields of endeavor"? You're an old field of endeavor.

View your organization's objectives not as a paternalistic pronouncement of top management's good intentions for all its corporate sons and daughters, but as early warning of the way the organization is moving. Don't wait for them to move you—beat them to the punch. Because if they do the moving, you're the one who is likely to suffer in the process. They say to cut costs—then you and your group find and cut the costs. Better your scalpel than their ax. At the same time, you and your group now begin to make your case that the costs can't be cut from your group. Encourage them to look elsewhere for their 10 percent.

The boss is responsible.

Closely related to the previous myth is the one that says management will make the decision and then management must bear the consequence: "I made a detailed presentation of the factors involved in that decision. I showed him clearly that unless we reversed the material flow our mill would have severe quality problems. He didn't agree. As a result, our current quality problems are his problem, not mine." Unfortunately, that is not the way the world works, logical as it may seem. The resulting problems will be the mill superintendent's problems, and if he persists in the above attitude his manager will one day be explaining to corporate executives that he has solved the quality problems by firing the mill superintendent. The buck can't be passed upstairs. Bucks are passed down, not up.

A boss who doesn't understand must be made to understand. If the boss still doesn't understand, you will have to make the wrong solution work, because you still remain responsible. You may have told your boss that the deputy director is totally incompetent, but if the response you get doesn't lead to removal of the deputy director, you'd better discover ways to be successful with an inadequate deputy director. Even in cases in which you are genuinely stymied by your boss's inability to see the light, you should still act as if it is your reputation that is on the line.

A general manager in a large corporation was responsible for a medium-size research facility. Early in his work with the facility he became convinced that the facility could never survive unless it was also involved in production of some of the items it was developing in its research laboratories. He couldn't convince his own management of the need. On the contrary, they insisted that the facility was for research and for nothing else. Instead of capitulating, he and his management team were so certain of the correctness of their decision that they began implementing it without corporate management's knowledge. Pilot workshops and technical laboratories were all expanded until they were at the edge of being production lines. Sales volumes rose from twenty or thirty prototypes to five hundred or one thousand "prototypes."

Later, during a period of economic downturn, corporate management was looking for a method of cutting costs. The general manager pointed out that with only another slight surge of growth his research facility could become a full-scale production division. The products were there. The facilities were there. The customers were eager and waiting. No longer would the corporation have to invest in the facility, but the facility could begin to return a profit to the company.

His facility became a division, and he became a vice-president. The point is that he recognized that even after management's decision, the buck was still his. Had the facility failed, he would have failed with it. Indeed, if his surreptitious expansion plan had failed, he would have faced a potentially career-closing disaster. His risk was great, but at least by pursuing the plan he pursued he knew he was living in the real world.

The boss isn't responsible. You are. You are even responsible for your boss's mistakes in your area.

The organization chart shows all key relationships.

Some hold to the theory that as long as I please my boss, everything will be all right. They have a vision of the organization as a gigantic ladder with one person reporting to another. That is true enough as far as it goes. But the names of some people who "report" to your management do not appear on any related organization chart. Old friends meet your boss in the airport over drinks in the bar and report on the casual trip they took through your operation. Your boss and the head of civil service regularly ride to work together in the morning. The head of civil service will undoubtedly take occasion to comment on the blistering letter you wrote in which you pointed up his inadequate procedures. Old Joe, long ago sidetracked to a back-row desk because of obvious professional incompetence, entered the agency with, and was a beer-drinking buddy of, hatchet man Sam, the deputy director of the budget review office. Your treatment of Joe may well affect how you are treated by Sam.

One plant manager of my acquaintance did everything possible to ensure that the general manager understood all his intentions, approved his plans, and was completely up to date on results. In the course of pleasing the boss, the plant manager alienated the maintenance superintendent, the engineering manager, the personnel officer, and the accountant. He never could understand why the regional management located in another state should bypass his manager to send him blistering comments and hostile evaluations. "How do they even know what I'm doing, much less have an opinion about whether or not I should be doing it?"

This makes a poor detective story. You have already guessed that the butler didn't do it. The accountant complained to his buddy, the regional vice-president's accountant, that "that idiot has lost complete control of his costs." The engineering manager reported directly to the vice-president that the Environmental Protection Agency would stop complaining if they could just get that plant to clean up its stack and stop trying to play it at the edge of the standards. The personnel director continually used that manager as the source of humorous anecdotes on how not to handle people.

Organizations are not run by the organization chart. Decisions are made based on a multitude of reports coming over the informal grapevine. If the word is out that you are incompetent, you are doomed, even if your boss continues to give you favorable reviews. On the other hand, if people know that your judgment is to be respected, breaks and opportunities will come your way with or without your boss's approval.

One more short story. In a federal agency the new commissioner of a bureau immediately launched a feud with the agency's administrator of planning and research. Since they both had substantial power bases, their quarrels made an impact on the peace and working capacity of the agency. Yet nothing seemed to alleviate the commissioner's need to try for the jugular whenever an issue arose between him and the administrator. In other instances, although feisty, he was not that unforgivingly combative. No explanation was ever given or obtained of his feelings during four years of battle.

Except perhaps this: One day over lunch the commissioner casually mentioned to the others at the table, a propos of nothing, "I called Harry ten years ago when I worked for another agency. He told me he had no time for flunkies, and hung up. I wonder if he remembers that." Probably not. Harry probably could see no way someone that low on that organization chart could ever have any impact on someone that high on his. Harry was lucky. The commissioner could have been assigned as his boss.

Honesty is the best policy.

Although earning the reputation of a chronic liar, or even an occasional fibber, will be your death knell in any organization, being known as perpetually honest won't help you either. A consultant initiated his rela-

tionship with a federal government official by saying: "Don't tell me anything you're not prepared to have everyone hear. I keep no secrets." His
client listened carefully and decided to take the consultant's advice. He
told him next to nothing.

Sophisticated managers will enjoy watching you get into hot water by
telling the truth when silence is more appropriate. They will also do their
best to be sure that you don't know enough about their operation to be
able to get them into trouble with your loquaciousness.

The ability to be silent is as respected and useful as the ability to speak
straightforwardly. There can be no single policy to govern the use of your
tongue. You must respond to the demands of the immediate situation.
Others will come to decide if they can trust you to be honest when
honesty is needed and to be silent when silence is demanded. As Bambi
said, "If you can't say something nice, make sure you don't mind if the
whole world quotes you."

"Always" and "never."

Everyone knows that universal statements are seldom true. Still,
groups within organizations consistently ascribe certain behaviors, attitudes, and values to other groups, as if such all-inclusive statements have
validity. "They will never cooperate." "They always turn out shoddy
work." "They don't like us." Or, on the other hand, "You can count on
them." "They always do the right thing." "Those people have their
heads screwed on right."

The unfavorable universal statement about another group has the negative effect of closing you off from the potential benefits of working with
them. Sometimes they will cooperate. With a little prodding, they may
very well turn out excellent work. Although they are not your friends
today, one strategically held lunch date might change that. With the
change comes the potential for receiving more assistance in getting the
job done.

In contrast, the favorable always–never statement may lull you to
sleep just when you need to be most awake. The day you decide to
count on them and not check their work may be the very day they fail to
live up to your universal judgment that "they always do the right thing."
The day you presume they'll come into the management meeting sharing
your position will be the day they come in prepared with devastating,
clearly enunciated arguments against doing it your way.

A related myth held by some is that you must take a position vis-à-vis
other groups in the organization. You must decide if you are with them or
against them. Again, this myth is seldom enunciated directly. If it were, its
foolishness would be patent. Can you imagine holding a serious meeting

to decide if we, as a group, will endorse the capability of corporate marketing or denounce them to all who will listen? Or holding a serious meeting to decide if we feel that the training branch should continue to receive our support or we should begin a whispering campaign to undercut their relationships with the rest of the agency? Although these meetings aren't held formally they are held informally, and while other departments aren't denounced publicly, they are often denounced surreptitiously.

To what good? Your group wastes energy in making universal statements that will hold little resemblance to the complex reality faced by the other group. Your group makes a negative prophecy about the competence of the other group and then feels a commitment to make sure it is fulfilled. Your group alienates another group. No matter how bad they are, they probably have something to offer.

Other groups in our organization owe us support and loyalty.

Logically this is quite true. Often their very mission is to support you. They should do it automatically. I encourage you to feel a loyalty to your organization and to spring to the assistance of other groups within your organization.

However, on the whole the world doesn't work that way, and if you expect it to, you will experience disappointment and failure. The planning group becomes enmeshed in its task of neatly connecting all the boxes, circles, and triangles on the chart. The organization effectiveness group becomes lost in a study of the effects of peer pressure on productivity. The print shop decides to dedicate its resources to effectively turning out the company paper. All of them, and for that matter, all of us, quickly become enmeshed in our own agendas, forgetting the purpose for which we were hired in the first place. Even the pure and innocent line manager is guilty of this. What manager has ever suggested that for the good of the stockholders his or her function and group be terminated? Or take a budget cut? Or even sacrifice next year's growth plan?

How do you get others to help you when they've forgotten that they're supposed to owe you that support? The clarion call to duty will gain you only their apologies, not their assistance. The planners will readily admit that they exist to help you plan, it's just that right now that they're much too busy. They are sorry, and you're back where you started.

Although other groups in your organization do technically owe you support and loyalty, don't expect it as your right. If you are to receive what you need consistently, you must strategize to get it.

In the next two chapters I will present two major approaches used by people who do not subscribe to these myths. Generally, these managers and their employees hold that the organizations in which they work are complex and sophisticated networks of human ties and economic pressures. They avoid any simple statement or set of statements that attempts to define or describe organizational life. Instead they rely heavily on organizing their own desires and then aggressively and assertively managing the interface between themselves and others to make sure they get what they want. They replace the belief in myths with belief in themselves and their capacity to get others to give them what they need. In short, they are self-reliant.

Before going on to the antidote, however, it will be useful for you and your group to see if you have the disease. Since most of the foregoing myths are recognizable as soon as they are enunciated, it is difficult to decide by reading them if you have allowed yourself to be victimized. "Of course not. I don't believe that." The following questionnaire asks you about your behavior, not your beliefs. The freer you are of the myths, the more you will agree with its statements. Fill it out for yourself. Try it out on the group you manage. It will provoke discussion about the group's stance toward the rest of the organization.

THE BEHAVIOR OF SELF-RELIANT WORK UNITS

SA = Strongly Agree   A = Agree   D = Disagree
SD = Strongly Disagree

1. We keep our résumés up to date.
   SA   A   D   SD
2. We chose our work with our own career development in mind.
   SA   A   D   SD
3. We keep one eye open for our next employer either in this organization or in another.
   SA   A   D   SD
4. We have sources of income other than this organization.
   SA   A   D   SD
5. We're interested in doing other things besides working here.
   SA   A   D   SD
6. We don't put up with nonsense for the good of the corporation.
   SA   A   D   SD
7. We actively seek friendly, even close, relationships with powerful people in the organization.
   SA   A   D   SD

8. We pay attention to the image we are creating with others in the organization.

   SA   A   D   SD

9. We form liaisons, informal mutual assistance pacts, with people we like and see as likely to go places within the organization.

   SA   A   D   SD

10. We work extra hours frequently.

    SA   A   D   SD

11. We expect others to work extra hours whenever the job needs to be done.

    SA   A   D   SD

12. Since we realize that often what is good for the whole organization may not be good for us, we identify our own needs and work for their fulfillment.

    SA   A   D   SD

13. We know our management's needs, wants, and desires and work actively to ensure that they get what they want.

    SA   A   D   SD

14. We never try to pass the buck to the boss.

    SA   A   D   SD

15. We actively identify and use all sources of influence in attempting to make things happen.

    SA   A   D   SD

16. We don't rely on our boss or our boss's boss to carry the message for us.

    SA   A   D   SD

17. Sometimes we're straightforward. Sometimes we're surreptitious. Sometimes we're silent. We choose our degree of candor to fit the situation.

    SA   A   D   SD

18. In describing others we don't use such words as "always," "never," and other words and phrases that denote that we feel we have complete understanding of their responses.

    SA   A   D   SD

19. We hold no formal or informal positions as to the work of other groups within the organization.

    SA   A   D   SD

20. We don't gossip about other groups.

   SA   A   D   SD

21. We never express disappointment at other groups that have failed us.

   SA   A   D   SD

22. We have strategy for gaining the loyalty and support of every other group that is important to us in the organization.

   SA   A   D   SD

23. We don't let people hide behind faceless titles, such as "the corporation," "the agency," "the board," but we penetrate these masks to confront the people who wear them.

   SA   A   D   SD

Now that you have completed this inventory, keep it in an obvious place for a couple of days. Refer to the questions between phonecalls, appointments, breaks, and other work. Compare your evolving day to the questionnaire. You may find reason to change some of your answers.

14

Defining success

I have treated the problems of being self-reliant in their natural order. The first problem for you, the manager, is yourself. Are you self-reliant? If you are not, there is little I can say that will make much difference in your performance as a manager or in your subordinates' effectiveness as a work group. For this reason, Part I aimed at initiating your own personal growth toward self-reliance. Only after that did I discuss with you methods for molding your own group. All managers mold their groups in their own image. Once you have taken a self-reliant stance, your group will have begun to do things in more self-reliant ways. With the help of Part II we have hastened an inevitable process.

Since only wise people appreciate self-reliance in others, the final step in achieving self-reliance in yourself and in your group is developing the quality of assertiveness. Your group can't expect the rest of the organization to arrive with bouquets and raises just because you're self-reliant. On the contrary, you probably won't be liked precisely for that reason. Frank Sinatra most certainly "did it my way." However, although he has money, and he has the admiration of many, he has the affection of very few. Most people are other-reliant. They strongly object to anyone living or working in a self-reliant manner. Such behavior awakens their own fears of being abandoned by those who sustain them and of having to take their own risks. Most people quietly take delight whenever Sinatra gets the least bit of egg on his face.

On the other hand, most people prefer and sympathize with Dick Van Dyke whose desires for the affection of other people cause him to behave like a cocker spaniel. They may not particularly admire Van Dyke, but they know they don't need to fear his disturbing the equanimity of the crowd on which they depend.

So too with your group. Your only redeeming feature may be your success. Don't expect to be liked.

"Those guys down in the print shop have certainly gotten cocky and demanding. 'I'd try to get that whole group fired if they didn't give me such quick turnaround on my orders."

"I don't know who they think they are not joining everybody else for the coffee break."

"Those #$*# down in quality are holding up another shipment, and this time they say they're going to put an inspector in the middle of our area until we stop making consistent mistakes."

In most large organizations much ineffectiveness is forgiven if you just remain "one of the gang." However, it is precisely this behavior that you and your group are preparing to forsake in order to be more effective. You will be forgiven very little in exchange for much admiration.

You will have to pursue success adamantly. But what is success? It is precisely the absence of an answer to this question that turns many work units belly-up over a period of years. They lack the statement of the ideal toward which they are striving. They lack yardsticks of their own accomplishment. If you don't know what you want, you can't very well concentrate on achieving it. This lack of purpose reduces your chances for success. For instance, can you be a top-notch quality control department and still be loved by production? Not likely. One or the other goal must be given priority. If you do not have your goals clearly articulated and before you at all times, you risk putting your self-interest to one side in favor of pleasing others.

This vision or dream that needs to be articulated is more far-reaching than the normal, ordinary objectives. These are the life dreams of your people. What are they living for? What do they want said of them when they are done with work? Everyone has such desires, although most of us are too shy to mention them. Indeed, the vast majority of us have given up on our dreams in the commonplace routines of our jobs.

The engineer who wanted to use his analytical mind to create radically new guidance systems now routinely accomplishes his functions within an elaborate work-breakdown structure. The social worker who wanted to heal the pain in the lives of others now brusquely fills out the right forms for poverty clients. The teacher who wanted to devise new methods for educating the preschool mentally retarded, now does the job by someone else's book, long ago having given up on a creative approach to educating.

Where are their life dreams? Just beneath the surface. Ignored, but ready to be rediscovered, if the rediscovery will only lead to achievement and not to further discouragement and failure.

In an earlier chapter you were encouraged to explore your own motivation. There I explained how being in touch with your own motivation would lead to your personal success. For the same reasons, combining and pursuing these dreams will lead to your group's success. The bulk of this chapter is devoted to methods for discovering life dreams, and to building a work-unit definition of success that springs from these dreams and uses them as the motivating force for a successful group. Before going into the "how to do it," let's take a look at "why not to do it at all." It is in these "why nots" that you will discover the resistances you and your people may have to such a conversation. To my mind the good outweighs the risks. However, you must judge for yourself. If you agree with me and decide to go ahead, proceed with caution. The following problems are by no means trivial.

PROBLEMS IN SHARING LIFE DREAMS

You will be mocked.

Your real desires are probably a step or two beyond your capabilities. Certainly they are at least at the edge of your potentiality. Often they seem silly to you—what if they seem silly to others? The risk is very real. Anyone with sensitivity hesitates to unveil secret hopes and ambitions to people who may not treat them tenderly. Don't attempt the following exercises unless your group has demonstrated genuine feelings of friendship for one another. Even then, expect that people will gradually test the ground with less than their ultimate desires. Only if the results are favorable will they tell the group what they really want out of life.

Some groups thrive on the jock attitude that if you're going to be a real member of the gang you always have to be prepared for this type of joshing. Such a group once argued vigorously with me to remove from a manual I was preparing the word "delicate" to describe relationships. They felt that relationships are not "delicate" but can withstand any and all tests. Some people have no sense of delicacy. If you are working with such a group, my heartfelt sympathies. Do not attempt these exercises, until they emerge from adolescence.

You may be held back deliberately.

If the group members are at cross-purposes, they may use these exercises as an opportunity to hurt one another. What better avenue for causing someone pain than to discover that person's deepest desires and then get in the way. In order to participate in these exercises, both you and your group must have reason to suspect that the others are favorably inclined. The best index is that others have helped you get what you want in the past. If they have, then you can easily confide in them. If they've not only not helped you, but have deliberately blocked your efforts, then obviously you can't speak freely with them. If you have no track record of being helped or being hindered, you must proceed cautiously.

You may talk about it, only to realize again that you cannot fulfill it.

One reason we don't share our dreams readily in the first place is that it only hurts to discuss something, or dream about something, we have no hope of having. Long ago we buried the dreams in favor of picking up our check and making minimal waves within the organization. Do we want to look at the dreams once again? What are the chances of our getting anywhere with them? If you can offer a fair chance that the ideal or a part of it may be attained, you may be able to encourage people to talk openly. If you can't offer a fair chance, try to avoid the topic and certainly don't schedule the meeting.

On the other hand, don't decide too quickly that you're powerless to assist your group in realizing its personal expectations. Together you may make an extraordinarily strong force. Dreams that no one of you can put into action alone may be implemented by all of you working together.

You may have to leave the group.

The police sergeant who really wants to be a chicken farmer, the bureaucrat who wants to run a restaurant, the account executive who hopes to run a boys' camp, are living and working lives far distant from their real desires. If they are serious, they should leave the group they work with and chase their dreams. They are aware that any frank conversation with you or with members of the group may bring them that exact advice. This Y in the road is precisely what they have been attempting to delay or avoid for years. They will prefer not to have the conversation, although in their case you are well within your rights as manager to inflict it on them. Usually people who are suspended between their real goals and their employment work at a level of energy that reflects their divided attention. Everybody's lot will be improved if they get off the fence.

It may become clear that your fond dreams need to be modified to cover all aspects of your desires.

The reason the sergeant puts aside his dream of becoming a chicken farmer is that he enjoys the hard-won power and prestige of his position.

Chickens would show him much less deference than the average citizen does. They would be even less responsive to his wishes than the men and women of his police unit.

People who run boys' camps are paid as much as one-half of the salary and commissions of a poor account executive. That is quite a drop in pay to contemplate for the price of fulfilled dreams. G.S. 12's either retire with substantial incomes or go on to becomes G.S. 14's and then retire with even more substantial incomes.

On the other hand, only some of the people who start a restaurant can relax with a moderate income. In order to succeed with a restaurant she will have to work twice as hard as when she was a bureaucrat. Even then the failed restauranteur may go broke and end up reentering the job market at either the same level or at a lower level than she left it.

Most of us prefer to keep our dreams a little distant from the cold water of reality. The conversations contemplated here will have that dash of reality, and therefore members of your group may prefer to avoid them.

Reality, of course, cannot be ducked. But it can be tampered with, adjusted, and modified. The sergeant can use his salary to begin setting up the chicken farm. The account executive can become the manager of the company-sponsored Junior Achievement program. The restaurateur can be given programs to manage that challenge her entrepreneurial skills and ambitions. But before holding these meetings it is best that everyone be clear that although uninhibited life-goal discussions will be encouraged at the beginning, reality will demand that the dreams be modified.

Your dream may be a threat to another person's position.

You may wish to upgrade your group's work to a point where many cannot go. You may wish to perform tasks yourself that others are already performing or are working toward. The risks you are willing to take may threaten another's needs for security.

I watched the majority of the professional staff of a religious social service agency turn immobile with fear as a young, charismatic bachelor described the stance the agency should take to fulfill its religious mission. Gently someone pointed out that he would be risking continued funding from the policy makers of The United Way. "To hell with them," was his retort, oblivious to the spouses and children of his colleagues who would be deeply affected if his dream were actualized.

HOW TO DEFINE INDIVIDUAL SUCCESS

The more involved they are in pursuing their dreams, the more your group will be able to stand up to the sometimes harsh demands of organizational life. They will be able to achieve at a level that commands the respect of others in the organization, and more importantly, the respect of the achievers themselves. Here is an exercise for your group.

In order to get at the dreams you must take time. A rough formula is at least two days for a group of five to nine people, three days for a group of ten to fifteen. If you have more than fifteen people you'll have to divide them into smaller manageable groups. The primary goal here is to put aside time to be together. Time to talk to each other. Time to listen to each other. Time to really get to know one another. Time to relax and trust one another. There is strange corner in what it means to be a successful contributor to our economy which says that everything can and should be done quickly. Presumably such "contributors" count their lovemaking as successful only if it was achieved within a certain time limit. People with that attitude will call everyone together in one conference room and ask them to let you in on their inner desires within three minutes. It can, of course, be done, but only if they are willing to ignore the quality of the effort. Such facile conversations breed more emptiness instead of the desired fullness of understanding.

Some time ago professional managers learned to replace the goal of cheapness with the goal of cost-effectiveness. They recognized that the cheap solution often costs more in the long run because it breaks down under even the slightest stress. It is also time to replace the word efficient with the word time-effective, or at least understand the word "efficient" in its root meaning of "time-effective." Too little time used is time wasted.

Here is the process for the meeting. Have each member of the group answer the following questions preparatory to the meeting.

—What have been the major events in your life until this moment?
—What do you hope will be the major events in your future?
—Which things have you enjoyed doing most so far? What did you enjoy about doing them?
—Which of the things that you've done have you liked doing least? What did you dislike about doing them?
—Which things would you most like to do in the future? What is there about that that interests you?
—Which things would you least like to do in the future? What is there about these things that you particularly wish to avoid?

The meeting should be held in a setting conducive to relaxed and lengthy conversation. The room should be geographically distant from the normal work site, and the telephone should be monitored by someone outside your work group. Continuous interruptions should be made difficult. The chairs are to be comfortable. There should be no smoking but opportunities for smokers. The setting should be cheerful. A dank basement or a sealed gray wall conference room will produce thoughts as dank and as gray as the setting itself.

Allow enough time so that you can also give the group leisure breaks of 15 to 30 minutes. Often it is during these breaks that people seek more private moments with each other to share and discuss what is happening in the meeting itself. In order to do this it is best to meet for twelve hours at a stretch, meals included, or even better, to use a retreat setting with overnight accommodations.

Self-Description

During the first part of the meeting, each person should lead a serious conversation about their answers to these questions. At least an hour should be used with each person, and there must be considerable give and take if the conversation is to have any meaning. The major points the person has made should be summarized and left for display on one of the walls. This is their self-description.

The Ideal Job

Next, you lead a conversation about this same person. This time, the person simply listens without commenting. The topic is: "What would be the characteristics of an ideal job for this person? What things should be avoided?" Leave a summary newsprint of this conversation next to the summary done under Self-Description. Continue to the next person's self-description, until each person in the group, including yourself, has had a chance to have their job desires explained and summarized.

Comments

Allow some time for people to comment on their own final set of characteristics. What would they like to see changed in the statement you and the group have made of their ideal job? What would they like to see added?

Potential Job Change

Lead the group in brainstorming changes that can be made in each person's present duties or in the present operating methods that should provide more fulfilling work for them. List these changes next to the other newsprints on the person. Ask each person if he or she is satisfied and discuss with each other things that might be added.

Actual Job Change

This is the hardest part. You make an agreement with each person for some of these changes. Voice any concerns you may have. Be clear about what you expect in return. Recommend that they feel free to come to you later on after these changes have been instituted and their usefulness determined, to talk with you about any changes you do not feel ready to make at this time. With each person, be sure to give enough so that the person feels helped by the change, and so that the change does actually have an impact on their willingness to work, their sense of job success, and their feelings of job fulfillment. What might some of these end results be?

Perhaps one member of your group enjoys writing. You agree to delegate most of the group's writing to him, and agree that all group publications will bear his by-line. Someone else may get the greatest enjoyment from being on stage. You will have her prepare and run throughout the year an orientation session to your group services for other units in the organization. Perhaps she enjoys organizing, dividing, and planning work. You will put her in charge of preparing the daily work assignments for the group. The end results of this "dreaming session" are limited only by your own creativity and that of your group.

As your people find themselves doing more of what they want out of life, more closely approximating their life dreams in their daily work, their energy will increase and their senses of success will grow.

The best way to ensure that all understand these changes and that all are deeply involved in them is this group meeting methodology. However, if circumstances are such that holding such a meeting is impossible I advise that instead of attempting to use shorter more compacted meetings you design for yourself an approach using similar questions and following the same general flow in which you meet with individuals. Even in a work setting that has tight time pressures you should be able to make significant progress through the judicious use of lunch hours, travel time, and coffee breaks. What I have given you is the rudiments of an approach to tailoring jobs that will give people a feeling of success on a daily basis and with that a feeling of vigor as they approach each day's tasks. And with that vigor the strength for being self-reliant, carving a sufficient place for your group in the organizational jungle.

DEFINING YOUR GROUP'S SUCCESS

At a less-intimate and less-personal level, your group also needs some image of what they want this group to look like and be like in the future.

This differs from normal goals, which indicate what this group is to accomplish. In defining group success you involve the members in plotting the group's future, not simply its tasks.

The other-reliant group hopes that the organization cares enough for its success to provide it with the capabilities it will need to survive the future. The self-reliant group plans and strives for its own future, realizing that no one is more likely to care for them than they are, nor more likely to plan for them, nor more likely to succeed for them than they are.

Since the future is too fuzzy to lend itself to precise descriptions, don't attempt to portray exactly what the group should look like. Institute a series of ongoing conversations about the future in which everyone shares and in which everyone learns. Although this topic is serious, it does not involve the type of personal reevaluation as the previous section and will not require the same type of intense, lengthy meetings.

However, be quite clear in your own mind that underlying the discussions are the same issues that were discussed earlier under How to Define Individual Success. It is important that the more personal discussions be held before these; otherwise, you'll find that you do not understand the content of these discussions.

For instance, Mary Jane doesn't think the group needs a writer. She lays out rational argument after rational argument to prove this. It seems obvious to you that the group does need a writer and you can't understand her stubbornness. Unless you remember that Mary Jane wants to be a writer and is much less likely to have the opportunity if you decide to hire a full-time person to fill the role. Or, it helps to understand George's insistence that the group double in size when you remember that George wants to be a supervisor. Obviously, if you try to hold these conversations without holding the previous section's conversations you court confusion. It is similar to playing pool in the dark. You will hear a lot of noise but will not know what is happening, and very few balls will drop in the pockets.

Bring your group together over a period of a month for a series of two-to four-hour meetings. The meetings will be spent completing a chart for the future. Figure 4 shows how to set it up. But it's more effective to create your own, if you are to cover all aspects of your group's life. Have your group help develop the categories using Figure 4 as a reference. The time frames in this chart may not fit the nature and style of your organization. Perhaps change comes to your group quickly and one year is a long time; or perhaps five years is a short time in your organization and 15 years is considered a long time. Alter and develop the chart to fit your situation.

Simply having some agreement among yourselves as to your future

together will help all concerned as they go about establishing both themselves and the group in the organization on a daily basis.

It is best, however, to take this one step further and review it at the
same time as you set your yearly goals and objectives. If you intend to
double the group's size within the next three years, now is the time to get
key management personnel to agree to the new shape of your group,
and initiate the search process for the first of the new employees. If you
foresee a substantial upswing of new services being delivered to new
clients and a sharp decline in the old services, now is the time to institute
the retraining program necessary for your present staff so that they will
have the capacity to meet the new needs. If in order to succeed you will
need massive expenditure for capital equipment, now is the time to discover how to attract these capital expenditures to your group. "Who
needs to be convinced?" "What needs will we fulfill if we use the equipment that we cannot fulfill without it?" "Why should anyone want us to
do that?" These are questions you should begin answering now.

As you set your normal objectives also set objectives and lay out plans
to keep your group progressing along the lines of this dream. The dream
should be reexamined once a year. At that time develop a new year
three and see to what extent you've fulfilled the goals of year one. Don't
be afraid to make changes, even radical ones. As the world shifts, so

Figure 4. Future planning chart.

Factors	Year 1	Year 2	Year 3
Size			
Functions			
Capabilities			
Mix of personnel			
Equipment			
New markets			
Declining markets			
Training			

do your targets, your desires, and your activities. The point is not what direction you have chosen, but the fact that you are self-reliantly choosing your own directions and having chosen a direction, continually move. It is stopping that will spell your end, since it is in stopping that you will signal that you have ceased to have your own dreams and have ceased to establish your own direction. In that case your group will have joined most groups adrift and at the whim of other's desires. The waters of most organizations are so tranquil that you won't sink, even without a rudder. But, you won't get anywhere either.

15

How and why
to look successful

Among the myths likely to debilitate your chances for success none is more deadly than the quietly arrogant statement, "People will just have to take me as I am." Of course, even those who utter it most adamantly mean it only minimally. They don't intend to forgo all manners, niceties, and customs by which we humans oil our relationships with one another, even though they may intend to forgo some.

In our society at least, admiration is given to the person who contravenes social dictates in favor of "being himself." Yet, even though we admire these "real" people, most of us limit the extent to which we are willing to follow the example of these paragons of independence. Perhaps we note that what they have is admiration, but not success.

Treated tolerantly as eccentrics, they are shelved when the real decisions are made. Mary's incisive and caustic insights may be both accurate and humorous, but now that we have laughed, we will retire to the board room without her. Harry's T shirt may be a sign to all that he still identifies with the boys on the loading dock despite his present status as a manager, but we have no intention of inviting Harry in his T shirt to the Café Exceptionale for a lunch meeting. Let him brown-bag it with the boys. We'll make our decisions without him. The radical unwillingness to conform to the unwritten laws of the organization is often read and responded to as a declaration of isolation from other people.

This chapter discusses the need for your group to "sell" itself to other groups, including management, within your organization. The first section involves altering your image so that you appear more pleasing to others. The second section is on altering your needs so that others will not see them in terms of your wants, but in terms of their own.

In many ways, this is a chapter about self-effacement. Continually we will be looking at "What do *they* want?" and relegating to second place "What do *you* want?" Such an effort can't be taken at all by the isolationist since that person wants no contact with others, pleasing or otherwise. However, such a program can be taken on by the other-reliant person. It is the other-reliant approach to the selling of self that most of us fear and wish to avoid. It is toadying and apple-polishing in tone, a mixture of the 'umbleness of Uriah Heep and the shrewdness of Shylock. It is self-effacement to the point of self-denial in favor of others.

Selling yourself and your group doesn't mean to abandon the work initiated in the preceding chapters of this book. Who you are is more important than how you look. No amount of cosmetics or marketing pizazz will make up for a poorly integrated person or a shoddy product. However, even a capable person and a worthwhile product need selling. "You" or "your group" are the real issue, but before getting to know you well, people have only the image you have given them of yourself. They must respond to that. If the image is abhorrent enough, they may decide that getting to know you better isn't worth the price.

There is a story of a Roman Catholic priest and an Anglican priest who first met through reading each other's poetry in journals. So much did they admire each other's style and thoughts that they began to correspond. They soon became fast, if geographically distant, friends. After a few years, they planned to meet in a London restaurant, which was to be their first chance to sit down and chat. The Roman Catholic priest arrived a little early, a proclivity that comes from attending monastic seminaries with strict timetables. The Anglican was apparently arriving a little late, a predisposition that came from having to diaper babies and kiss wives before going out the door.

As the Roman Catholic priest was killing time with his soup, he glanced into a mirror bordering the room and saw the elegant figure of the Anglican, who was looking at him with horror. Before he could turn in greeting, his fellow poet had vanished through the door. The Roman Catholic priest inspected himself in the mirror—short, fat, unkempt, soup stains on his cuff—and said, "He liked the letter, but he couldn't stomach the envelope."

In a way, these two had an advantage, although it proved their eventual undoing. It's very rare to see the letter before the envelope. Most who contact your group will see the envelope before the letter.

HOW TO CHANGE YOUR IMAGE

Since undoubtedly within your group you have at least a few people who will find it extremely repugnant even to consider altering their image, here are some arguments for it.

Others can make you become the person they see you as

An interesting experiment is often run by social psychology teachers with their students. One student is sent from the room. Meanwhile, the other students are instructed that for the rest of the hour they will not treat the student who is being experimented on as having opinions of any value. The teacher will also take a deliberately negative attitude toward that pupil.

The student is then invited back into the classroom. As the class progresses, other students don't react to his opinion but pass it by as if they hadn't heard it. The professor fails to call on him, unless he is the only person left to be called on. Then he calls on him only reluctantly, making apologies to the rest of the class for taking up their time. The average college student who is the subject of the experiment very quickly figures out what is being done to him and has a good hunch as to the intention of the experiment. Nevertheless, almost inevitably, he begins to act as others "expect" him to act. He becomes uncomfortable, apologetic, and what is even more remarkable, his opinions begin to deteriorate in actual worth as he increasingly becomes too confused and frustrated to think straight. The bottom line is: If you aren't valued, you become less valuable.

In the world of organization life, the first ten minutes you or a member of your group spends in the room is the time you can make the strongest impression. After those first few moments, others begin to color everything you do with their initial impressions of what you are like, and you frequently begin to behave in a manner similar to their perceptions of you.

If the image you convey is one of strong, successful, competent people, others will tend to regard you that way. The more you establish that image in the early stages of the relationship, the more they begin to help you round it out. They begin to ignore your faults, miss your mistakes, and generally give you the benefit of the doubt. In their minds you are competent, and since a competent person couldn't possibly have said what you just said, obviously they must have mistaken your meaning.

On the other hand, if the image you convey initially is one of weakness, failure, and incompetence, those you meet will be quick to disregard even the most accurate of your insights. Every slip will be duly noted as they seek to reinforce their image of you as an inadequate person and second-rate professional. Soon you begin to stutter and become clumsy both in words and thinking as you realize that everything you say seems to be missing the mark. As people continually respond to your best ideas with blank stares, these same ideas no longer appear valid even to you. Your self-confidence begins to ebb, and their expectancy that you will not produce creative and useful approaches to problems is soon realized. The downward cycle is complete.

You respond to your own image

Grandmothers have given succeeding generations of small boys and girls the advice to whistle when afraid, take on a jaunty air, bounce along as if not having a care in the world. The psychology is accurate. Whistlers soon begin to respond to the image they have created and begin to feel almost as secure and comfortable as they appear.

Actors report that after they have donned the clothing and makeup of a particular character, and have mouthed the words to be used in various situations, they begin to identify with and share the feelings the character is purported to have. After playing the part for awhile, an actor may even complain to the playright about the inaccuracy of various lines, as well as the unlikeliness of some behavior. Particularly in the great American art of the soap opera, the personalities of the actors and the characters become so intertwined that a writer often becomes unnecessary. The actor knows what the character should say.

Each of us is an actor to some extent as we rise in the morning to prepare ourselves for the day. We put on the clothing and behavior to fit the part we customarily play. We say: "I am this type of person. I shall therefore wear this suit, smile this smile, say these words, comb my hair thus, and drive this car."

However, just as with an actor, the process can work the other way. Instead of choosing behavior that fits our self-image, we may choose different behavior, and our self-image will change to fit it. This is the accurate insight upon which a number of self-help books are predicated. Not only is behavior a product of self-image, but self-image is also a product of behavior.

Perhaps you feel too sedate, think of yourself as old, lacking young ideas, unable to innovate. If you sell your Dodge Dart and start coming to work in a Datsun Z you will begin to feel differently about yourself. If you multiply the effect by dressing a little more flamboyantly, combing your hair more stylishly, and begin redecorating or at least realigning your office, you'll begin to feel that fifty isn't so old after all. Of course, you can push this effect to the point of ridiculousness, where you look like an old man or woman trying to be a teenager.

Perhaps you go home at night kicking yourself for getting trapped into discussions with other managers that are obviously coquettish and flirtatious. You hate the "little girl" feeling that comes over you when others make playful advances, and you would like to stamp out the "simpering" behavior with which you respond, a behavior that encourages even more such advances. Granted that many organizational settings are infiltrated with sexually adolescent males. Still you and your image of yourself are part of the problem. There are women who are not receiving the advances.

Embedded in your image of yourself is the facet that says you're a cute little girl who should wriggle with pleasure at the compliments of the opposite sex. It's hard to chop out that piece of your personality directly, but you can get at it indirectly. How are you manifesting it in your dress and behavior? Change that and you can change your self-image. With your altered self-image you will bring about permanent changes, not only in the responses of others to you, but in your responses to them. With the demise of the "bangs" and the miniskirts and the introduction of sober suits and a briefcase, every glance at yourself in a mirror reminds you that you are a person who isn't to be trifled with, a person with ideas, a person with a mission, not a high school cheerleader.

All images are on purpose

The person who says, "They'll have to take me as I am," claims falsely to be above those who choose the way they will appear to others. All images are on purpose, even his. The businessman who is always brusque is deliberately, although perhaps unconsciously, trying to tell others that he is a very important person, far too occupied with his own tasks to pay attention to the likes of them.

The superintendent who scoffs at the idea of wearing a suit and tie as pretentious attempts to impress people with an inflated image of himself, wears dirty overalls to show what a good sport he is. The secretary who squeals that she doesn't know why men keep flirting with her spends hours in front of the mirror and dollars at the shopping center to make sure that they continue to do so.

Images can even be chosen for the affront they give others. During the latest period of teenage rebellion, young people grew beards, wore their hair long, and refused to bathe with any frequency. For some, that image was chosen deliberately to offend the older generation. Now that we old people have stumbled along in their footsteps, and long hair and beards are accepted fashion, the next generation of the young may have to shave their heads to similarly offend. And if that is what is necessary, some will do it. As a matter of fact, some already have.

Whole groups of people will often choose the same symbols to indicate how dedicated or energetic they are. One group I worked with used as their creed the early hour at which they showed up at work. In case I hadn't been virtuous enough to be present for their early arrival (and I seldom had), they took pains to notify me of it during the course of the day. "I was in at five. Had a few things to clean up before the shift started."

For another group it was the number of messages they had received during their absence from the office. They turned down lunch because they had to return telephone calls, presumably to people who were skipping lunch in order to receive their return call. And they went from meeting to meeting throughout the day carrying in a highly visible manner a stack of the official telephone message cards which, during dull moments, they would shuffle like a deck of cards and stare at gloomily as if there were no hope of their ever completely moving the mountain of responsibility from their shoulders which their capabilities forced them to carry.

What are the drawbacks to making a conscious effort to control your own image? One major pitfall is that you may overplay your hand. If your group is the publications unit of a large corporation, you might decide to forgo bluejeans in favor of joining the rest of the corporation in more traditional professional regalia. Although a move from sports shirts to ties will be mildly noted as an improvement by others, a complete switchover to vests and suits will probably send the rest of the corporation into shock. Trimming the beards may help your relationships with other groups. Removing them altogether may also remove the dash of eccentricity that others admired and respected. Changing your image radically can cause more problems than it solves.

You may even outdistance your ability to respond to your new image. The idea is to give others a more accurate impression of the kind of quality they can expect from you, not to delude them into thinking you're able to deliver more than you can. Such a delusion is bound to collapse sooner or later to the deep disappointment of all concerned.

You have three fundamental choices. You can be other-reliant, and wait for others to signal to you your worth and value. This will give you time to develop an image that fits their perceptions. Or you can be isolationist, tell yourself you are valuable, not consider your image, and let others respond as they will. Or you can be self-reliant, assess your own worth and value, and decide the best way to show others quickly how you perceive yourself so that you can begin immediately to influence their perception of you.

Once you and your group are agreed that a look at your own image and the decision to change your impact on others will be useful, you may find some of the following variables worth exploring.

Clothes make the man—or woman

Various types of clothing are worn customarily by specific segments of our society. Some outfits are chosen for practical reasons. For instance, carpenters wear clothes that allow freedom of movement and keep out sawdust. Some clothing is chosen for purely symbolic reasons. Although a tie serves no function other than keeping ketchup stains off the table, woe to the male manager without one.

What is the general type of clothing worn by your group? What would other people consider the type of work and style of person who wears such clothing? My experience has been that the higher you rise on the organization chart, the more likely it is that the people you meet will be dressed in an unassuming but well-tailored style. However, that varies from organization to organization. One way to see what messages others pick up from the way you dress is to see who else in the organization you most resemble.

Your work area counts

Is your work area neat, or is it cluttered? Is it cheerful, or is it gray? In some organizations neatness says to others that you have your work life under control. In others it means you don't have enough work. In some organizations a cluttered work area says to others that you're so busy you have no time even to bring order to things anymore. In others it means you can't handle your job.

Cheerfulness tells them you're a creative and happy person. Grayness says that from you they can expect methodical, straightforward work. Each of these images is perfectly valid, and each can be the sign of a successful group of people. But each says something to a particular group of people. What do you want to say to those who enter your work space, and what are you saying now?

After a brief meeting that was held to discuss their group image, an engineering unit of my acquaintance decided to hide their chess boards. This group was beginning to earn the reputation of the "goof-offs who play chess all the time" to casual passersby. Their manager was receiving heat to "do a little disciplining down there," even though contrary to what it looked like, no one actually played chess except during lunch. Their reluctance to continually put away and set up their boards may have been practical, but it made those who didn't know the situation think they put chess ahead of their engineering duties.

What kinds of products?

Obviously you want your finished products to reflect the quality craftsmanship of your group when they reach your marketplace. But how about your interim products—those papers and prototypes that are passed around your own organization? Are they a fair representation of the capabilities of your group?

When I was working for a large corporation as an internal consultant, I was asked to quickly write up a summary and make recommendations based on a meeting some ten of us had attended. We were all in a bit of a hurry, since the group was to meet again the next day and move on to action. When I returned to my office, my regular secretary wasn't available, so I had to give the work to a much slower typist. Toward the end of the day, she appeared with a manuscript that was still far from perfect. Since I knew that this was simply a rough document for review among friends I had her duplicate it and distribute it in that condition. The next day we held our meeting. I began by apologizing for the condition of the text and gave the above explanation. Everyone understood the problem. Nevertheless, two years later I was given an assignment to take responsibility for the Training and Development work within the area to which this group was assigned. One package I received was the files on the area used by the last person who had held that responsibility. His files contained a photocopy of my rough document. Every error had been circled and every typo pointed out before the document had been photocopied. To this day I don't know how many people refer to that document when they recall the quality of my work. I do know that under no circumstances will such a document ever go out with my name on it again.

What is the quality of the products that leave your office? Are your people allowing slipshod efforts to go out the door using as an excuse that "It's only for good old Sam?" Products can come back to haunt you, as mine came back to haunt me.

How much intimacy?

One consulting firm of national reputation tells even its most junior members always to refer to the president of client organizations by his or her first name. Their theory is that if their consultant doesn't have that degree of intimacy, their consultant can't be of any value. On the other hand, they don't encourage even their most senior consultants to establish old buddy relationships with clients. Few agency or corporate leaders are looking for companions in their consultants, and most will be repelled at the mere suggestion of that type of closeness.

How do people in your group regard their relationships with the higher-ups in your organization? Are they able to indicate that they feel competent to have a dialog as professional equals, or do they by their style of address indicate that they feel there is and should be a tremendous chasm between their lowly selves and these, the powers that be?

On the other hand, does your group tend to become overly intimate with others? Do you let them know too much about your internal difficulties? Are you too revealing of your group's expectations? On the whole, do you try to become too friendly? Many people really enjoy listening sympathetically to your troubles. Part of what they like is the sense of their own superiority to you and to your group, since they don't have troubles to match these. Along with their sympathy, they also pass their judgment upon you. In their eyes, you have become losers. They'll remember your self-proclaimed status the next time you suggest a joint project.

Mannerisms may be harmful

One corporate research department always held the area involving research in human factors in low repute. The other managers felt that the psychologists who managed that group didn't give their all to the corporation and didn't care if their own groups succeeded or failed. When the psychologists were confronted with this feedback it was their turn to become upset. "What are you talking about? We care as much as the next person. We work just as hard, if not harder. You don't even see us most of the time, so how can you judge whether or not we give our all?"

With a rare degree of honesty, the other managers developed for the psychologists their portrait of "a manager who really cares." Did it include any of the usual functions of management, such as planning, organizing, controlling, staffing? No, for no manager actually saw another doing any of that. Did it include such results as return on investment, or the ratio of contract to development dollars, or goals met and achieved, or clients brought in? No, for success or failure in those areas was as much a product of the environment as of the manager's effort and caring.

The portrait was a one-sentence profile: "Managers who really care are seen hurrying through the halls carrying a sheaf of papers and looking anxious." The psychologists habitually sauntered through the halls, had their hands in their pockets, and didn't look worried.

Of course, this profile is a silly way to measure anyone's performance, but it is the way their performance was being measured. Although they fervently wished the world worked differently, the psychologists weighed the relatively small effort involved in hustling through the halls against the relaxation it would bring all those who thought they weren't earning their pay. When I was a construction laborer we had one rule only: "Do not sit down." The corollary to this rule for the psychologists was: "When goofing off, carry something."

I have listed only some of the ways in which I have seen some of my clients judged, either favorably or unfavorably. In order to take a hard look at the image your group projects and to do something about it I recommend a four-step process, which should be taken during a meeting of about four hours' duration.

Call a short conference on image control

The first step is to talk to your group about the arguments for consciously controlling your image. (Refer to Figure 5 throughout this discussion.) Begin by asking them to list the times they feel they were badly misjudged or that the group was misjudged. After a number of examples have been given, go back to each example and see if you can uncover what aspect, behavior, or symbol your group presented to bring about the misjudgment. Try to help them understand that the issue is not one of justice. It is, of course, unfair for others to mistake the female deputy director in the meeting for a secretary, simply because she carried a notebook to the meeting and kept track of what was going on. They

Figure 5. How do others see us?

Areas in Which We're Seen/Judged	Present Behavior	Present Impact	Desired Impact	New Behavior
Clothing				
Work areas				
Products				
Intimacy				
Mannerisms				
Others defined by group				

wouldn't make a similar decision about a man. However, unfair as it is, if she wants them to start thinking about who she is, getting rid of the notebook will help.

I know a college professor who has, through a decade of her teaching career, disclaimed any knowledge of how to type. Her first move in entering a new assignment is to remove any nearby typewriter from her area on the grounds that she doesn't know enough about them to prepare an envelope. In actual fact, between high school and college she worked four years as a typist and can still turn out 70 wpm when needed. However, she has formulated and is responding to the professional woman's third law: "Professional women with typewriters are usually treated as typists." In order to obviate constant battles about her true role she is forced to deny herself the convenience of having her own machine.

Where is the justice that prevents others from trusting one of your most able people to do disciplined work just because he or she is fat, and in their minds "fat" and "undisciplined" are one and the same? However, if this person wishes to remove the second tag, losing weight is one way to do it. It isn't fair, but then, very little else in life is.

Second, have your group draw up a list of those areas in which others see and judge you. You may come up with some areas that haven't been considered here.

Third, for each area ask yourselves the following questions. (1) What do people see when they observe you? Be specific about the observed behaviors, no matter how hard it is to face. "Leaning against the walls talking to each other" as opposed to "walking briskly" or "misspellings and typos" versus "clean copy." (2) What kind of impact do you think this has on them? "Frightens them"? "Makes them nervous about our competence"? "Offends their uptight value system"?

Fourth, repeat the third step, but this time do it in reverse. (1) What impact would we prefer to make? After that question is answered in all categories, (2) which of these behaviors should we change in order to begin making that impact?

The first time through don't bite off more than you can chew. A few behaviors changed in a couple of areas is quite enough for the sake of the experiment. After a month, conduct a review and evaluation meeting. Ascertain how the group finds it is sticking to the new and promised behaviors. Do they see any changes in others brought about by their attempts at image control? Remind them that just as it took years for them to build their old image, they must expect to stick with their new behaviors over some months without expecting much effect. If all is generally going well, I then recommend that you once again address the chart you drew up and select other behaviors as the target for next month's effort at change.

SELLING YOUR PROGRAMS

In Chapter 14 you were encouraged to develop a clear picture of where your group wants to go—what they want from life and what they want from work. However, don't expect everyone in the corporation or agency to rush to your aid, however clearly defined your destination. They're in a hurry to get to their own and won't care about helping you unless they see it as a means of getting them what they want, not of getting what you want.

If you have trouble gaining support from those groups that are theoretically designed to support you, don't feel that yours is an unusual organization. Most have the same problem. The issue is further compounded if you believe the myth that: "Others in the organization owe me help since we're all on the same side." That should be true, but isn't. If you want help, you'll have to invent strategies to get it.

In some way you must sell others into believing that your product is good for them. Instead of emphasizing its importance to you, point out its importance to them. Is it hard to get the corporate organization development people to do any work within your area, because they're too wrapped up in their research projects? Work out a strategy that makes your area their next research project. Of course, they should help you because you are already being assessed to pay their salaries. But since they are not, consider seducing them into your area by playing to their needs.

Are the people ahead of you in the production flow consistently failing to supply you with a product close enough to specifications for you to work with? Of course there are various forms of muscle and penalties that you could apply. However, consider working out an arrangement in which they will gain if they supply you with the appropriate product— perhaps something as simple as acknowledging every product that meets specifications by presenting them with a report of that number at the end of the day. If they are consistently rewarded for doing it right, they are going to help you, not for your sake, but for their own.

Did your husband influence you to marry him by explaining the delights he had in store for you of getting up at 2 o'clock in the morning to feed the infant, or did he mention instead his intentions of putting everything his energy could produce into making your life happy? Did your wife even hint that one of your future roles was to keep her yard immaculately mowed, or did she indicate the neatness, tidiness, and overall excellence of living quarters you could expect if you were to marry her?

There is no harm in putting a little sugar on the pill. After all, there are both sides to the issue. Don't emphasize the demand your needs will place on others. Emphasize the reward you are prepared to give them. Such a strategy will make it much more likely that you will get what you want.

No one in the maintenance group of one plant could make a dent on the purchasing department's policies and procedures. Purchasing went their own way oblivious to the needs of maintenance, which often had to drive in to the local hardware store to buy needed parts that purchasing had failed to stock.

One maintenance foreman finally made a major breakthrough. He pointed out that if they got him the parts he needed, as part of the same process he would help them clean house of the parts he had no use for. When purchasing realized that cooperation could mean a 20 percent cost saving, they suddenly came up with more time to discuss its procedures with maintenance. They saw that management would see them more favorably as a result of this joint program.

AN EXERCISE

Unless they are experts in marketing, many groups have not thought through what they have to offer other groups in the organization when they are seeking cooperation. A short exercise that can be fun and at the same time productive involves gathering your group for a two-hour meeting. During the first half-hour, list on newsprint all the groups in your organization that represent a key to your group's success—include precisely what it is you need from them. "Precisely" is important. Don't just say "cooperation"—say "24-hour turnaround" or "ignore small errors" or "use of stenographer." In the time that remains, list what you have to offer each of these potential sources of help that is of equal value to what you need from them. Don't sell short what you have to offer. It may not seem to you that your approval or disapproval means much to others, but it probably does; giving it can motivate them to cooperate. So also can a monthly memo to their bosses documenting their successes. Notice that once again I recommend positive reinforcement. Reporting the other group's failures will start a war and is for last-ditch use only.

You may even come out of this exercise with a few action plans to nail down collaboration from the formerly recalcitrant.

Here are two books to consult on how to enhance your image. The first is about modifying your behavior by changing your thinking. The second is about changing your impact by the way you dress.

Maxwell Maltz, *Psychocybernetics* (Englewood Cliffs, N.J.: Prentice-Hall, 1960).
John T. Molloy, *Dress for Success* (New York, Wyden, 1975).

PART IV

ABOUT BEING HAPPY

A few words to you as a person that had to wait 'til now: Yes, Parts I—III will help you become a successful and self-reliant manager. But what's the point, if self-reliance doesn't make you happy? These last two chapters are about just that. Chapter 16 tells you how to make sure your job suits your capabilities, and Chapter 17 talks about playing. Then comes a short postscript, which puts this book into a larger context.

16

Creating
your promotion

Some managers treat their jobs the way acrobats treat their swings. A job is simply a temporary perch until the next and higher trapeze comes by. They neither care for their job, nor for the group they manage, but immediately look ahead to see where they can get from here.

Many managers err on the other side. As they enter a job they look like a bear preparing for winter hibernation. At first they stir up a great deal of activity as they rearrange their cave to suit their individual needs, inclinations, skills, and insights. "A real go-getter," everyone says, as systems are changed, furniture moved, people reinvigorated. But once the cave takes on its final shape, these managers begin to enter the great sleep that will last until retirement and be broken only as occasional small details get out of line and require momentary awakening and attention.

The major contribution you make to your group is the changes you bring to it in trying to make it a happy place to work in. Since you have had the good sense not to destroy what was there when you arrived, the group now has the advantage of its past strengths and the new values you have brought them. But there comes a time when you and your group become one. They have learned what you have to teach them and you, if you are a quick-witted manager, have gained from what they knew before you arrived on the scene. Two and two have been added and the result is four. Together you may struggle and bring the sum to five, but to add up to eight, the group would need a new manager or some other major change.

There is even a serious risk that the gains made through your work may deteriorate as you and your group, assured that you have conquered all conquerable horizons, drift off into the land of nod.

There should come a time when you decide that the situation is in hand, at which point you start to look for your next job. Here, as in all other cases, you should not wait for anyone else to decide that the time has come. Be self-reliant, and make your own decision.

There are a number of factors that may block your management from seeing the usefulness of moving you on to another position. One factor could be your success in this job. A manager I worked with had a similar problem. He had convinced his management that the plant he ran would benefit greatly from a complete overhaul of its process. One day he was contacted by the executive who had the responsibility for his type of plant in the corporation. This executive had decided to veto the new project. The plant was the only successful one of its kind in the company, largely because of the manager's efforts, and the executive didn't want to risk any change.

At a slightly later date, this plant manager had a chance for a promotion. The major argument against him was he was doing his job so well that the executive doubted he could get anyone to replace him. Of all the similar plants in the corporation his was the only one that showed a profit. The executive didn't want to trifle with success.

Since management tasks and skillfulness vary widely, it is impossible to predict with any accuracy the point at which you should think about moving on. Three years in most management jobs will be, to my thinking, the minimum required to do any kind of job well, particularly if you intend to institute more than surface changes. For instance, most of the strategies suggested in Part II of this book will not have any special impact on the way your group operates for at least two years. On the other hand, I can't imagine a management job that remains challenging for ten years. By then you will probably be in a rut.

ARE YOU READY FOR A MOVE?

It may be time to create your promotion. Here are some questions to help you decide if you should begin to look ahead. For each question put a T for "then" to indicate what the situation was two years ago. Then put an N for "now" to indicate the present situation. The more your N answers move toward the left side of the scales from the T answers, the more likely it is that you should be looking onward.

1. Normally when you come to work are you bored or are you excited?

|⎵|⎵|⎵|⎵|⎵|⎵|⎵|⎵|⎵|⎵|

bored   excited

2. Do you ever worry about the job?

|⎵|⎵|⎵|⎵|⎵|⎵|⎵|⎵|⎵|⎵|

never   always

3. Do you have to seek advice on what to do in your job?

|⎵|⎵|⎵|⎵|⎵|⎵|⎵|⎵|⎵|⎵|

no   constantly

4. Are you engaged in, or do you need, any training to do the present job?

|⎵|⎵|⎵|⎵|⎵|⎵|⎵|⎵|⎵|⎵|

none   much

5. Are you finding the mannerisms of the people you work with irritating?

|⎵|⎵|⎵|⎵|⎵|⎵|⎵|⎵|⎵|⎵|

extremely   do not
annoying   notice

6. How much reading do you do about your present job?

|⎵|⎵|⎵|⎵|⎵|⎵|⎵|⎵|⎵|⎵|

none   a great deal

7. Do you discuss the day's happenings with your spouse or close friends?

|⎵|⎵|⎵|⎵|⎵|⎵|⎵|⎵|⎵|⎵|

never   daily

8. Have you instituted any new ways of doing the work recently?

|⎵|⎵|⎵|⎵|⎵|⎵|⎵|⎵|⎵|⎵|

no   many

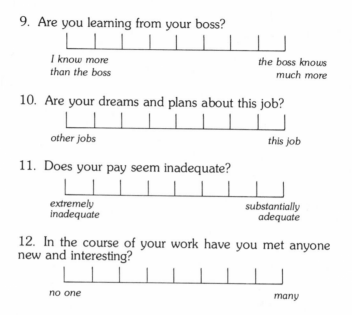

9. Are you learning from your boss?

I know more   *the boss knows*
than the boss   *much more*

10. Are your dreams and plans about this job?

other jobs   *this job*

11. Does your pay seem inadequate?

extremely   *substantially*
inadequate   *adequate*

12. In the course of your work have you met anyone new and interesting?

no one   *many*

If you decide that the time has come to move, there are ways to go about finding a new position that will not only increase the likelihood that you will get that next job, but will also help energize you in this one.

Selecting multiple targets

Go back to the exercise in Chapter 14 that helps you review your own needs and desires. Sit down with a close friend or a spouse and work your way through the exercise, applying it to your own needs. Try to come up with a profile of the kind of job that could excite you. Then, and only then, should you look around to see where that job is. Don't make the mistake of looking at the job market first. The deficiency in that approach is that you will not be as creative as you will if you use the approach I suggest.

If you go to the supermarket knowing that you want bananas and find no bananas there, you will then go on to another supermarket. But if you go into the fruit department without a clear idea of what you want, since your eye isn't stimulated by the bananas (they aren't there), you will select something else, which you didn't really want.

The first instance requires more energy, but you get to eat what you want to eat. The second is easier, but you wind up eating what you didn't want to eat. Using this self-reliant process, a probation officer may want to make lots of money in the next job. This realization will probably take the probation officer out of the corrections field.

On the other hand, using the more "other-reliant" process, the same person will keep plugging away from one unsatisfying probation job to another without knowing why, never having sat down, independent of the confusing stimuli in the present context, to identify and come to grips with the real needs.

Once you have prepared your profile, select a variety of jobs that could prove agreeable, and begin slowly and patiently to explore them. Don't fall into the trap of setting your sights on only one goal and expecting to achieve it. For every job there are several candidates, most of whom either have qualifications equal to yours or whose capability so resembles your own that the person hiring them can't distinguish their talents from yours. Therefore, if you set your sights on one job, the odds are excellent that you will be disappointed. You should keep four or five places in your sights at once, and as soon as you have been turned down for one or found it inadequate to your needs, add another to your list of targets.

Getting assessed by key people

Once you have an idea of the general characteristics of the job you want, ask other people to help you work out your strengths and weaknesses with regard to that job. The first reason for doing this is the obvious one of learning them and instituting your own program to capitalize on the strengths and do something about the weaknesses.

A more subtle reason for the same project is that you enlist the help of others in promoting your promotion. Have your boss assess your potential. Have other key figures in your organization assess your potential, particularly those you respect and are on good terms with. You then become their project. It isn't just you who are looking for a promotion but, because of their involvement in assessing you, they too are looking for your promotion.

"Harry took that course in financial management as I told him to. He really is ready for a promotion. Sam is retiring, maybe I should offer Harry that job."

A third reason is that this method puts the word out in no uncertain terms that you are looking for more challenging work. If your own management wants to keep you, they know they had better deliver that work before you find another organization that will. These words should never, of course, be explicitly stated by you. If they are believed, your management will resent being intimidated. If they aren't believed, your management will resent being bluffed. On the other hand, if you initiate a wide-open growth and promotion campaign, the same message will be spread subtly, politely, and definitely. Of course, if this strategy is to be success-

ful, you will have to be the kind of manager your superiors don't want to
lose.

Trying it out

Although you cannot move to the new position while you still hold the
old one, you can identify aspects of the new job and work out projects
you might handle while you remain in your present job. For instance,
you may be interested in managing the long-range planning group. You
can volunteer to take on some special assignments that involve planning
for areas in which you have particular expertise.

As a result, you will learn more about planning technology, you will
demonstrate that you can handle large planning tasks, you will test for
yourself whether or not planning is as interesting as you thought it would
be, you will indicate your own aptitude for the task, and you will have
something new and exciting to do to relieve the boredom you are
beginning to experience in your present job. That's a lot of result from a
small move.

Another method for trying out the new job is to select and take courses
that are relevant to it. Focus on courses that have a strong experiential
component. That is, select courses that have you do things, not courses
that have people talk to you. Not that you can't usefully listen to some
words, but there is no better way to learn to do a thing than to do it
under expert guidance.

Using your professional organization

The grass may actually be much greener on the other side of the fence.
You may fare much better in another organization. Use your friends in
professional organizations to search for a new job in other companies for
you. If you have had the good sense to become actively involved in a
professional organization this strategy will probably occur to you automatically. However, if you do not belong, join now and get yourself
known.

The professional organization is an invaluable tool if you wish to avoid
becoming a company person with all its drawbacks, which include personal and professional narrowness, lack of job mobility, and overdependence on the company.

STRENGTHS FOR CLIMBING

Since the arrival of the Peter principle it has become quite fashionable
to sneer privately at those managers we have identified as having
reached their "level of incompetence." True as that tragedy is (it affects

both the person and the organization), there is another problem we commonly ignore, one that has a more insidious but no less devastating effect. It is the tragedy of those who have never reached their "level of competence."

The incompetent person in the vice-president's chair is an obvious problem. But what about the person who should have been there but is parked on a much lower rung in the organization? That's the one whose failure is seldom seen, and whose effect is difficult to calculate.

"Joe does a good job on the loading dock. Such a bright man. I have often wondered why he was never promoted."

Nobody knows what might have happened if Joe had been the vice-president of sales during the slump year. "Mary is an excellent technician. Her reports represent penetrating analyses and sound recommendations. I often think she knows the agency's business better than her own management does."

And what would have happened if she had been the deputy director during the congressional investigation of 1974? Who will ever know?

How far you can go in your present organization or in any organization depends on the four factors inherent in your personality structure, which to some extent govern your progress. Of course there are other factors in the situation itself that will have a significant effect. But there is little that you can do about them, and since they vary from situation to situation I will not discuss them here. The factors you can usefully study are ambition, thick skin, risk-taking, and competence. By examining the chemistry of these four factors within yourself you can predict whether you will be a low achiever, a failure, an underachiever, a high achiever, or an overachiever.

Low achievers lack competence but have the conscious or unconscious wisdom to avoid the situations that will demand competence. Such people rarely fail as they have never stuck their necks out. Furthermore, if they were to try, they would soon fail. They have selected a position in the organization, and they will maintain it.

The failure's level of ambition involves taking risks higher than their basic abilities allow. The failure leaps blithely on the tightrope only to fall again and again. The low achiever possesses the same capacity but has the good sense to keep both feet firmly on the ground.

Underachievers lack the drive to fulfill their own potential. The underachiever consistently selects a position that is certain to incur little risk in accomplishing whatever task. For some underachievers, it is their fear of risk that forces them to keep their talents minimally employed. Perhaps for some it is an absence of ambition. And for others some mixture of the two.

Achievers appropriately match their moderate competence to moderate risk situations just as *high achievers* match their high competence to higher risk situations.

The higher the ambition, the more likely you are to tolerate higher risk positions as a means of achieving what you want out of life. The thicker your skin, the more likely you are to experience the risks as not so risky after all. This will allow you to pursue more demanding tasks. What are these two characteristics?

Ambition is the hunger to go beyond the point for which nature intended you. It is the stuff of which *overachievers* are created. It is the desire to have more responsibility than the rest of the world would give you based on your capabilities. It is the desire to be paid more money than other people with the same inherent talents, the desire to have more power than others who have the same wisdom. The greater the degree of your ambition, the more you will press yourself to take the risks that will put you in a higher management bracket than your competence allows.

Of course, ambition is not without problems. Along with the higher position will come longer hours, distance from your family, absence from social and athletic activities, and the potential for such psychosomatic responses to the added stress as ulcers, obesity, and high blood pressure. However, ambition is such that if you have it, you've got it, and it will not go away easily.

To some extent you will have to come to terms with it and allow it to be a factor in your career decisions. Many eagerly allow their drive to carry them forward and accept the cost as expected expenses for pursuing a career. Others, less willing to disregard other aspects of themselves, learn to moderate their ambitions, living with less than they desire of money and stature in order to keep their peace of mind. Either way, if you are an ambitious person, you have to sacrifice something. As the saying goes, "You pay your money and you take your choice."

Another factor in becoming either a high achiever or overachiever is how tough your skin is. To what extent do the opinions of others matter to you? That is the extent to which you will be limited in the risks you are willing to take. If you have thicker skin, you will be willing to take the risks that others cannot take, since failure doesn't have as strong an effect on you as it does on them.

Failure for thin-skinned people implies some diminution of themselves as people because they are regarded with pity by others. Failure for you means that you simply failed, nothing more nor less, and certainly holds no diminution in your respect for yourself as a person. You will be happier with the fact that you tried than you will be saddened by the fact that you failed. Studies of the careers of people who have been unusually successful show that many experienced titanic failures in their professional history. Some highly successful owners of businesses have suffered through as many as three or four bankruptcies. However, they realized that to fulfill their own ambitions they had no choice, even after failure, than to set their sights high and try again. The fact that the opinion of others did not have that great an impact on their feelings of self-worth made the new beginning much easier.

I have a friend who lost the election for mayor of a major city. For some weeks after the election he had to endure the pitying looks of others who were concerned about the emotional impact on him. However, he knew the gamble when he rolled the dice. Two years before he had won. This year he had lost. But what he had learned from that loss made it all the more likely that next time around he would win. He viewed the failure with equanimity and was quite willing to risk it again, because it meant little to him what others felt about him—although whatever they felt, he would be delighted to receive their vote.

There is a rung on the management ladder where everyone is stretched beyond his or her competence. No one is competent to govern most large federal agencies. Nor is anyone competent to run an operation with 6,000 employees. No one can run a conglomerate. Certainly no one is capable of being President of the United States. The size and dimension of some tasks exceed the capability of any person, unless that person is willing to risk major failures on occasion and endure minor failures day by day. The top positions in management are for overachievers only.

As you look forward to finding a new job and plan your career growth you must have the answer to two questions:

1. To what extent are you ambitious enough to exceed your own capabilities and make the sacrifices necessary to succeed?

2. To what extent is your skin tough enough so that you can afford to take the risks implicit in trying for the upper rungs of the management ladder?

If you don't make the decision consciously, your chances for success or personal happiness are diminished. It doesn't matter what answer you give, but it does matter that you find an answer that matches your own needs. As with all other decisions about life you may be forced by your own character structure or by circumstances to remake the decision in the course of your career, but daily ambivalence will not wash.

Perhaps after ten years of climbing the ladder you will decide that the top is too demanding for you. Or perhaps after ten years of standing still you will recognize that you will never marry and have that family, and you will decide to accelerate your career. These decisions will be accepted as legitimate by your co-workers. But if you announce your intention today to become vice-president of sales, and tomorrow you leave the meeting to take your son to Little League, you will find yourself risking your chances in all forums.

One of the sharpest and most ambitious people I know suffered from such a division of effort. Although he was passionately interested in business, politics, and his own family, the people involved in each endeavor felt he was short-changing them in favor of the other two areas. He ran himself ragged trying to please them all, rather than deciding on their relative priority and living with the fact that one person can't be totally successful at everything.

STAYING WHERE YOU ARE

You may take a long look at your own capabilities, weigh them against the risks and stresses of working toward a promotion, and conclude that your present position adequately meets your needs and priorities.

If you take that course, you must also decide how to conquer the problem of creating a rut in your group. If your decision to remain in the job was based on the fact that your competence is still being tested adequately by its challenges, becoming stale won't be much of a problem. However, if you could go further, but are unwilling to push yourself, then you owe it to yourself and your organization to develop a strategy for staying fresh in the same position. There is no point in being bored 40 hours of every week and 22 days of every month.

The on-the-job hobby

An optometrist I know fought the boredom of routinely fitting hundreds of people with glasses by conducting his own independent research into the problem of crossed eyes. He saw every otherwise dull patient as a potential source of data for his study. And if the person in the chair didn't fulfill that function, well then perhaps the next person would. If a given issue of the professional magazine had nothing to say about the problem of crossed eyes, whatever tidbits he acquired in the course of reading proved useful to his more routine patients.

His hobby brought him national recognition and the concomitant pleasure of having his expenses paid and receiving a modest stipend two or three times a year for traveling to a convention center and addressing an audience of fellow professionals.

If you manage the shipping department, your hobby might become the application of hydraulics to lifting or material flow processes. If you manage a training department you might make a study of innovations in audio visual equipment or the psychology of learning. You can imagine the practical knowledge you would have to pass on to others based on your on-the-job application of the principles learned in your new avocation, not to mention the interest this would add to the job itself.

Training and promoting others

If you don't want to incur the risks and stresses of moving up the ladder yourself, you might consider turning your group into an academy for those who do. Of course, this shouldn't be done at the expense of getting the work done, but in the process of getting the work done. The company will gain well-trained managers, you will have an added source of interest at work, and your group will have a constant flow of fresh, upward-bound people with new ideas for getting things done. Furthermore, the long-term benefit of this course will make your life easier and easier as your pupils become your executives.

Opening up to new ideas

If you do not plan to move, make sure that your group doesn't remain the same. Remember when you first came on the job and you ran into that old timers' group? They may have been janitors, or they may have been executives, but they had known one another for 30-odd years. They knew the job backward and forward, and they bristled at suggestions, requests, or changes from anyone, but particularly anyone with less gray hair. Although you may not believe it, if you allow your department to grow old with you, that is who you will become.

Even if you aren't inclined to train and promote others, make sure that your group experiences healthy turnover. Each new person should be regarded as new blood and a potential source of valuable change. Meet with them every so often during the first couple of years they are with you to gain a new perspective or insight into various aspects of the job. Tell them outright that you've put them in charge of making sure you don't ossify and become old and rigid.

Fresh eyes see new things. Invite peer managers to come down to your area, spend a significant period of time browsing around, and offer you their suggestions and criticisms. Whatever you do, don't argue with them about whether or not their ideas are good or bad. You aren't expected to do everything they suggest, but do listen to whatever they say. The minute you begin to point out their errors in judgment about your area, they'll either stop telling you what they saw or end up arguing with you about what is right or wrong in your area, which defeats the whole purpose. You asked for their judgment, so accept it graciously.

Whenever a major change is in order—be it technical or personnel—

take advantage of the time to solicit ways to do things better from all employees. People often hesitate to recommend radical change because they don't want to rock the boat and risk their own security. But by definition, a major change means that the boat is being rocked. People become more open to change as long as that's the trend, will they or nill they.

A university controller met with the group that reported to him and asked, "Since Sam's retiring will mean some changes around here, do you have any suggestions for other changes?" Each interview ran to two hours, with the subordinates doing all the talking and the controller writing everything down. Several of the suggestions for useful change were common to practically all the interviews, including one to reduce the department by three positions. In a static period his subordinates may have hesitated to tell him anything. During a period of change they were eager to see their own ideas implemented.

The lateral transfer
Another possibility, if you don't want to go up, is to go across. The increase in pressure will not be that much, and your competency won't be tested to the same degree as a step up the management chain. However, you will have to shake up your thinking as you face a new group of people and a different task. They too will benefit from the expertise you bring them from your old job.

ON QUITTING

There does come a time when you should quit, both for your own sake and for that of the organization. The best situations calls for you not to quit because of your distaste with your present organization, but because other opportunities have appeared, new doors have been opened, and, with regret, you must move on. Unfortunately, this isn't always the case. The time may come when you simply don't like being where you are because of the nature and shape of that organization. You have little idea where you are going next, but you know you have to go somewhere else.

Continual boredom and frustration, as well as constant anger, are among the symptoms that the time has come to move out. Particularly if you find yourself wasting your time and your family and social circle are complaining about what is happening to you on the job, don't struggle to endure it—get out. You have only one life. Don't waste it.

Before you make a move

However, before you make a move toward quitting, check to make sure that the cause of frustration is peculiar to your organization and not common to all organizations, or to all organizations in your chosen field. For instance, slow responses from management can drive you up a wall, but most organizations suffer from the same problem. If that is the basis of your frustration, reconsider whether or not your organization is worse than others. Keep track of how long it takes management to respond, and ask a number of your friends in other organizations to help you out by doing the same. Then compare notes. There may be no point in moving.

Usually if you ask your friends for sympathy, they will give it to you, ignoring the facts in the process. I listened to someone complain at a party that management was trying to reduce her vacation time from four weeks to three weeks. All her friends at the party were in similar jobs in other organizations, and all of them offered support and agreed that her management had no right to be so restrictive. They neglected to mention that most of them, in quite similar circumstances, were receiving only two weeks' vacation. She had asked for sympathy, not the facts. Rare indeed is the friend who will give you the facts under those circumstances.

Imagine her shock and dismay had she quit based on the support she received at the party to enter one of her friend's organizations. If you are sitting in the frying pan, make sure your buddy isn't sympathizing with you from a cozy position smack in the middle of the fire.

Incidentally, the fact that you hear grumblings is not a sign that an organization is in real pain. Human beings always complain. To diagnose the extent of organization health, you have to find out what people are muttering about. When you hear or participate in grumbling about the company cafeteria, attune your ears to the infinite distance between complaining that all you get is hot dogs and the fact that the steak is often too rare for your taste. When discontent is in the air about the decision-making process, listen to the difference:

"No decisions are ever made."
"The decisions they make around here are no good."
"The boss makes all the decisions."
"My input in making decisions isn't given enough weight."
"Decision-making meetings seem to last forever."
"I am asked to take part in decisions for which my opinion isn't needed."

My experience indicates that all company cafeterias are lousy, but some are lousy because they are dirty and some because they choose poor background music. No decision-making process is complete, but some are lacking because the decisions are poor and others because of the overinvolvement of the complainer. Before you decide to leave the organization, compare its level of grumbling with that of your next organization. Your present organization may be a gem.

Do not threaten to quit. Your manager may give in to your desires for fear of losing you, but the threat will only have that effect a couple of times. After that, it will have worn out and your manager will know you aren't serious. Furthermore, your boss will resent having been forced to give in on that issue and will look for ways to regain any lost ground. If you can't make reasonable progress with your boss without making such flamboyant threats, you do have a problem, and you should consider quitting. However, get your ducks in order, find your next job, pack your briefcase, and then go in and calmly announce the fact. Don't be deterred by any temporary change of heart on your boss's part. Your boss hasn't experienced a conversion. The organization won't change overnight. Don't unpack your briefcase. Keep going the way you were headed. If you don't, everyone will figure you were just bluffing anyway. And perhaps they'll be right.

The definitive move

There is a moral undertone to the question of quitting. "Not quitting" has been elevated to the status of a virtue. How often have you heard it said of some prize fighter who spent the last three rounds having his face turned to hamburger that "At least, he didn't quit." As if there were some virtue in what a dispassionate viewer would simply consider an irrational act. If there was no hope of winning anyway, he should have quit.

Granted, one can quit too readily and too easily, but a person can also quit too late. There is a type of bulldog that becomes deadly if given the right hold—once they have the opponent by the neck, they hold on through any punishment until the opponent falls lifeless to the ground. Unfortunately for their success as fighters, if they get the wrong hold they maintain it with similar single-mindedness. They will continue their grip on a leg as they are torn to pieces.

Often, in our struggles with life, we grab it from the wrong angle. A good quitter is a person who doesn't let go during minor difficulties if there's a good grip, but knows how to let go quickly and cleanly when the grip just isn't right. Once you have decided that you are unhappy where you are, spare no horses—get yourself somewhere else. Life is short. Working hours are long. Move to happier surroundings.

> *What Color Is Your Parachute?* If you are a job hunter or a career changer you should read this practical manual. Even if you aren't,

you may want to read it anyway. After you see the options available to you, you may decide to seek another job or career. The second book I recommend will make you work harder than the first, but it will provide a sounder product. Both books share the same philosophy, but this one contains no philosophical chats—just exercise after exercise designed to orient you to your next job.

Richard Nelson Bolles, *What Color Is Your Parachute? A Practical Manual for Job Hunters and Career Changers* (Berkeley: Ten Speed Press, 1975).
John C. Crystal and Richard N. Bolles, *Where Do I Go From Here With My Life?* (New York: Seabury, 1974).

17

How to
enjoy work

If you are a grim person, and perhaps even if you aren't, you may have visualized the self-reliant manager as carrying on a desperate struggle in which a moment's relaxation could cost the victory. The self-reliant manager works not with the plodding determination of a plow horse turning one furrow and then another, but with the gleeful energy of a gnome moving from one source of fascination to another. The self-reliant manager plays at work.

In our society few people know how to play. Only very small children enjoy themselves by doing what they want to do. But even children have the spirit of fun stamped out as quickly as possible. Two small boys have no sooner picked up a bat and begun to knock the ball around the backyard than a group of enterprising parents take them to the playground, outfit them in uniforms, and teach them how to do it right. They learn the correct way to hold the bat and that each is assigned a position where he must stand and pay attention to the game.

They learn not to respond to their feelings of boredom by watching birds fly by or by going home to mom for cookies and milk. In short, they learn that bats and balls are not to be played with when they feel like it and abandoned when they lose interest, but are objects for grimly determined work. Every year middle-age adults risk heart attacks at tennis schools in the name of improving their game. Instead of playing in the spirit of fun and relaxation, they drive themselves so that their return to the home courts will mean winning a few more games than last year.

Certainly competitive athletics has its thrills. I was deeply moved by the 1976 gold medal won by the American women's swim team. Every person on that relay team swam her best time ever in order to win the championship. The spectacle was fantastic, but I certainly wouldn't mistake it for play. Both the training that got them there and the effort they put into winning were work, not play. And yet, after watching the Olympics, millions of Americans will now think of swimming not as floating, flipping, and flopping lazily in a clear lake, but as pounding down constraining lanes in a chlorine-saturated pool. For them, swimming will no longer be play, but work.

It is no wonder that managers who have never learned how to play (even when they are supposed to be playing) don't know how to play when they are working.

The difference between work and play is not in what is done but in the underlying attitude. Just as hitting a tennis ball can become work, developing equations for computer architecture and sweeping halls can become play. Of course, there will be days when no change of heart or approach will make a difference, and you will dislike being on the job. But there can also be days, and many of them, when the job itself becomes your entertainment, quitting time comes too quickly, and you look forward to picking up the task tomorrow.

Here are some pleasant tricks you can play on yourself to increase the likelihood that you will enjoy work. Each is based on one way in which work differs from play. For a summary of the differences, see Figure 6.

Figure 6. How can your work seem like play?

	If Work	If Play
The choice	Must do	May do
Flexibility of approach	Low	High
Results of failure	Catastrophic	Tolerable
Stakes	Real and high	Artificial, changeable
Purpose	Extrinsic	Instrinsic

Find ways to take vacations when you want them

Work differs from play because it is something that must be done; play is something you choose to do. As soon as the choice is removed, it becomes less likely to be fun to do. The same person who might run five miles nearly every day out of sheer joy, runs only reluctantly when the track coach says that to remain on the team that distance will have to be run every day.

In most jobs, the organization makes an attempt to control the hours during which you are fulfilling your function. The first step in being able to choose to do your tasks is to carve out room for your decision by discovering ways to choose not to do your tasks.

For instance, when it feels like work to go to the job, call a meeting in some agreeable spot. Breakfast and luncheon meetings are good alternatives—different surroundings make for a pleasant break in your habits. It's not uncommon to accomplish more in the relaxed atmosphere than in the office.

Another possibility is to take tedious work into charming surroundings. Do you have to draft a boring report in order to ensure that your management meeting is properly recorded? Take your notes and pad to the municipal art gallery, pick a comfortable place, and have a go at it. In the summer, a picnic table in the park may be the ideal place to tackle a humdrum assignment.

I have arranged meetings with business associates by the pool at the local Marriott Inn. It's a pleasant summerlike place in the middle of Minnesota's winters, and nobody seems to mind two nonpaying guests discussing business poolside.

Leave major segments of the day unplanned

If you don't have the luxury of leaving several hours open, plan for only one or two days at a time, and leave major segments of the time after that unplanned.

Work is defined as work when your time is programmed and all options are taken from it. Even if your choice involves picking one tough job over four equally tough jobs, it is better to be able to make the decision at the moment itself than to have it all arranged ahead of time. Don't worry about your natural inclination to skip the important jobs. Eventually even the worst of tasks will challenge your interest or feed on your guilt and you will do it. This method has the added benefit of improving your ability to make decisions in using your time to best advantage. At the moment of choosing, more facts will be available as to how the time can best be spent.

Expect and allow for less than first place

If you have chosen competent competition, you will not be first 50 per-cent of the time. The fun of games occurs when you allow yourself to play hard and yet be comfortable with the fact that winning isn't neces-sarily being first. Of course, our spirit of playing as a nation is such that only a rare few enjoy the game unless they are number one. Vince Lom-bardi said that "Winning is the only thing," and that statement elevated him to the role of national saint and prophet by many sports buffs. Chris Evert stands grimly on the base line and pounds out ground stroke after ground stroke. No one asks her if it's fun. I presume it isn't. It doesn't look like fun. Yet she is the top seeded women's player, and as Vince said, "What else is there?"

The paper in my city announced after the marathon event of the 1976 Olympic games: "Frank Shorter loses bid." Frank Shorter had just cov-ered a more-difficult-than-normal marathon course, in a rain, faster than he had ever run before. What did he lose? The gold medal. One person ran faster than he did.

So different are self-reliant values from those expressed in that news-paper headline that I have an announcement to make. In the 1976 Mother's Day Four-Mile River Road Race, I won 113th place. It took ef-fort and training, but I won it. As a matter of fact, without reaching down for an inspired kick on the final bridge I might have lost 113th place to whoever that was who came puffing up to my shoulder. Some of my friends wanted to give me sympathy on 113th place. It took them time to realize that I was and I am genuinely proud of it.

Two years before I would barely have been able to walk that distance. Compared to myself, I am gaining. And with these words, I am putting out a warning to whoever was in 90th place: "Look out, I'm coming after your title in '77." The athletes in first, second, and third place are running a different race, no more fun nor (I hope) no less fun than my own. But I'll be darned if I'll classify myself as a loser because they crossed the finish line 15 minutes before me.

In the race for 113th place I was the winner. If you're a self-reliant per-son, winning depends on who you are and where you start from, not whether or not you are first. One reason so few people enjoy games is that they have learned from the example of professional athletes that they should not allow themselves to be anything less than first.

If you want to enjoy your job, you can't expect to be first at everything you do. You must learn to enjoy your second, third, and fourth as well as first places. It is the salesman who is capable of enjoying the sale he nearly closed who will be able to move on lightheartedly to the next client and close the next sale.

Daniel Lord, a prolific writer of a few years ago, commented on a school classmate of his. The classmate's writing style was far superior to Dan's, and the level of his thoughts put him beyond Dan's league. Yet the man never published because he knew that what he wrote was not the very best. He edited and re-edited, and when he realized he was still short of perfection, he put the manuscript not in the mail but in the file. Dan, on the other hand, didn't mind writing the third best book on a topic. It was different, it was a contribution, and it was his.

The person who prizes being first at all costs may well lose the ability to try anything for fear of failing at it. Certainly the unwillingness to allow for lower places causes unnecessary strain. The overriding need to be first means that the win itself contains little satisfaction. The win becomes just another failure averted, and the winner must trudge on to setting up the next win quickly for fear of failing at whatever venture is about to be pressed upon him.

Look at your job in perspective

The need to win increases as the stakes become higher. In games the stakes are artificial. You can behave as if they are high, or you can behave as if they are low. The stakes are whatever you decide to make them. Usually we behave on the job as if the stakes are both real and high, although most often the stakes are artificial and are therefore only as high as we decide to make them.

Only rarely will you get fired if you do something wrong. I have participated in programs to identify and remove marginal managers and have found that only with great reluctance will anyone initiate the removal of even the most hopeless of cases. I presume that anyone who has had the wisdom to make it to this chapter of this book is sharper than a "hopeless case." If it gives you pleasure to pretend that you actually risk your job with each individual decision I will not willingly remove that pleasure from you. But remember that you are pretending. Very few of your decisions are likely to affect your future employment, and the insistence that they are puts unnecessary pressure upon you.

Enjoy the job itself

Work is something you do in order to have something else as a reward for doing it. Play is done for the sheer pleasure of being involved in the doing itself. Rod Dixon, an Australian middle-distance runner, was asked what he would do when he gave up his racing career. "My plan," he said, "is to return to the small town in which I live and enjoy myself by running in the surrounding hills, fields, and beaches." For Rod the pleasure in running was not in winning the race. That was an added, incidental pleasure; the pleasure was in the running itself. He would continue to run without the race.

The point that the process is more important than the goal has been discussed before, but deserves a second look as we near the end of this book. The intellectual operations in playing chess are little different from those involved in developing a market plan that will be approved by management. The planning can be enjoyable in itself. The physical stress in swinging a hammer and in playing handball is about the same. Carpentry can be fun in itself. The emotional stress in putting on an amateur play and in developing and presenting a lecture is quite similar. Teaching as a process can be enjoyable.

What blocks the enjoyability of these processes is that we have trained ourselves to see them as things to be done in order to accomplish something else, instead of things to be done to give ourselves pleasure. Carpenters don't rejoice in the heft and feel of the hammer, in their power and dexterity as they drive the nail, but think of the house they have not yet completed and the paycheck that is coming at the end of the week. Teachers don't rejoice at their own cleverness in beguiling their students into paying attention, but focus on the need to pass knowledge on, and again on the paycheck at the end of the two weeks.

Goals, of course, should be selected because of the reward to be obtained from their achievement. But, since you will spend infinitely more time pursuing the goal than achieving it, you should also select your goals based on the enjoyment you will experience in the pursuit.

Enjoy managing itself. Look again at Chapter 4 for more hints on how to motivate yourself to do this. If you don't like managing, for heaven's sake, your sake, and everybody else's sake, do something else.

Put yourself in the center

In a sense, this is what the whole book has been about. People who play do so because they like what they are doing. Otherwise they would stop. The person who works does so because someone else likes what they are doing and is paying them to do it. Self-reliant managers put themselves in the center. They do what they do because that is what they like to do. If that is not what they like to do, they do not do it.

Such a playful attitude may seem like certain death in the organization that pays your salary. However, in the long run, only those who have put themselves in the center will succeed. At the beginning of your career, or during a career reassessment period, you may distress everyone you know with your seeming ambivalence, as at first you seem to pursue one job, and then you announce your interest in another. But those who sacrifice themselves because others say they should be willing to do what they find distasteful wind up the marginal failures I mentioned at the beginning of this book. Not only do they not enjoy their work, but their work benefits little from their efforts. For, because of their distaste, they are only half-present on the job.

A philosophical approach to play is discussed from a unique point of view in two books I think you will find interesting. Becker discusses the fact that a major block to our enjoyment of life is our ostrichlike attitude to its temporariness. Leonard sets for himself a much simpler task than I've set for myself in this chapter. He teaches the reader how to play while playing.

Ernest Becker, *The Denial of Death* (New York: Macmillan, 1973).
George Leonard, *The Ultimate Athlete* (New York: Viking, 1975).

The coming of a new order

I recall sitting in a hotel restaurant some years ago with a manager who was both a friend and a client. We were eating a meal between sessions of a teambuilding event. He was commenting on what a satisfying life I must lead as a consultant. "You have so much influence over people's lives," he said. "True enough," I responded, "but of course, not half as much as you do." He was astonished, and even after we argued, remained unbelieving. The point that I tried, unsuccessfully, to make with him was that while I gave advice, he acted.

I said to people, "Let others in on your decisions." He invited them in the office to discuss specific approaches on specific proposals. I said, "Know what people feel." He attended their spouse's funeral. I said, "Let people know whether or not they are doing good work." Daily, he complimented some and pressured others. I said my words, and then was gone for as long as a year. Nearly every workday morning he reappeared to influence his group. Who, then, is having the most influence?

Managers generally sell themselves short in terms of their impact on people. You must remember that most people spend half their waking hours being managed. In my opinion, the single most influential group of people in the United States is its managers.

Teachers, of course, have much to say, but they present their message to children. Children live in a protected fantasy world, even college-age children. They can choose to believe or disbelieve the teacher without much consequence one way or the other, as long as they put the right words on the test paper. But when they leave school and plunge into the world, which refuses to treat them kindly, their relearning process is directed by their working manager. The immediate superior doesn't hold classes, of course, but indirectly and subtly passes on a personal conception of the way the world works.

Preachers are allowed the privilege of saying almost anything within the confines of their sanctuaries. Outside their sanctuaries their authority is considered suspect. They too are seen as living a protected life, offering advice far distant from the clamor of the battlefield. What they consider of central importance often has little to do with what the world is trying to accomplish.

Even writers' words can go over our heads. I think of this as a practical book and yet I'll wager you've found numerous instances in which using my advice in your situation would cause nothing short of an explosion.

I am not against these three groups of people having impact. At one time I was both a teacher and preacher and now I am a writer. But when the real decisions are being made, we aren't there, the manager is.

Our society is much too complex to ever again be moved by a charismatic leader. Charismatic leaders provide single, clarion answers. They may have the "right" answer for some of the people, but they will never have the right answer for all or even most of the people. What is needed in Virginia is not needed in North Dakota. What's needed in New York is not needed in McGregor. What is needed at Honeywell is not needed at the Federal Home Loan Bank Board. Tomorrow's answers will be worked out from situation to situation by society's on-the-job social engineers, the managers.

It is my opinion, for the reasons given in Chapter 2, that we are entering a new order, an order that will have as its basic unit the self-reliant person. I don't believe that any one person will issue a gospel to attract everyone else to valuing and implementing self-reliant approaches. I do believe that manager after manager will be attracted to the pragmatic consequences of self-reliant strategies. Managers, even more than political leaders, educators, clergy, writers, philosophers will gradually turn this nation into an even better place to be working, as yeast in dough. Quietly, but thoroughly and completely.

Along with the practical benefits of this leavening will come side effects, which are extremely important in themselves. I expect that people will develop a keener self-awareness, greater personal strength, and enhanced respect for themselves. I predict that along with that strength they will gain the capacity to see strength in others, since they will no longer need to hold others down. With that respect I also anticipate warmer, closer, more loving relationships, and a greater peace among people.

A tall order indeed! One that humanity has worked toward for some time. But managers do not need to keep this vision before them for it to happen. They need only focus on tomorrow's goals and select the best strategies for achieving them. These strategies will be self-reliant strategies. As I outlined in Chapter 2, the world is changing. Self-reliance is becoming the answer. There is no urgency about focusing on this vision, but knowing it is there, knowing it is possible, and knowing that others share it may make your daily tasks lighter and your daily decisions easier. It will also help you to know that you are working with the tide, not against it.

Five years ago a manager friend of mine was known as "that kook out in the research department." Now the rest of the corporation is trying to find out what he is doing that makes his group so much more effective than others. His formula in brief is: "Nobody is asked to bow to anybody at any level. All are expected to stand tall."

I am glad that you read my book. I hope it is of use to you. Stand tall!

Your last stop on the reading list is Teilhard's optimistic vision of where humanity is headed. As a manager, you may be too pragmatic a person to enjoy the style of this overview. It is both philosophical and abstract. No matter. If Teilhard is right, we are inexorably going the way he points out. He has had such impact on others that his thinking will impinge on your life from the strangest angles. The book you have just read, for instance.

Pierre Teilhard de Chardin, *The Future of Man* (New York: Harper & Row, 1964).

Index